D1206282

COLETTE AT THE MOVIES

COLETTE

COLETTE AT THE MOVIES

CRITICISM AND SCREENPLAYS

Edited and introduced by
Alain and Odette Virmaux

Translated by Sarah W. R. Smith

FREDERICK UNGAR PUBLISHING CO.
New York

Selections translated from the original French
Colette au cinéma
© 1975 by Librairie Ernest Flammarion, Paris
Copyright © 1980 Frederick Ungar Publishing Co., Inc.

Printed in the United States of America

Design by Anita Duncan

Library of Congress Cataloging in Publication Data

Colette, Sidonie Gabrielle, 1873-1954.
      Colette at the movies.

      (Ungar film library)
      Translation of Au cinéma.
      Filmography: p.
      Includes bibliographical references.
      1. Moving-picture plays—History and criticism
—Collected works. I. Virmaux, Alain.
II. Virmaux, Odette. III. Title.
PN1995.C61713   842'.912   79-6148
ISBN 0-8044-2125-0
ISBN 0-8044-6086-8 pbk.

CONTENTS

TRANSLATOR'S NOTE

One of the great writers of her generation, the French novelist Colette through her early film criticism and screenwriting had as important a role in the development of cinema as its first defender in America, Vachel Lindsay, or her great co-workers in France, Louis Delluc and Germaine Dulac. Until recently, her writings on the subject remained scattered and inaccessible, but in 1975 they were collected and introduced by Alain and Odette Virmaux, who published them under the title *Colette au Cinéma*. It is also thanks to their efforts that we once more have available two important works that were long presumed lost: her dialogue for Marc Allégret's *Lac-aux-Dames* (1934), based on a novel by Vicki Baum, and her original scenario for Max Ophuls' *Divine* (1935), loosely inspired by her own *Envers du Music-Hall* (1913). As is the case of much of the screen writing by our own William Faulkner—see Bruce Kawin's *Faulkner and Film* (Ungar, 1977) —these films are not only interesting in themselves but throw an important light on the themes with which the novelist was preoccupied in her fiction.

With one indicated exception, the selections from Colette's writings on and for the movies presented here are given in their entirety. The introductions by Alain and Odette Virmaux have been edited for the American reader.

My thanks and appreciation go to Stanley Hochman, Film Editor of Frederick Ungar Publishing Company, and to Lee Hochman; to Professor Martine Loutfi of Tufts University; and to Jane Larson and Karen Henry, my typists.

Sarah **W.** R. Smith
Tufts University

Colette is shown below with director Yannick Bellon during the 1950 filming of a short documentary on the novelist, who wrote the script and did the narration. On the right is Jean Cocteau, whose The Blood of a Poet, *made twenty years earlier, established him as an avant-garde filmmaker.*

INTRODUCTION
COLETTE AND THE CINEMA
by *Alain and Odette Virmaux*

Between the author of *Gigi* and the screen, the whole world knows confusedly that there was some relationship. But what it has done for Colette's writing, the cinema has done—should one say unfortunately?—for the work of many other writers. The justification of our anthology is not in the fact that Colette's writing has repeatedly been adapted to film, but rather in the fact that Colette was excited and interested by the cinema, in all its aspects, throughout her life.

She appears in the *Dictionnaire du Cinéma* published by Seghers not because of the films based on her books, but as a writer of scenarios, dialogue, and criticism—an active presence in the cinema. Without ever abandoning writing, Colette concretely participated in the cinematic activity of her time. Her contribution to the formation of a true language of film is undeniable and her name is often cited by historians of the screen. Thus, for a long time it has seemed logical to us to collect the texts—scattered, inaccessible, forgotten, or thought to be lost—that demonstrate her role.

One objection suggests itself: most of her writing about film does not appear in her *Complete Works*, published from 1948 on, during her lifetime and under her aegis. That is, she willingly left out of the *Works* almost everything that is to be found in this volume, almost everything that interests us now about her relationship with film. There are a few exceptions to this rule—notably "Backstage at the Studio," collected in *Paysages et Portraits* (*Landscapes and Portraits*). But her criticism and *chroniques*, scenarios and dialogue for films were pitilessly thrust into outer darkness. Maurice Goudeket tells us that Colette eliminated many similar uncollected pieces he submitted to her: "Even if many of these

1

pages seem to me today unjustly rejected," he writes with frankness in *Près de Colette* (1956, *Close to Colette*), "they cannot appear without the public being given notice that the author did not give her approval to them."

Authors are not always the best judges of their own work, as Goudeket also writes; but, in addition, Colette could not have suspected, a quarter of a century ago, the interest that would be excited by such work. At that time the history of the cinema was not yet being studied in any organized fashion, and film scripts and the dialogue of films were seldom published. But several years after Colette had died, it became evident that she had been a pioneer in cinema criticism; her testimony in favor of Thomas H. Ince's films was unearthed, and the disappearance of the dialogue she had written for *Lac-aux-Dames* was deplored. The writer's role is seen differently today than in 1948; we no longer think that certain subjects are unworthy of an author's pen or of "great literature," and we don't entirely see why such a quantity of supposedly "minor" work must be kept to one side, especially when these "minor" works overflow with verve, passion, and evocative richness.

Of course, the cinema was not the great love of Colette's life; one can at best say that at times it occupied an important place. At three times principally: between 1914 and 1919, as she was writing her criticism and *chroniques*, her first adaptations for the screen, a scenario —the period of her Roman visit, what one might call her Musidora period; then between 1931–1935, the period of *Lac-aux-Dames* and *Divine* and her subtitling of *Maedchen in Uniform* and the American *Papa Cohen*; finally in 1947–1953, the period in which her own works were adapted in series for the screen and in which Yannick Bellon did a film on her—her apothesis into a cultural object for the screen. The last of these three periods does not interest us here, since the writer was reduced to an almost total passivity; in the two previous periods, however, Colette took an active role in creating the cinema of her time.

We do not mean to say that Colette's interest in the cinema is limited to these periods; rather, they are the most obvious manifestation of her continuing interest. One needs only to leaf through her correspondence to find references to visiting "darkened theaters": going to the cinema in 1914 with Marguerite Moreno, seeing Griffith's last film in 1921 with Léopold Marchand, discovering *The Blue Angel* in 1930, praising *Les Anges du Péché* to which Bresson had taken her in 1943. Maurice Goudeket recalls Colette during her last years staying with him at

Deauville and going to the movies in her wheelchair; and we may recall that in the famous apartment in the Palais-Royal, books had to cede enough room for a television—and this at a time when the possession of one was a rare luxury, not the banal and ritual fact it has become today.

Her interest in the moving picture was always high. Doubtless this helps to explain the favor with which she welcomed the many proposed adaptations of her works to the screen. We hear, through her correspondence, of many that did not come to a successful conclusion: a *Chéri* in 1922 and again in 1926–1927; abortive projects with Henri Diamant-Berger, Germaine Dulac, and Emile Vuillermoz, described in the *Letters to Marguerite Moreno*, others in the *Letters to Hélène Picard*. And when a project finally became concrete, it was after innumerable preliminaries: *Le Blé en Herbe*, made in 1953, had been under discussion since 1947, and we learn that even while writing *Gigi* (1944), Colette had thought specifically about what the cinema could do with it, although the film would not be made until years later. But in spite of setbacks or delays, interest in the cinema flourishes throughout her correspondence. Sometimes it takes the form of disdain for "this sort of work in which one gives birth far from the eye of the spectator" (to Marguerite Moreno, August 17, 1928). But the screen remained a familiar preoccupation, always present: sworn at, but never for a minute condemned or proscribed.

There are other proofs of this fidelity. Anyone may watch cinema; anyone's books may be turned into films; these facts are not always explained by a profound and distinterested love for cinema. But not everyone has fought for the cinema, and Colette did so even outside those periods that we have designated as devoted especially to the screen. She allowed her name to be lent to two film conferences, in 1922 and in 1926, the latter on "Photogenic Qualities of the Animal." Her non-filmic writings are full of rapid allusions, glances, fugitive comments on the cinema; she speaks in *Aventures Quotidiennes* (1924, *Everyday Adventures*) of memories of Eleanora Duse, revived by seeing her in *Cenere*; in a *chronique* published in *Excelsior* for July 31, 1916, we read of a taxi hurling itself down the rue de la Paix "with that blind petulance, that capricious contempt for danger that we admire in the cinema, when the enchanted taxi swims through the flood, hardily penetrates a Norman chateau and leaves it again by the dormer window." Under her pen, the cinema became an ordinary fact of life; here as elsewhere Colette was far ahead of her time.

But let us leave these minor aspects of her involvement with the cinema to come to the essential. And the essential is not the adaptations of her own works made by others. Colette did not conduct herself like other writers, who surrender totally the rights to their films. Rather, she most often took a direct hand in the adaptation. It was not by chance that she took advantage of her Italian trip, during the First World War, to be present during the making of the first films based on her work: *Minne* (1916) and a first version of *La Vagabonde* (*The Vagabond*, 1917), with Musidora. For the second *Vagabond* (1931), her contribution is even more clear. She writes to Hélène Picard in 1931, "I was forced to make quick revisions in the scenario of *La Vagabonde*; it was so dull I couldn't avoid it." Even at the end of her life, when she was imprisoned in her apartment, she followed with interest the cinematic transpositions of her books. Her collaboration, not always credited, in the screenplays and dialogue of the films made from her books is well-known (see the article "Colette" in the *Dictionnaire du Cinéma*). She devoted to these enterprises a passionate interest that was maintained until the release of the film. Her interest is evident in the case of Claude Autant-Lara's *Le Blé en Herbe*, which had its world premiere in January 1954, only a few months before her death; though she could not attend, she recorded a message which was played before the film was projected and which was reprinted by *Figaro*. A clever publicity stunt? On the contrary, everything suggests that the desire to cash in on her literary fame counted for little in her conduct.

This does not mean that her contributions to the cinema were disinterested. All her life Colette was obsessed by the fear of "running short"; she never hid it. If she had been sheltered from want, she would have signed fewer contracts. Undeniably the cinema was to her a source of revenue; sometimes her commitment to it was determined by money or the lack of it, as for instance when she left *Film* in 1917 "because there was no money in it" (*Lettres de la Vagabonde*). But she would not have given so durable and so varied attention to an often despised mode of expression if she had not felt for it some sort of profound adherence.

Her work directly for the screen provides evidence of this. The most relevant piece of that work is unhappily, at this writing, considered to be lost: this is the scenario she wrote for the actress Musidora—star of Louis Feuillade's *Les Vampires* (1915–16)—and which was filmed in Rome in 1918 under the title, *La Flamme Cachée* (*The Hidden*

Flame). Barring its improbable rediscovery, we will know nothing more about the film than what is given by several summaries in the press and by Musidora's memories of it, published in *L'Ecran Français* (No. 241, Feb. 13, 1950) and in Francis Lacassin's *Musidora*. According to Lacassin, the film concerned a student, Annie Morin (Musidora), who marries one of her fellow-students, a millionaire, but loves another, a poor man. In the hope of remaking her life with the latter, she ruins her husband, hoping to drive him to suicide. But she herself dies in an explosion, after having offended and driven away the man for whom she should never have hidden her love. Whatever the merits of this film may have been, the mere fact that Colette consented to work on it is significant. Several writers who esteemed the cinema, Apollinaire among the first, tried to write screenplays; but not until Jean Cocteau's *Sang d'un Poète* did a writer really succeed in expressing himself on screen. By writing a scenario that became an effective film, Colette made herself a special case. Her involvement with the cinema is both earlier and more historically important than would be suggested by the credits of Max Ophuls' *Divine* (1930), which advertised that it possessed "the first scenario written directly for the screen by COLETTE."

Though *Divine* is based on an earlier book, *L'Envers du Music-Hall* (1913, *Music-Hall Sidelights*), the addition of a story line to the film can allow us to speak of it as an original work. Such is not the case with *Lac-aux-Dames*, for which Colette merely wrote the dialogue (although it is likely that she also had something to do with the conception of the film—see our notes). Less personal still was the task of writing subtitles for *Maedchen in Uniform* (1932) and an American film, *Papa Cohen* (1933), the latter of which has sunk with hardly a trace.

But there remains a final category of work, less known than the adaptations or even than the scenarios and dialogue writing: this is Colette's own writing about the cinema. Not the incidental allusions to the screen, but writing consecrated directly to film. These pieces were all written for one or another periodical. Some of them are scattered through other writing and treat cinema as one of the multiple kinds of current events. Thus "Colette's Diary," begun by her in *Le Matin* in October 1913 and including several topics every Thursday under the title of "A Thousand and One Mornings," devotes one to "The Film" on March 19, 1914, and another to "The Scott Expedition on Film" the following June 4. In *Excelsior* one similarly discovers a review of *The Cheat* in August 1916 and a dialogue, "Bel-Gazou and the Cinema," in December 1917. Most of these have never before been published in book form; hidden in the mass of other topics, they have been almost completely forgotten. Colette continued this practice of dealing with the cinema from time to time among other topics; her *Jumelle Noire* (*Black Opera Glasses*), the collection of her dramatic criticism, was to include several sketches about the cinema: "Cine-actors" (1934), "Black and White" (1935), and two descriptions of Mae West.

But not all Colette's writing on the cinema has this dispersed, fragmentary quality. A much more coherent series appeared in 1917. At this period she was reviewing films for one of the first specialized magazines of cinema, *Le Film*, edited by Henri Diamant-Berger. It was a brief association: barely three months (May–July 1917), seven articles, about fifteen films—after which she surrendered her place to Louis Delluc. Did she really leave, as she wrote to Georges Wague, "because there was no money in it"? It may be noted that at this time her associations with periodicals—with the exception of *Le Matin*—seldom lasted long; at the same time she was still taking an interest in the cinema, writing *La Flamme Cachée* and her article about its filming, "Backstage at the Studio," reprinted here; she was perhaps also writing a series of sketches that appeared above the signature of "La Femme de Nulle Part" ("The Woman from Nowhere") in *Le Film*. The next year she would publish four *chroniques*, also collected here, called "A Short Manual for an Aspiring Scenario Writer," in which the tics of films of the time would be lovingly dissected.

It remains for us only to discuss the limitations of Colette's interest in the cinema. Unlike Cocteau, Pagnol, or Malraux, she was never tempted to get behind the camera. Furthermore, her attachment was above all to the silent screen. It was in the silent era that she pleaded publicly for certain films, that she wrote an entirely original scenario, that she took the most interest in the work of the studios, that she was most attentive to the evolution of a cinematic language, that she took part in conferences on the cinema. After 1930, there is nothing comparable. Her attention is less vigilant, a fact that approaching age does not suffice to explain. The cinema—now the "talkies"—comes to her; she is asked for more adaptations, for collaborations, for work-to-measure for the cinema; her pen is appealed to. And her support remains effective, convincing, even decisive. But Colette has ceased to be a part of the avant-garde of cinema. Her writing contributes to the functioning of cinema but no longer directs its evolution.

Colette's "pre-cinematic" instinct has often been praised; "She has a camera at the tip of her pen," wrote Gabriel René in *L'Ecran Français* (1950). Similar praise has been lavished on the instinct that always allowed her to choose evocative detail and to invent efficacious and well-chosen dialogue. It has even been said that her novels are made to be filmed and that some of them seem actually to be early versions of shot breakdowns. But it is useless to say that Colette "instinctively understood" cinema; one could apply the same argument as well to Flaubert. It seems to us more legitimate simply to say that the cinema accorded well with Colette's sensibilities. To the extent that it offered her the diverse image of an animated, changing, multiple, and constantly renewing universe, it suited perfectly her insatiable appetite for discovery and sensation. It was much closer to her spirit than the static world of the theater. It fascinated her because it brought her the world, nature, men, continents, the spectacle of life in all its forms: the growth of plants, the first natural actions of an animal or a newborn infant. As regards the screen, she was less a specialist in dramatic art than a journalist, or better yet, a simple person, attracted by the film as by a special form of the living world itself. But this is to say that Colette the viewer, critic, and creator of film was only one more aspect of Colette the writer.

Very logically, Colette herself became a filmic object. Yannick Bellon made a film about her in her last years: a homage, of course, a way of fixing the living image of someone who was life itself and who had become a cultural quasi-monument, but also the result of a long attraction and a persevering communion between Colette and moving images. This film thus also has a symbolic value, but the vision it gives us is that of the official writer, laden with years and honors, almost embalmed alive. Looking beyond this inevitable portrait of a consecrated image, our purpose is to go back to the period when neither Colette nor the cinema were valued objects of cultural consumption; when the relation between them was still living and still to be defined; when both were still applying their energies to the conquest of their respective selves.

In 1948, Jacqueline Audry (left) directed the first film version of Colette's novel Gigi; *it featured Danièle Delorme (right) in the title role. The novelist is shown in conference with the star and the director in her famous room overlooking the Palais-Royal gardens.*

COLETTE THE CRITIC

The pieces collected here form the most substantial part of Colette's
writings on the cinema. Several have been omitted as being already
collected; criticisms of a few minor films were cut from this English
edition; and there may be one or two pieces that have so far escaped
us. However, any eventual discoveries are not likely to change the
basic shape of Colette's cinema criticism as it is presented here.

Among the texts you will read here are several that appeared
successively in several periodicals. Both the first part of "Backstage
at the Studio" and the succession of articles making up "A Short
Manual for an Aspiring Scenario Writer" were given by Colette, at
intervals of several months, first to *Excelsior*, then to *Le Film*, finally to
Filma; one of them, "The Femme Fatale," even appeared twice in the
latter magazine, with a change of title and several cuts. We need not be
surprised at this example of "backstage at the typewriter"; it is not
likely that the specialized periodicals paid their contributors well, if at
all, and we may remember that Colette wrote in *Letters from the
Vagabond*, in 1917, that "there was no money" in *Le Film*.

Film criticism, properly so-called, represents only a part of the texts
in this collection. Since Colette assumed the task of film critic for only
three months, she found herself chained to those films that happened
to be showing at that time. This explains why she wrote nothing on a
major work of the period. Nothing on Griffith—whom we know she
followed, if not appreciated—nothing on Chaplin, or Mack Sennett, or
Sjöstrom or Stiller, or Max Linder or Feuillade. To make up for this
lack we find only a eulogy for Abel Gance and his *Mater Dolorosa* and
commentary on several films directed or produced by Thomas Ince:

Civilization, Civilization's Child, and *The Despoiler.* Gance, of course, we know primarily as the maker of *Napoléon.* Ince is far less known than his two partners, Sennett and Griffith. Their production house, Triangle (1915–1918), drew film out of the trap of facility and raised it to the level at which it was conceivable to speak of it as a new art. However, unlike Sennett and Griffith, Ince's reputation has not been maintained by a legacy of universally recognized "classic" films.

Moreover, the films directed by Ince and about which Colette had to write between May and July 1917 were perhaps not among his best, with the exception, of course, of *Civilization.* At a time when the United States had just entered the war on the Allied side (April 1917), France was sent films that would demonstrate or support a sort of bellicose ardor. From this comes the sometimes painful naiveté of the scenarios, of which Colette's sarcasm allows us to get a fairly precise idea; see for instance her ferocity toward *The Despoiler.* This mocking lucidity did not prevent her from doing justice to the real merits of these works and to the evident superiority of the American productions over a European cinema still engrossed by imitation of the theater. Jean Cocteau's later eulogy of another Ince-produced film, *Carmen of the Klondyke* (1918), confirms Colette's lucid judgments, which have been cited by Georges Sadoul and Jean Mitry in their discussions of Ince.

In fact, the regular work of cinema criticism and the obligation to take notice of often mediocre work did not suit her temperament, and she must have given up without undue regret. She was more at ease and put more into her work when she could exercise a freer choice and draw the attention of the public to the merits of an unrecognized film. Thus *Film* praises her warmly for having "launched" *The Scott Expedition to the South Pole* in 1914 and, above all, in 1916, *The Cheat. The Scott Expedition* was one of the first great documentary films and opened the way for a whole school. As for *The Cheat,* it is well known that Cecil B. De Mille's film had an extraordinary effect in France; for Louis Delluc, Cocteau, and many others, it was the avowed source of their passionate obsession with the art of the film; according to Jean Mitry, "the French cinema between 1919 and 1924 rested entirely on *The Cheat.*" It is clear that Colette played a decisive role in this phenomenon. The story of *The Cheat* is a banal society melodrama; why was it so admired and so imitated? Because the film represented a significant advance, that of a film which invented its own language rather than relying on the stilted and petrified language of the theater. *The Cheat* imposed its own style of "interiorized" acting rather than the earlier excesses of expression. From this came the lasting fame of Sessue Hayakawa, the Japanese actor with the impenetrable masklike face. Need we say more about Colette's discoverer's instinct? She was the first to understand the importance of such a change of direction, and she encouraged the cinema to forge its own autonomy.

One often has the feeling that she was most interested not in examining films one by one but rather in studying the "phenomenon of cinema" as a whole—most especially the way in which it was received by the public and its potential for making an impact on the spectator. She looked less toward judging films than toward attentively measuring the way in which they were received and understood. For example, she frequently relates the reactions in the theater during or after the showing of a film, the gossip about films, the variations in the popularity of the stars. She often shows herself attentive to the procedures, habitual or otherwise, of cinematic expression: in a review of Ince's *Not My Sister*, not included here, she attacked the mania for what we now call the "shot-countershot"; in discussing *Civilization* she admired an ellipsis effect and the projection in silhouette of the shadow cast by an unseen spectacle. She is extraordinarily sensitive, above all, to details: lighting, acting, set decor, costuming, diverse accessories, familiar animals. Often she finds that a scene has missed its mark because of a badly conceived detail—an actor badly framed, a ridiculous hat—and she then mentally recreates the scene in the same way that Gide, in his *Journal*, completely reconstructed the films he had just seen.

Little by little Colette returned to her preferred genre, the *chronique*, or bylined column, as she had practiced it for several years in *Le Matin* and *Excelsior* under the title of "Colette's Diary." This *chronique* was a sort of sketch-pad composed of several brief and distinct rubrics, a formula toward which her criticism in *Le Film* tended. To read them one by one is to observe how Colette chafes at restricting herself to a mathematical recitation of all the latest films. Into the middle of properly so-called criticism, she introduced unexpected subjects: "Film and Fashion," "The Friend of Film" (which brings backstage gossip on stage), "They're All Going to the Cinema" (which describes a musical revue about the cinema). In short, one should hardly be surprised that after these sorties she quickly passed the honor on to Louis Delluc and that later she came back to *Le Film* as the author of works, reprinted from *Excelsior*, which this time were real and avowed "chroniques," such as "A Short Manual for the Aspiring Scenario Writer."

These latter texts explode with brio and verve. They constitute a stunning satire on a certain kind of theatrical cinema, the sort whose knell was first sounded by *The Cheat*. But to be appreciated, this satire should be considered in the context of Colette's whole attitude to cinema, an attitude fundamentally quite coherent, even though it is a hundred miles from being organized and thought through. The author of *Backstage at the Music Hall* aided in the birth of an entirely new sort of cinema, a cinema based on American films and on the first documentaries; she hailed the appearance on screen of natural settings, the outdoors, simplicity, real life. Similarly, in "A Short Manual for the Aspiring Scenario Writer," she denounced the laughable conventions and the pretentious artifice of a studio-based cinema still trailing at the heels of the theater. But before this she had manifested her sympathy—in "Backstage at the Studio" and even in "Film"—for the unappreciated labor on the sets, the obscure fauna that dwelt there, the obstinate illusion that reigned there. Apparently diverse, but in fact complementary, attitudes; it was because she looked forward to a different type of cinema that Colette could condemn, but tenderly, an outmoded and superseded form.

The deep unity of such a position is assured by her wit. The "Short Manual" overflows with a teasing pleasantry that bears witness first to her prodigious knowledge of the world of films, then to an uncommon skillfulness of pen. It is an art of dialogue developed with brio, of telling detail, of well-managed progression, of the selection of words that always hits its mark. These pages seem made to illustrate in advance the astonishing advice for a writer that Colette was to give to Marguerite Moreno in 1924. They are also a fine example of craftsmanship.

We notice, finally, in looking at the "Short Manual," how much of the chronicler's talk is based on the known or supposed responses of the public—the reaction of someone who has studied the public. Colette's discussion is always oriented toward the goal of the enterprise, how the public will react. This gives to her writing on the screen an air less esthetic than sociological, if the word isn't too heavy for this Burgundian who was so far from "intellectual" and, so often, so Parisian. This caring for the public, acquired in her diverse professions, confers on her writing a competence and a seriousness that mask themselves behind an obstinate refusal to be grave or eloquent. The vivacity of her pen speaks volumes; we must not mistake it for lightness.

FILM

Colette's first known film article was published in *Le Matin* on March 19, 1914, under the title "Le Ciné"—a professional slang word just coming into use.

This sonorous hall of brick, iron, and glass is only a small corner of the enormous factory of cinema, of *film*, according to the professional nickname, for the spectator says, "I'm going to the cinema," but the actor or the mime says, "I make *film*."

Footsteps resound as if in a train station; walking, one must bump up against and skirt around a strange collection of animal cages, baskets in which captive hens cackle, cardboard rocks, staircases in false marble. A "set" part of the hall assembles the shore of the Adriatic, climbing roses, the pergola of an Italian villa, a balustraded terrace on which, suddenly, a noble couple seat themselves: the nobleman in purple velvet, his companion in a stiff brocade bodice, murmuring to him— not tenderly: "Say something, will you? Say something! We look as if we're waiting for the Metro!" The mauve light of the lamps flattens them; they have the black lips and glittering eyes of mulattos, eyes underlined with deep blue.

Another blinding star lights, not far away from them, a grilled enclosure in which, against a Louis XVI salon wall-hanging of striped Pekin silk, two lions and a lioness move about, dazzled and humiliated under so much light. The lioness, crazed, leaps and falls with all her weight on a *film* employee, rolling on him. The man is freed, the grille opened. "Why?" he asks. "She didn't do it out of anger." And he stays in the cage.

Here, one has no sense of the time of day. Under this brilliance, it's impossible to know whether it's light or dark outside. One doesn't know if these people who cross the hall and climb the platforms are coming to work or leaving. Men, many women, not a few children—hurried people, furtive, who go away, tired, carrying a package under their arms, as if they were leaving a dispensary; blonde chorus girls, made up for the music hall that awaits them; a young woman in the scratched boots of an animal trainer; Chinamen, baby-actors who yawn under their knitted shawls; two little-girl-actresses, habitués of the Parisian theater and *"film."* These last have the cool assurance, the lively and experienced eye, the reserve, that are appropriate to their careers. They are resting on a cardboard lawn, and the lioness's leap didn't draw the slightest shriek from them. They are chatting. The younger, who looks eight, is saying to the elder, aged ten to twelve:

"Yes, my dear, this time it's real, I have a contract at the X— Theater . . . it was signed this morning. I'm quite pleased with it, especially with the way it came about. You can imagine, passing an audition like that, just breezing through it, with nothing prepared. . . . Naturally I knew a monologue and a little story, but I only knew them, I didn't *have* them, I hadn't really *explored* them . . . Oh, I would have managed all the same; when one has to manage one always manages. But I wasn't very much at my ease when I went in to see the director. And then, *oh la la!* I shouldn't have worried! Nothing, my dear—he asked for nothing, not a line! I got a contract on my looks, love, my looks alone!"

THE SCOTT EXPEDITION ON FILM

Consulting the programs of the Parisian theaters for the first week of June 1914, we note at the Théâtre Réjane a "cinematographic film," *Toward the South Pole.* But according to Louis Delluc in an article in *Le Film* (June 3, 1918), the spectacle was "foundering in indifference." It was Colette who first noticed and "launched" the work, called sometimes *Toward the South Pole*, sometimes *The Eternal Silence*, sometimes *The Scott Expedition.* Her review appeared in *Le Matin* on June 4, 1914.

In 1910, polar expeditions excited a passionate interest in the public. Striving toward the only still-virgin corners of the globe, they took over where the wars of colonial conquest had left off, but the nationalistic aspect of these enterprises was masked by their "sporting" character. In histories of the cinema, the film of which Colette speaks is attributed to Herbert G. Ponting, who was the cameraman. As such, he accompanied the second Scott expedition. The first polar expedition had taken place between 1901 and 1904; in 1910 Robert Scott tried again—bringing film into the adventure (Gaumont had obtained the exclusive rights to the film)—with the announced intention of being the first to reach the South Pole. He was overtaken by the Norwegian explorer Amundsen, who reached the pole in December 1911, one month before him. On the return journey Scott and his companions perished from hunger, cold, and exhaustion. Near the bodies were discovered not only their expedition diary, which became a Bible of the active life for young Englishmen, but also the films that the explorers had continued to shoot almost to the end. The first films sent back by the expedition had already been shown in London, with considerable success. The tragic ending of the adventure and the successive versions of the film since the macabre discoveries of 1912 impressed the public greatly. The "definitive" film was shown in London in 1913 and in Paris the following year. Its merits are not solely due to its pathetic context, and Georges Sadoul considers that it opened the way for a whole genre, and particularly to Robert Flaherty's *Nanook of the North* (1922).

In two details of this review, Colette suggests the atmosphere of French film of the period. Early in the article, with three film titles she defines the productions of the French cinema: two-thirds frequently painful burlesque, one-third tearful melodrama—on the level of facile tear-jerking or deliberate vulgarity. "Rigadin" was the hero of a series of films—starring a vaudeville actor, Charles Prince—made between 1911 and 1914. At the time, his success was rivaled only by that of Max Linder, but Rigadin's comedy was more frankly trivial.

Another detail emphasizes the inappropriateness of the adjective "silent" as applied to the early cinema. Nothing was less silent than the films of this period. It is generally known that in many theaters the film benefited from a musical accompaniment. But few realize that some films were accompanied by spoken narration, a procedure that Colette seems to think was far superior to intertitling. Her reaction is significant: the monotony of the narration, due no doubt to the routine imposed on the reader, did not detract from the emotive power of the film, which, on the contrary, was intensified by this colorless voice. Note also Colette's allusion to a rose-colored landscape, which probably refers not to the hand-coloring practiced in the films of George Méliès and others, but to the use of dyed films that gave different colors to differing scenes.

When *Rigadin Gets Married*, when *Grandmother Goes to the Beach*, or when a *Kidnapped Child* sets a ravisher with a plaid tie against a stage child with the eyes of an old *rouée*, Paris runs to it, posters shriek it from the walls of every suburb, and the following week, the grateful provinces and foreign countries inherit these "sensational films."

But when Scott and his companions, before perishing at the South Pole, capture for the inhabited world living images, animated portraits of an unknown land, it attracts a bit less attention in Paris than the last visit of a foreign ballet—that is, not much. Still, a spectacle such as the one we saw yesterday honors—should we say rehabilitates?—the cinema, which is in the process of losing our respect. In two too-short hours, the marvel of this age, the cinema, recovers its freshness, its miraculous quality—ceases in short to be merely a tool of vaudeville and grotesque imbroglios. Some day, there will doubtless be no other method of instruction for children and infants than film. Yesterday evening, we found a universal lesson in what we saw. The narrator's colorless voice, untouched by the privations, tortures, agony, of the Scott expedition, read, briefly and coolly, the most beautiful possible resumé of that heroic adventure; but our emotions awakened and grew under that monotonous and convinced voice of the believer, who let fall so frequently the words "Snow . . . lost . . . impassable . . . death . . . honor. . . ." I said our emotions, not our sorrow. So much terrestrial beauty, though it is desolate, enchants us; and so much courage, though defeated in the end, fills us with enthusiasm. And how many seated travelers, chained vagabonds, leaned forward yesterday, like me, toward the salty water, biting and dark, that rocked the blocks of ice split by the prow of the ship! To know how the snow flies at thirty degrees below zero, to touch the fluff of a penguin chick that has just broken its shell, to see the behavior of penguins, their gestures like those of little pot-bellied notaries with short arms, their familial gentleness; the wet and half-frozen velvet that covers the olive-shaped body of the mother seal and her sucking baby; these things belong to us now, they are in us, as is the surprising image of the walrus chipping steps with his teeth in the ice of a glacier . . . We know how the Arctic gull builds her nest and sets her eggs, we have seen her scarcely trembling under the eyes of a man watching her. We will not forget that the innocent beast, the animal that has not yet suffered through man, greets him familiarly, questions him, treats him as an equal, on these shores without beach or land, as if in a harsh earthly Paradise. . . .

The volcano Erebus, whose broken summit not fifty pairs of human eyes have seen, we have the privilege of possessing in purplish rose, its smoke flattened by the polar wind . . . For this rose and black smoke, this menacing and magnificent image, to come to us, men—the same men that we have seen black with cold, their faces peeling—had to set out on a voyage, gripped by a mortal curiosity, by the pride of discoverers. One man had to wait immobile for nine hours in a sack of reindeer skin for the playful walrus to dive, emerge, plunge again and show under the solidified water its beautiful dog's eyes . . . Another had to bury himself under a snowstorm that was covering the birds' nests . . . A third, a fourth, had to raise the tent; melt together the snow, the bouillon, the frozen cocoa; cook the meat for the sled dogs, the dry blood for the ponies . . .

And Scott, with his long, wise, adventurous face, had to ride away from us over the white desert, slowly, his hand on the bridle of his horse, waving—toward whom? toward *us*?—in a last, an inestimable gesture of "Au revoir." He had to perish, along with all those whose crevassed cheeks still laugh on the screen; and by preserving the films, the snapshots, the manuscripts, they were thinking only of *us*—us, their fame, their immortality—until their deaths.

THE CHEAT

This review first appeared in *Excelsior*, August 7, 1916, under the title "Cinema"—a title Colette used several times; to avoid confusion, we have given it the title of its subject. *The Cheat* was directed by Cecil B. De Mille in 1915 from a scenario by Hector Turnbill and starred Fannie Ward, Sessue Hayakawa, Jack Dean, and James Neill. It is a sombre story of a society woman who is branded by a rich Japanese whose mistress she has refused to become; she is avenged by her husband who kills the Japanese and is triumphantly acquitted. This racist subject did not prevent the film from being banned in several American states and from having generally poor success. In Paris, on the contrary, the general public was overwhelmed with enthusiasm, but for dubious reasons. As Louis Delluc said, "No one actually wanted to see anything in it except the Japanese . . . Hardly anyone thought of its absolute cinematic newness." Hardly anyone except Colette, whom Delluc greatly praised for discovering and "launching" *The Cheat*. The film "inspired nothing but pro-Japanese polemic; first, and alone, she proclaimed in the daily press its artistic value" (*Le Film*, June 3, 1918). Like Delluc, Leon Moussinac, Alexandre Arnoux, and Jean Cocteau, she noted its importance in the evolution of the cinema, but she did not go so far as to consider it a masterpiece.

The success of Sessue Hayakawa, whose talents at miming Colette praises here and in "The Friend of Film," was so durable that in 1944 the actor was able to successfully produce his own play based on *The Cheat*; there were, in addition, numerous other remakes of the film, and a lyric work was created at the Opéra-Comique in 1917 on the same subject. Hayakawa pursued a long and brilliant, if uneven, international career in film; among his best-known roles is that of the Japanese commander in David Lean's *Bridge on the River Kwai* (1957). He died in Tokyo, November 24, 1973, at the age of eighty-four.

In 1916, it was not yet clear that America would take over the market for films and the cinematic art; Colette's warning seems like a prophecy. After *The Cheat*, Chaplin, Pearl White, the Western cowboy Rio Jim, Griffith, and Ince were to conquer an empire that had previously been European and particularly French. Her solution, the establishment of classes in film acting, was brought forth in the context of the tireless efforts she had made to persuade her friend and teacher Georges Wague—the Brague of *The Vagabond*—to set up a pantomime class at the Conservatoire. Several months before this article appeared, in January 1916, her efforts had succeeded, and it is interesting to note that when she speaks here of training the cinema actor, she emphasizes the importance of mime. Wague's pantomime class was to become in 1933 a class in posture and in theatrical and cinematic mime. It is possibly due to counsel such as Colette's that in 1918 *Excelsior* announced the creation at the Conservatoire of two professorships of cinema.

Note Colette's early interest in filmic fashions, set design, and props, which were to receive fuller treatment in "Film and Fashion" and "A Short Manual for the Aspiring Scenario Writer," and her reference to the routinization of film music, of which the frenetic repetition of the same few musical phrases in the sound versions of old comedies can give us some idea.

In Paris this week, a movie theater has become an art school. A film and two of its principal actors are showing us what surprising innovations, what emotion, what natural and well-designed lighting can add to cinematic fiction. Every evening, writers, painters, composers, and dramatists come and come again to sit, contemplate, and comment, in low voices, like pupils.

To the genius of an Oriental actor is added that of a director probably without equal; the heroine of the piece—vital, luminous, intelligent—almost completely escapes any sins of theatrical brusqueness or excess. There is a beautiful luxuriating in lace, silk, furs—not to mention the expanses of skin and the tangle of limbs in the final melee, in which the principals hurl themselves unrestrainedly against each other. We cry "Miracle!"; not only do we have millionaires who don't look as if they've rented their tuxedoes by the week, but we also have characters on screen who are followed by their own shadows, their actual shadows, tragic or grotesque, of which until now the useless multiplicity of arc lamps has robbed us. A monochrome drapery, a sparkling bibelot, are enough to give us the impression of established and solid luxury. In an elegant interior there is no sign (is it possible?) of either a silk-quilted bed in the middle of the room or of a carved sideboard.

Since our French studios don't hesitate to lay on special trains, hire crowds, dam rivers and interrupt railroad service, buy villas and dynamite ships, I wish their magnificence would extend to furniture, women's dresses, men's clothing, to accessories that are stylish, complete, and irreproachable, to everything that the assiduity of the public has given it the right to demand.

Is it only a combination of felicitous effects that brings us to this film and keeps us there? Or is it the more profound and less clear pleasure of seeing the crude "ciné" groping toward perfection, the pleasure of divining what the future of the cinema must be when its makers will want that future, when its music will finally become its inevitable, irresistible collaborator, its interpreter; when the same slow waltz or the same comic-opera overture will no longer accompany, and impartially betray, a tragedy, a love duet, and an attempted murder?

Is wartime not the time, you think, for these frivolities? I disagree. America is building conservatories solely for cinema actors, who will study in them for two years. French commerce, French art, the French economy itself, will have something to worry about and suffer from after the war because of the progress the American cinema is making. Here as elsewhere, a special art of acting, the secret of onscreen walking, onscreen dancing, must inevitably be taught to classes of young actors.

I offer these young actors, as their first model, this Asiatic artist whose powerful immobility is eloquence itself. Let our aspiring ciné-actors go to see how, when his face is mute, his hand carries on the flow of his thought. Let them take to heart the menace and disdain in a motion of his eyebrow and how, in the instant when he is wounded, he creates the impression that his life is running out with his blood, without shuddering, without convulsively grimacing, with merely the progressive petrifaction of his Buddha's mask and the ecstatic darkening of his eyes.

CIVILIZATION

This is Colette's first article for *Le Film*, for which she wrote only from May 28 to July 21, 1917. It was not Louis Delluc but Henri Diamant-Berger who introduced her to *Le Film*, the magazine with which Delluc would be so closely associated; he joined it after her, but became almost immediately its editor-in-chief (July 1917) and succeeded her when she abandoned the "Criticism of Films" column. In the beginning of 1917, Colette had spent several weeks in Rome for the filming of *The Vagabond* with the actress Musidora; she describes this in "Backstage at the Studio."

Her criticism of Thomas H. Ince's *Civilization* appeared May 28th in *Le Film* and was republished shortly after in *Filma* (in the issue of June 15–30, 1917) as part of a collection of articles on the American director. In May and June of 1917 *Civilization* was obviously the "film of the year" in France, due to the recent entry, in April 1917, of the United States into the war. For its presentation in Paris, the original pacifist film was given a warlike slant. Indeed, the editing was even manipulated to aid the change, as Colette's initial surprise at seeing new and different sequences testifies. Today, in spite of the furor it created on its first release, *Civilization* has aged terribly, although historians agree that it exercised some influence over the work of, for instance, Abel Gance. The film depended on a naive acting-out of symbolism and allegory, which was that of the painting and sculpture of the time; Colette grasped perfectly the ludicrousness of this procedure and understood that the true interest of the film lay rather in its realistic scenes and the visual power of its evocation of the horrors of war. The torpedoing of the ocean liner, which Colette singles out, contains an extraordinary and still gripping early use of fast cutting.

Civilization (1916) was directed by Ince, assisted by Raymond B. West, Reginald Barker, Scott Sidney, John Parker Read; scenario— C. Gardner Sullivan; photography—Clyde de Vinna, Irwin Willat, and Robert Newhart; sets—Robert Brunton; music—Victor Schertzinger; actors—Charles French, Enid Markey, Frank Burke, Lola May, Howard Hickman, Hershell Mayall, George Fisher; a Triangle production. The Vitagraph film *The Battle Cry of Peace* (1915) was directed by J. Stuart Blackton and starred Norma Talmadge; a pro-war propaganda film, it hypothesized that after winning in Europe the Germans invaded North America, where German troops committed the worst possible atrocities. Its spectacular effects (New York bombarded by the German fleet, skyscrapers tumbling under the shelling) and its prowar stance made it a sensation in America.

I saw *Civilization* for the first time three weeks ago in Rome. Here in Paris I looked in vain for certain scenes that have been cut in deference to French taste. In their place, we have been given a stirring parade of the allied armies and the portrait of Marshal Joffre. After all, why not? It's becoming general practice to accommodate films to the suggestions and desires, sometimes judicious, of foreign distributors. Three different endings are not too many for the same scenario. "Leave out the adultery for the English,"they counsel. "Beef up the death scene for Italy, and let's not forget a little nudity for Russia!"

Will the film of tomorrow be a sort of Esperanto, as intelligible to the Eskimo as to the Argentinian, or will it be necessary to make an unhappy love story for Italy and Spain, an action film for New York, a sugary vaudeville for Rio de Janeiro? We will return to this point.

Civilization, like *The Battle Cry of Peace*, has the merits and defects of a big American film. That is to say, in the course of two kilometers of excellent shots you will find the unexpected side by side with the unoriginal, the most naive trick photography superimposed on a sumptuous and novel effort of set design. Delicious details abound—a chubby baby barely able to walk but already holding down a role, a dialogue between a performing dog and a little girl—because there's everything and there's too much.

A wealth of minor actors, each of whom in his or her moment is equal to a great artist; mediocre major actors, with the exception of the inventor of submarines, that *illuminatus* weighed down with crime, whom a tardy Grace touches and who dies as an apostle of peace. Why should I tell you the plot? You already know that it has to do with a menacing Kaiser, a menaced nation, a war and a peace. Mysticism, with all its risks and perils, plays a very large role. It is not my business to discuss its Protestant artlessness, which puts symbolism within the reach of the smallest child; this is not the time to use the screen as a religious battlefield. I regret only the manifest tangibility of a handsome Christ who converses, in all simplicity, with a fat Kaiser-Pilate in front of a Book of Reckoning, while Hate, a robust, chained being, writhes at their feet.

I will admit I gave more attention to the tableaus in which the Americans are past masters: the scenes of crowds, bombardments, and battles. A people that imagines war so intensely is worthy of living it, at our side. There are a hundred scenes that one could not praise more highly. One particular cavalry charge, flying on clouds of dust and smoke, surpasses our most winged imagination. Explosions of undersea mines, ambulances blown up, famine, clinging mud—nothing is forgotten in the breathtaking and no doubt salutary assembly of all the horrors of war. Frenetic cuts—sixty a minute, at certain moments—strive to, indeed do, give us an impression of tumult, earthquake, and ubiquity. He is an artist—whoever he is—who composed groups like the miserable mother clutching her three children, while there parades before her an invisible army whose shadows, helmets, and obliquely-pointed bayonets stripe her trembling knees with shadow.

You must see the torpedoing of the liner, a tableau of minute and veridical horror, in which the sinking ship appallingly empties its lifeboats, too heavily laden with women and children, into the blue and black agitation of a sea where pale heads swim, struggle, and disappear, heads with soaked, slick hair, hands that claw at sky and water.

Let us leave all these unpleasantries and note, to smile at it, that the finish of *Civilization* shows us a Kaiser who repents. Who repents! The American sense of humor is not dead, after all.

THE DESPOILER

Another anti-German propaganda film, directed in 1915 by Thomas H. Ince and Reginald Barker, with Charles French, Enid Markey, Hershall Mayall, Robert McKim, J. P. Lockney, and John Gilbert; photography —Clyde de Vinna; scenario—J. G. Hawks.

A German colonel (whew!) gives his Kurdish troops the chance to (can I say it?) pillage a convent. But by a strange coincidence (you guessed it), his only daughter has taken refuge in that very convent. The Kurdish chieftain rapes her. Has she suffered enough? You think so? Not at all. She kills the satiated Kurd, and when her father arrives at (I hardly dare say it) the pillaged convent, roaring, "Who has killed my faithful Kurd?" she covers her head with a veil and accuses herself, solely so that her father can say, without recognizing her, "Have that woman shot!" So it goes; and the makers of this film intend us to think that the punishment is the father's.

This Germano-Kurdish *fait divers* includes good photography, attractive crowd scenes, and some close-ups designed to produce inappropriate laughter in the public—see the "indecent lust" (*sic*) of the Kurd for the young girl, and the nun who sedulously spies on said indecent lust. As for the young girl, in my opinion she justifies neither indecency nor lust.

MATER DOLOROSA

In 1917 Abel Gance had already made fifteen films, including the experimental *Folie du Docteur Tube* (*Dr. Tube's Madness*, 1916), but his great films were still to come—*J'Accuse* (*I Accuse*, 1918), *La Roue* (*The Wheel*, 1923), and *Napoléon* (1925–1927). *Mater Dolorosa* was his first big success—"the most popular French film in 1917–1918,"

according to René Jeanne and Charles Ford; indeed, it was so successful that Gance proposed a sound version fifteen years later. Today one
finds it hard to understand the grounds for that success, so painfully
bad is the scenario, which centers around the blackmail practiced by a
jealous husband on a formerly guilty wife—he takes their baby from
her to make her confess and name her accomplice. "One trembles,"
film historians Maurice Bardèche and Robert Brasillach say, "to think
that a betrayed doctor would not save his child so as to punish its mother,
whom he believes unfaithful; and the whole floats in a sea of images so
ridiculous as to attain the grandiose." We must admit that the public
of the time took a lively pleasure in such pathos. But one can explain
Colette's admiration only in the same terms as for *The Cheat*—because
of the new and vivid language of the film. Her judgment is corroborated
by Delluc's, who praised *Mater Dolorosa* for remarkable "effects of
chiaroscuro which bring out the play of the physiognomy." Note also
the reference to Henri Le Sidaner (1862–1939), who specialized in
paintings with twilight effects.

    Mater Dolorosa (1917): direction, scenario—Abel Gance; photog-
raphy—L. H. Burel; starring—Emmy Lynn, Firmin Gémier, Armand
Tallier, Gaston Modot. In the 1932 remake, Roger Hubert was the
director of photography, and Line Noro, Jean Galland, Samson Fain-
silber, and Antonin Artaud starred.

    This review first appeared in *Le Film*, June 4, 1917.

After sessions in the Italian cinemas, seeing *Mater Dolorosa*
here is a not insignificant pleasure. May this film quickly
traverse the Alps, to combat among the great producers of our
friendly ally the scorn in which our French productions are now
held! For four months I have been seeing what France gives the
Roman filmmakers. I closed my ears to the words like "boycott,
inertia, clumsiness, parsimony" that were hurled at us; I
would also have liked to close my eyes to our films. I sighed
with boredom and even with humiliation. Vaudeville with stories
from the Bibliothèque Rose; comic films that inspired tears;
dramas in which the censor tolerated, heaven knows why, a
classic pimp inspiring and guiding a young lady in a short dress
and long stockings; "new" films that had been kept in storage
for three or four years and that hadn't benefited from it; everything including those very Parisian idylls filmed in that lovely

—and vertical—light of the Midi, that would change blonde Venus into a Hottentot.

"What's the use? One might as well let them go on . . ." I would be the last to agree. Let us send beyond the sea and the mountains films like *Mater Dolorosa*. Here, the coordinated result of two efforts, the interpreters' and the director's, appears in its full beauty. It is thanks to that effort that we forget that Gémier, with his narrow mouth and his light, narrow eyes, is utterly unphotogenic. The screen, cruel to fading beauty, is also capable of betraying the best talents. Some hand has given Gémier help here, turning his face toward the most favorable light, using close-ups not as one would play with binoculars but to underline a paternal smile, a wrinkle of masculine sorrow. It is the same hand that groups, brings closer, disentangles the three actors of the intimate drama: the husband, the suspected wife (Emmy Lynn), and the child. Gémier—I should say the husband—has been reproached for the inflexible rigor with which he separates, in order to make her confess, a young mother from her child. The film gains, all the same, from Emmy Lynn's lovely tears and from the child's scenes, which one can hardly resist. And I applaud a new use of the "still life," the touching use of props, as in the fall of the veil on the floor. We will eventually succeed in creating significant decor, sets full of undertones, an agreeable anxiety suggested, at the right moment, by a shot of a scene without actors. An empty chair at the bottom of the garden, a rose abandoned on a deserted table—did the great painter Le Sidaner need any more to hold us, dreaming, in front of a little table? I know very well that's Le Sidaner. But have patience. The miracle of cinematography is in young hands, astonished hands, hands often inept, erring, paralyzed with routine. Patience!

While we're waiting, let us praise *Mater Dolorosa*. Let us praise Emmy Lynn, exhausted young mother, who surpasses everything she promised us in the theater. Agree with me, since I take so much pleasure in it, that the action progresses in scenes lit with a rare richness—gilded whites, sooty and profound blacks. And my memory also retains certain somber close-ups in which the speaking, suppliant head of Emmy Lynn floats like a decapitated flower.

THREE REVIEWS

The following three reviews—*Femmes de France*, *L'Étrangère*, and *Maciste alpin*—first appeared in *Le Film* on June 18, 1917. *Women of France* was directed by Albert Capellani and starred Clara Kimball Young and the director's brother, Paul Capellani. Capellani, after having figured as one of the pioneers of French cinema, left for America in 1914, where, as Colette presages, he was eventually swallowed up by the studios.

Women of France

While we in France are forcing ourselves toward the "American-style" film, Monsieur Capellani, in America, is devoting himself to directing a film he calls *Women of France*. It doesn't seem to me that being overseas has given him a taste for daring and original experiments or freed him from theatrical tradition.

The Women of France—why the plural?—are Clara Kimball Young, adorned with a bright smile and a bourgeois charm. Thirty-five hundred feet of bourgeois charm is a lot, even with the help of Capellani and a young American actor who is both very talented and a careful observer. It's long, this melange of military current events and boorish sentimentality. "Boorish" is an extreme word; but what is one to think about a famous Spanish surgeon who, out of jealousy, intercepts the correspondence between an engaged couple, forges fragments of letters, and kidnaps the credulous fiancée, while her husband-to-be has gone to close the eyes of his dying father? Find me many surgeons who would be capable of doing as much, even famous ones, even Spaniards.

And moreover, I hardly like it that the Woman of France, as proposed to the Americans, is so stupid as not to consider the existence of telegraphs and railroads in order to rejoin her fiancé when he absents himself the night before their marriage —and, later, so feather-headed as to consent to fly to neutral skies and the arms of an Andalusian surgeon.

Purely theatrical artifices, an unnecessary art-school, a superfluous little model, a thief who has nothing to do with the action, the false identity of the young wife-nurse, drag out an intrigue on which I am wasting time, since I can find nothing to say about honest directing.

An advertisement a good yard square, illustrated with photographs, that tells us the story, does not neglect to bring to our attention that "by using two copies of this, one underneath the other, you will get a handsome poster-photo" (sic). And, of course, the heroes of the film "leave to go to" London, "leave to go to" Paris, as it has become customary to say in all French films and also in the big daily papers.

The Stranger

Thirty-five hundred feet of film, sixteen pages of advertising on handsome glazed paper; a loss of money, a waste of time, I don't add—for obvious reasons—a waste of talent . . .

Maciste the Alpinist

Although he hardly figures in the histories of cinema, the character of Maciste holds an important place in the history of the popular film— so important that after a half-century of existence, he still appears on the European screen as a hero of "costume drama." A variant of Hercules or Tarzan, Maciste does not come from literature but belongs entirely to the screen. In Pastrone's monumental film *Cabiria* (1914), he makes his first appearance as a Roman slave accomplishing prodigious feats of strength. The character, incarnated by an athletic Genoese docker named Bartolomeo Pagano, had a success so dazzling that it brought him autonomy. Maciste became the hero of a long series of adventure films, all starring Pagano: *Maciste the Light Infantryman, Maciste on Vacation, Maciste in Love, Maciste's Revenge*, and so on. Most of these were made by Guido Brignone, as is the case with *Maciste the Alpinist*. For obvious reasons, the Maciste adventure chosen for French screens in 1917 was as warlike as possible; but this detracts nothing from the mythic power of this cinematic type, whose fame rivaled that of Judex or Rio Jim and whose longevity is unequaled.

Christus was among the films that enjoyed an extraordinary vogue during the First World War, belonging to what one might call the Catholic or rather the Evangelical vein that was flourishing in France (Zecca's *The Passion*, 1914), in America (Ince's *Civilization*, for which see above), and especially in Italy, with *Quo Vadis, The Last Days of*

Pompeii, Fabiola, and others. Rumor had it that in the middle of the war, the Vatican smuggled through Switzerland to Germany a copy of *Christus.* The film was made in 1914 by Guido Antamoro from a poem by Fausto Salvatore, "Il Canto della Agonia," and starred Alberto Pasquali (Jesus), Amleto Novelli (Pilate), Mastripieti (Judas), and Leda Gys (Mary).

Jean Daragon was the second husband of Marguerite Moreno, Colette's great friend; Carso (or Karst) is a natural plateau, not far from Trieste, on the frontier between Italy and Yugoslavia. It was one of the principal theaters of operation of the Italian army in 1916–1917.

Maciste, Italian Alpine soldier, this time places in the service of his country his good-giant's torso, his arms that rock cannon redoubts, and his jaw muscles that can bend iron. This ogre, who wouldn't harm a fly, saves women and children, uproots trees, knocks down a horse with the flat of his hand, and ties Austrians in bunches of four or five and brings them back to camp, a little like a housewife bringing home the leeks. The day in which his heroic adventures have Carso or Trentino as their theater will make the fame of this superb Maciste complete.

While we wait, we must congratulate Italy for discovering and developing a type, a force. Maciste will evolve on screen, both diverse and resembling himself, just as a robust musical theme renews itself in a hundred variations.

The direction, the choice of locations, the easy trickery of the feats of strength and collective acrobatics leave nothing to be desired, and a thousand grown-up persons were amusing themselves like children. We heard in the theater murmurs of "Terrific!" "Well done!" and even, from the women, "Isn't he handsome!"

A female observer—age eighteen, with needle-pricked fingers and dewy eyelids—added Sunday night: "From the back Maciste is Sacha Guitry, only better, but when he's fooling around, you would think he's Jean Daragon."

A difficult spectator, that same evening, found *Maciste* a bit light to follow *Christus.* "At least agree," said his neighbor, "that the ending suits the public better."

And let me also quote to you this dialogue between a young woman and her boyfriend, who was enthusiastically taking her to see *Christus:*

"You'll see," he said to her, "you'll see when Judas is about to embrace Jesus and . . ."

"No, no," begged the young woman, "don't tell me! Don't tell me! I don't want to know how it ends!"

FILM AND FASHION

This review, which appeared on June 25, 1917, in *Le Film*, is a first sketch for the following year's "Short Manual for an Aspiring Scenario Writer." Fresh from her Italian stay during the filming of *The Vagabond*, from which she had returned at the end of April or beginning of May, Colette is full of memories of Roman movie theaters, of filming, and of her very recent discovery of the powerlessness of the author who is present during the filming of her work.

Among the current news of her Italian trip is her enumeration of the most celebrated Italian and French actresses of the moment. Of Colette's little list, only Mistinguett and Fannie Ward, who get off relatively easily, did not work in Italy as "divas"—not yet called "stars" since America was only beginning to make its influence felt. The least known is Vittoria Lepanto, of whom Colette would speak again on July 21; she was part of the *Film d'Arte Italiano*, founded in Rome in 1909 by Charles Pathé to fight his Italian rivals. Francesca Bertini, who between 1911 and 1921 was the most glorious of the "divas," had made her debut in the same company; it is hard today to imagine her celebrity, but Delluc himself praised her lavishly in *Cinema and Company*: "Only in years to come will it be known how necessary it is to study the complete work of Francesca Bertini." Posterity has not supported his predictions; rather, the few films saved from that period seem ridiculous, and the "divas'" acting insupportable.

Between 1913 and 1925 Pina Menichelli was the Italian answer to the vamp. Her provocative personality—her posters advertised her as "born for films of insatiable and cruel love"—is well-defined by several of the titles of her films: *The Demon in the House, Royal Tigress, Vanquished Furies*, etc. Diana Karenne did not reach the same heights, but had a long and brilliant stardom as the elegant great lady, noblewoman, or queen of many a European film; for a time she had her own production company. Mistinguett started her career in the music hall, then was engaged by Albert Capellani for the *Societé Cinématographique des Auteurs et Gens de Lettres* (SCAGL), "The Filmic Society of Authors and Men of Letters," founded by Pathé, where she acted in realist dramas, melodramas, comic films in which she was sometimes associated with her young music-hall partner, Maurice Chevalier, and even in adaptations of classic books (*Les Misérables*, Capellani, 1914). The American actress in *The Typhoon* (Ince, 1914) is probably Gladys Brockwell; though made before *The Cheat*, *The Typhoon* was released in Paris after the success of the later film.

Musidora was both Colette's close friend ("my little Musi") and her first screen interpreter; she is better known for having been, before her Roman period, the famous actress of Louis Feuillade's *Vampires* (1915) and *Judex* (1916). The Surrealists avowed great admiration for her because of her work for Feuillade (see their play written for her, *Le Trésor des Jesuites*, in the special Surrealist number of *Variétés*, June 1929). The celebrated silhouette in the black leotard, source of so much scandal and so many dreams, was born Jeanne Roques in 1889, took her pseudonym from a poem by Théophile Gautier, directed films, and after leaving film in 1926 was a journalist and, from 1944 onward, a historical researcher for the Cinémathèque Française; she died in 1959.

Four months ago, in a Roman cinema, I was following with interest a dramatic film. Two sisters loved the same man; one confessed to the other, the second kept silent. And when the silent one went off, carrying a double secret, the public noticed that she had an X in black velvet ribbon across her fanny. Farewell dramatic atmosphere, farewell all curiosity about the ending; the bizarre and absurd detail of a dress design swept all before it, and the hearty Italian laugh burst out . . .

This unexpected comedy, which bubbles from a fantasy of eccentric or merely marginal style, has the power to destroy authors, directors, actors in the cinema. I have heard them groan or get angry, without looking for the remedy. For every Francesca Bertini, faithful to long and simple drapery, how many Vittoria Lepantos there are, embroidered with bats and topped with unbelievable chapeaux! Pina Menichelli gives shelter to brooms of white heron feathers, and the elegant Diana Karenne herself does not entirely avoid birds of paradise, though Mistinguett happily limits herself on the screen to straight dresses. Fannie Ward will before long regret the ruffles that suit her original style. Look at the American woman who plays opposite Sessue Hayakawa in *The Typhoon*; listen to the laughter at her hats and her hobble skirts. And do you think that Musidora—aside from the documentary quality she may find in it—will take very much pleasure, next year, in a particular scene in which the Vagabond appears in a barrel skirt and an Empress Eugénie bodice?

I am surprised that the cinema—"still young, already cumbered with routine, and badly served by unworthy partisans," according to the excellent phrase of Henri Diamant-Berger—has not yet found, or created, its own fashions. What a career, what success, and what pleasure will reward the first intelligent designer who wants to "dress the screen"! He will be required to have the talents of a painter, a sculptor; he will have to play with a master hand over the keyboard of tonal values. He will have to assure the future of a modern comedy by saving it from the ridiculous *derniers cris* of fashion; he will have to, at need, prevent Madame Tallien from parading under the wig of Madame de Sévigné. He will have to search out the beautiful fold, the weave that catches the light, the obedient drapery, the silken slash, the embroidery with visible design. He will have to lengthen the short bust of Mme. Such-and so, employ as well as possible Miss Someone-else's good legs . . . Thanks to him, perhaps, will we one day perhaps see a millionaires' ball in which the elegance has not been rented at five francs a day and there are no laced boots? Will this intelligent couturier contribute to the education of cinema—this *nouveau riche*, simultaneously lavish and miserly, which pays for autos and special trains for its actors but refuses them clothes and presentable shoes? I call the couturier to the rescue because the author's authority, alas! does not have any weight, as you may see in dialogues like this one, between the director and his principal actress:

"Miss X, you'll wear the pink tulle for the scene in which you pick peonies in the garden and give the pigeons grain."

"But, monsieur, that's an evening dress, very low and sleeveless."

"Who cares! It's the one that looks best against the dark leaves. And then, for the dinner, the dinner during which you break with your husband, the black dress with the train and jet beads."

"But, monsieur, why, when my husband is wearing auto clothes?"

"What's the diff? The light gray of the jacket against your

black velvet—it's stunning! Don't worry your head about it; just do your work; as for me, I'm creating Art."

I don't invent; I quote.

Up to now, designers, furriers, stylists, have only used the screen as a means of advertising, an incomparable one at that. I'm not against them continuing to look there for a guaranteed profit. But the time has come for one of them to put forth his full efforts for the screen, to leave his small seasonal ambitions and raise his "creations" to the level of a discovery.

SHOULD WOMAN FORGIVE?

La femme doit-elle pardonner? first appeared in *Le Film*, July 2, 1917, with *"Comment Allez-Vous?"*

Should Woman Forgive? when her husband, having encountered one of those "creatures of luxury and ecstasy" who sing "Tipperary" in music halls, starts off by sleeping out on Christmas Eve, disdaining the joys of Christmas and the Christmas tree, then goes on and borrows fifty thousand francs from his wife to finance the theater where the creature is going to make her debut? More than one Parisienne, well-versed in disguising cruel domestic drama as light vaudeville, would answer the sorrowing Madame Holmes, who tardily stretches out a hesitant hand to her husband, already en route on the long and too well known voyage of rehabilitation:

"Yes, of course, madame, pardon him. Pardon him, and above all make no scenes, especially because he has put himself in the wrong. The creature-of-luxury-and-ecstasy has just died, hit by a stray revolver bullet; Providence does these things—in the cinema. Pardon him, and no complaints! But get out of the habit of telling your mother everything. And then take care of your toilette, pay attention to what you wear in the mornings! And stop crying like that when your husband spends a night out. Spare one sorrowful thought for the creature-of-luxury-and-ecstasy and regret her death, since it's highly improbable that your husband would have long been fascinated by a lady who poured Ylang-Ylang, White Heliotrope, and Chanel No. 5 in her tea, and who showed a very uncertain taste in her choice of dress . . ."

I'll add, on my own account, that this American film—with good camerawork, sometimes arbitrary lighting—would gain from cuts and some reworking of the text. The subtitles of films certainly need to be taken in hand by some literary man who has lost his literary ambitions, or some journalist exiled from an important editorial post.

HOW ARE YOU?

A comic film in which there is an idea—hardly worth mentioning, you think? A macabre idea? Not at all. It would be, if this young man, who has been given only six days to live by a misdelivered diagnosis, really did die from the incurable disease from which an old neighbor is suffering, a disease which a skillful anatomist intends to study, an anatomist so taken with his art that he pays six hundred dollars in ready cash for the young man's remains (I thought I wasn't ever going to get free of that sentence!). But, since the young man is as healthy as you or I, and since in spite of the funereal solicitude of the anatomist—"How Are You?"—he gets married at the end, let me have my innocent amusement at this little story in which there is neither adultery, nor ravished women, nor an inventor whose discovery has been stolen from him, nor a kidnapped child, and which allows itself the singular luxury of being acted by neither Charlie Chaplin nor Mabel Normand nor by Him—oh restful charm of unknown faces!—but by happy young people who are not identified.

HER HERO

Son Héros and *L'Ami du Ciné* first appeared July 9, 1917, in *Le Film*.

Her Hero, by golly, is the man with the fists, because she is blonde, fragile, and capricious, and because her husband spends his time playing poker at his club. The hero's fists defend her from several of the dangers that prey on leisure—morphine, literature; and then, with an imperious and sweet force, that famous fist draws to the "hero's" heart the frail, blonde, and capricious young woman. Be reassured; it so happens that the hero is an honest man. He tears himself, just in time, from the lips of the frail, blonde, etc. and sends her back to the repentant gambler.

To hear it told so briefly, you might think that this story is blonde, frail, etc. Give the scenario to an American director and he will wring from it a sentimental drama in four reels and 3600 feet. *Her Hero* contents itself with about three reels and an irony that is not afraid of being comic. Different temperaments and different latitudes . . . No doubt because of the coming dog days I feel enormously grateful for what is called the French lack of seriousness.

The three characters in *Her Hero* live their lives, from beginning to end of the film, in "interiors," and it is a rather attractive tour de force to have given the decors and the lighting a diversity that pleases the eye. I emphasize the lighting (which recalls that of *Mater Dolorosa*), because, with the greatest possible ingratitude, I am about to reproach it with its very richness and ingenuity. Films d'Art, if from the expository sequences onward, from the antechambers and the boudoir where Madame is dressing, you indulge yourselves in these virtuoso plays of light, what can you do for a *crescendo*? And with this luxurious waste of hot whites and sooty blacks spilled over the calmest scenes, don't you risk impoverishing those moments when everything—light and shadow, music and silence—should work together to conquer the spectator?

THE FRIEND OF FILM

This is Colette's second excursion outside film review, after "Film and Fashion." This time, she goes back to a style of writing which is dear to her and at which she excels, the dialogue sketch.

In *Excelsior*, August 28, 1917, there is an announcement that "the film *The Cheat* is about to be staged" and that André de Lorde and Paul Milliet had written a music drama based on it, for which Camille Erlanger had written the music. The work was in fact given in 1921 at the Opéra-Comique, but it did not have the success its promoters had wished. "The Friend of Film" suggests that the principal roles could be filled by Mary Garden and Jean Périer, that is to say, by the creators, fifteen years earlier (1902), of Debussy's *Pelléas et Mélisande*. In fact, the roles of the musical drama *The Cheat* were played by Vanni-Marcoux and Marguerite Carré. Colette's energy is evidently being expended here on a marginal and futile subject. But her teasing dialogue permits us to measure again the extraordinary ebullition produced in France by De Mille's film. It is not without reason that historians of the screen consider this film, whatever its merits, as a decisive date in the esthetic evolution of the cinema.

They tell me the thing is decided: *The Cheat* is going to be made into an opera. The news was given me by one of those "friends of film" whose enthusiasm crushes me and whose conversation temporarily deprives me of any taste for cinema. I let him, with a combination of treachery and discouragement, declaim his joy at what he called "the latest conquest of the filmic art!"

"An opera? Really? Tell me about it."

"Exactly, an opera! Everything for film, everything through film; film as means, as end, and as example! And, you know, a great composer of the new school is writing the music. What a splendid drama!"

"And who will play it? Have they already found people worthy of taking over for Hayakawa and Fannie Ward?"

"Ah . . . that's the difficulty. What do you think of Mary Garden for the role played by Fannie Ward?"

"Mary Garden would be fine. And the Japanese?"

The friend of film leaned forward, with an anxious face:

"The Japanese, the Japanese . . ."

He looked at me steadily.

"It's strange," he said, "the Japanese . . . I don't conceive of that role, you understand, as being sung. Or let's say there'd be very little singing. One would need a great artist capable of mime. Gesture, stage presence . . . Very little voice. No vocal effects, no melodic phrases. Everything in *recitative*. But silence, you understand, above all, silence. Jean Périer, perhaps . . ."

"Of course. Besides"—I insinuated with a poisonous sweetness—"really, the Japanese has nothing to say in the story."

"That's quite right. My opinion exactly. He has nothing to say. The fist, the glare, that's the whole role. I see so clearly what's needed. I can see it as if I were there."

"I think you were there. Wait, one moment, I have an idea. Supposing that the Japanese, in your opera, were made evil, seductive, and . . . mute?"

"Mute?"

"Mute. As mute as a screen. He could, by mime, make himself understood just as easily—perhaps better—and then . . ."

"I've got it, I've got it!" the friend of film cried. "We'll get Hayakawa to create the role in the opera!"

"I hoped you'd say that."

"Magnificent! Magnificent! That takes a weight off me . . . It's foolish, perhaps, but the idea of hearing the role of the Japanese sung . . . and even that of the woman, if it comes to that, in the great scene, the struggle between Fannie Ward and Hayakawa, I can't yet imagine how they would exchange the lines 'Be mine!' 'No, never!' 'You swore it!' 'Pity, pity! oh, the villain—!' and so on."

"I share your apprehension. One could, though, get around the difficulty with those cries . . ."

"How?"

"One could arrange, for example, a silent scene, very rapid, in the style of that lovely scene in the film . . ."

"Of course . . ."

". . . and since the scene would be silent, there wouldn't be any difficulty in having it played by Fannie Ward . . ."

On my interlocutor's face appeared signs of suspicion. I hastily continued:

"And in the same fashion, for several essential scenes that it would be hard to bring on stage—the tragic crossing of the Japanese gardens, the shadow scenes through the paper walls, the telephone conversations—the logic of the drama, and veracity, would suggest that we bring into the opera . . . oh, very little, four hundred feet of the original film, five hundred, more if necessary . . . Oh! my goodness, since one were going that far, why stop, rather than . . ."

But I had gone too far. The friend of film must have suspected that my gravity masked a complete lack of good faith, and he dropped the conversation there. For the true friend of film, when given a successful film, doesn't rest until he has transformed it into a bad play, an ankylosed opera, or a dislocated pantomime-ballet.

THEY'RE ALL GOING TO THE CINEMA

After this review, published in *Le Film*, July 21, 1917, Colette resigned, to be succeeded by Louis Delluc. In the next issue of *Le Film*, under the signature of "The Woman from Nowhere," appeared a series of sketches in her manner; they are markedly inferior to work signed by her, and we have chosen not to reprint them here. Nothing in this review announces the end of her collaboration with editor Henri Diamant-Berger; all the same, this final piece of film criticism is longer and more elaborate than the preceding ones, and once again, Colette succumbs to the temptation to escape from simply reviewing films.

The first section concerns a boulevard revue put on at the Ambigu and entitled *Ils y Viennent Tous, au Cinéma* (*They're All Going to the Cinema*). This formula-phrase had been used in an advertising poster that for a long time had covered the walls of Paris as part of a campaign carried on for several years by the first large film companies; see, for example, the often-reproduced Pathé poster "They All Bring Their Children," which shows world-renowned figures of 1909 (Fallières, the Tsar, the Kaiser, the King of Belgium, the King of England), accompanied by their progeny, watching their own image on the screen. The revue itself was authored by André Heuzé, Gaston Secrétan, and Henri Diamant-Berger (which perhaps explains why it received such extensive notice in *Le Film*). It starred all the celebrities of the era—Mayol, Huguette Duflos, Mistinguett, Chevalier, Gabriel Signoret and Jeanne Renouardt (as Pierrot and Columbine), and finally André de Lorde, the "Prince of Terrors," so-called because he was, and would continue to be for another quarter of a century, the chief provider of Grand Guignol in horror drama. Like the project of turning *The Cheat* into an opera, this cinema revue demonstrates both the increasing audience for the cinema and its new stature; from here on it would be pillaged, be imitated, and become a source of inspiration.

The *Mysteries* and *Vampires* to which Colette refers are Louis Gasnier's serial *Mystères de New York** (1915), starring Pearl White, and Louis Feuillade's famous *Vampires* (1915–16), another serial, already referred to in "Film and Fashion."

Émile Vuillermoz is known today as a composer, music critic and

---

* *The Clutching Hand* and *The Exploits of Elaine.*

historian of music. However, in late 1918, he was to initiate a column of
film criticism in *Le Temps*, which would be a regular feature of that
paper until 1939. Colette's allusion proves that in 1917 he was already
known as an ardent defender of film, on behalf of which he would war
in numerous periodicals. The essential portion of his ideas about film
appears in the third volume of the collection *L'Art Cinématographique*
(*The Art of the Cinema*), published by Alcan in 1927, under the title
La Musique des Images (*The Music of Images*). He develops the thesis,
referred to here by Colette, of a parallelism between musical rhythm
and the rhythm of projected images: "A cinegraphist must know how
to write on the screen melodies meant for the eye."

Comparison between theater and the film has long been a favorite
sport of people of letters. With certain nuances—"a robust and capricious *offshoot*"—Colette saw film as a new development of the theatrical
art.

A cinematic revue? I don't see any problem, and more than
one advantage. Already revues, undifferentiated, have borrowed
from the films; *Vampires* and *Mysteries* in flesh and blood have
played hide-and-seek on the stage with their doubles on the
screen. Every week at the cinema brings us a little "revue" of
the news. Lloyd George and Viviani, Wilson and the bemedaled
nurses, the glorious "aces" of aviation, file past on the screen
to the sound of national anthems; from there to seeing them
wink toward the audience with a slightly more confidential air
or to hearing them detail for us, through the medium of a narrator drowned in shadow, the *Sister Republics Polka* or the *Waltz
of the Clouds* . . . is the chasm too great to cross? The revue at
the Nouvel-Ambigu tries to cross it.

I am accustomed to confide what I think to *Le Film*. A de-
served tribute of injurious epistles and friendly letters encourages me. I want to continue this practice and to scrape off
the amiable and quite new face of this revue the mask of
theatrical makeup which someone, I think out of *amour-propre*,
found it necessary to give it. The more the theater, which sulks
at film but uses it, seeks it out, the more film—its robust and
capricious offshoot—must flee it. To divert us, the "Cinematic
Revue" has no need of so many narrators of both sexes, of
couplets, of spoken commentary. See how during the performance the public favored the scenes in which the voices were

silent and the image simply unrolled; see how a face true to type, a comic or graceful gesture, made them laugh before the punch line or the refrain . . . Yes, I understand, you are after a synchronization of gesture, voice, and orchestra, while I still find "human, all too human" the sound of a colorless voice in a darkened hall. I am still at the stage of the "symphonic film" of Vuillermoz, who wants to orchestrate landscapes and to film imitative harmonies. We will speak of this again.

For the moment, I am stubborn enough to think that neither rhymes nor words add any powerful attraction to the pantomime of Signoret and Renouard, or to the sketch between Mistinguett and Chevalier, or to the striking close-ups—my dear, you could count his eyelashes!—of the prince de Lorde. And, authors of this revue, still intoxicated with the theater, you really must take note of the pleasure that the audience gets from scenes beyond the slim means of the theater—for example, in that seductive superimposition of images: diaphanous Pierrots dancing the farandole at night on the roofs of Montmartre and of the Sacré-Coeur.

But since you don't agree with me, and because the needs of your cause or those of an entirely praiseworthy patriotic propaganda require the aid of a human presence, a human voice, let them at least be, one and the other, the one exhaling the other, beautiful, pure, suave, and ephemeral, like a fountain seen between trees, like the cry of a hidden bird, making more beautiful the silence and the solitude . . .

CIVILIZATION'S CHILD

This piece was published with the preceding review. *Civilization's Child* (1916) was produced by Triangle, Ince's company, and directed by Reginald Barker, one of the directors in the Ince "stable"; the photography was by Joseph August and Clyde de Vinna, the scenario, by Gardner Sullivan; it starred William Thompson, Anna Lehr, Margaret Thompson, Joseph Dowling, Jack Standing, Dorothy Dalton, J. P. Lockney, Clyde Benson, and J. Barney Sherry. Louis Delluc also greatly admired the film and hailed it as a triumph of honest "popular art, which we have never had except under the pompous, specialized and imperious form of ecclesiastical luxury . . ."

The Shielding Shadow was another film made by Louis Gasnier, a French director working in America (thus, of course, it too is an "American film," in spite of Colette's confusion). It starred Grace Darmond and Léon Bary. Suzanne Després, a theatrical star of the turn of the century, made two great successes of Eugène Brieux'. *La Robe Rouge* (1900) and a revival of *La Fille Elisa* (1890), adapted by Jean Ajalbert from Elmond de Goncourt's 1887 naturalistic novel.

This is an American film I encountered by accident in the Maillot quarter one day of torrential rain. It was on a double bill with some imponderable *Shielding Shadow*. The next day, in fine weather, I returned to the same movie house for the American film. How old is it? Has Paris already seen it? I don't know and I have never heard anything about it, although because of the extraordinary quality of the acting it merits our astonishment and our consideration.

I don't know whether it will become fashionable. A sad and sudden ending, a lamentable story, and the somber and illogical cuts made by the French censorship work against it; and, of course, it is too much that out of five principal characters, four are blackguards, while the fifth—a seduced and abandoned girl from whom, later, are torn her poor and painfully reconstructed happiness and both her husband and child—dies as a result of their mistreatment, rather than triumphing at the eleventh hour.

But when the intimate drama calls together and assembles, on this narrow field, humiliated innocence, ferocious lust, and sorrow, everything is to be admired, studied, and retained. Rustic, beautiful like all women whose abundant soul overflows in their magnificent eyes, Anna Lehr is in the tradition of Suzanne Després in *La Robe Rouge* and in *La Fille Élisa*; I needn't say more. And with what strong and loving arms she can carry a sleeping baby . . .

The actor playing the "exploitative boss" is not unworthy of her—heavy, soft, with a mastiff's swinging jowls, small bulging eyes, agile, capable of rapid changes of nuance, with hands like a caressing monster—nor is the long, slow, hesitant Jew, whose boneless fingers, low shoulders, and dragging feet are as eloquent as his face. There is also a bad girl with craftiness lurking at the corners of her mouth and a velvet-eyed Slavic musician, a perfect combination of listless Gypsy and fortune hunter. You will see them, I hope. You will note the perfection of a lower-class gesture, of the way in which they eat, drink, wipe their mouths, hold their napkins, smoke, take off their shoes. You will agree that the poor girl, drunk on wine, really behaves like a poor drunk girl, and you will not deny that her stupor and unsteady gaze are equal to Hayakawa's performance when [in *The Cheat*] he faints from his wounds.

THE SHADOW

This piece on *L'Ombre* was published with the preceding. Dario Niccodemi was the Italian author of the play from which *The Shadow* was taken; Colette exculpates him from blame for the French intertitles. For Vittoria Lepanto, see "Film and Fashion."

The Shadow? What shadow? Is it the Valley of the Shadow, into which the heroine descends at the end? This film has already toured Italy; its posters ornamented all Rome this spring. It comes to us supported by a text of which I swear Dario Niccodemi is innocent, as far as the spelling is concerned.

One of my friends, an amateur of film, was congratulating himself the other day on being able to tell an Italian film anywhere.

"How?" I asked.

"By the quantity of furniture in the salon. By the luxurious dimensions of the rooms—Madame's small drawing room or the little room in which she does her hair almost never measures less than twenty-four feet by thirty. By the lack of gaiety in the male actors, who hardly manage a smile. Finally, by the fact that the Italian film always contains, whether it's good or bad, cinematographic or not, at least one idea and sometimes two; there are a good number of French films that couldn't say as much."

For the moment let us leave these categorical opinions aside. *The Shadow* shows us a husband who, granted, doesn't smile easily, but we must admit that given his wife, struck down by a sudden paralysis that has lasted six years, and a mistress, who having given him a child during those six years, daily presses him to marry her, he has some reason to look worried.

The difficult role of the young wife, paralyzed, then cured, then struck down again, this time fatally, is acted by Vittoria Lepanto, from whose sensitive face a good director could easily have drawn deep expressiveness. But Vittoria Lepanto has been left to her natural impetuosity, which draws her toward movement and emotion wasted in waves of superficiality. All the same, what qualities she has! And—if it were reined in—how much could be added by that vigor in her body, in her glance, even in her hair, by that slightly cannibal smile. At the moment of her resurrection, when the paralytic, after six years, stands again and staggers with joy, Vittoria Lepanto is a great tragedienne. She knows how to fall like nobody else, without holding back, with an entire and thrilling abandon of the body. If in her next film she is given an outstanding director, a designer, and a modiste capable of saying "Don't make us laugh!" to her sartorial fantasies, Vittoria Lepanto will be able to match the most highly praised stars, whether in Italy or elsewhere.

THE FRENCH CINEMA IN 1918

This was first published in *Excelsior*, May 14, 1918, and called "Cinema," then in *Le Film* for June 3, 1918, under the title "Colette at the Cinema," and finally in *Filma*, August 15–30, 1918, as "Luxury." The present title has been chosen as both more precise and more extended.

In *Le Film* this text is published with "The Femme Fatale," which appears later in this collection, and the following editorial note, doubtless by Louis Delluc, appears as preface:

It is with great joy that we present to our readers these intelligent and witty pages from the pen of our collaborator and friend, Colette. Colette's perceptive love for the cinema benefits all cinema. When you read these lines you will discover what observation, what a sense of appropriateness and proportion, Colette brings to her love for film. The best way she can be useful to us is by putting her finger on our errors and weaknesses, especially when we know that her criticism is neither biased nor hostile. On the contrary; remember the enthusiastic words of this same author when, before the war, she discovered and launched *The Scott Expedition*, which was foundering at the Théâtre Réjane in public indifference, and later, *The Cheat*, which was exciting only pro-Japanese polemic until, first and alone, she proclaimed its artistic merits in the press. After that have come her generous campaigns in our columns. Film has numerous and determined opponents, but with such friends we need not fear or even remember them.

Colette's continuing interest in the music hall is shown by her reference to the Grand Café Chinois-Théâtre de Ba-Ta-Clan (The Great Chinese Cafe and Ba-Ta-Clan Theater); founded under the Second Empire, it was the most important *caf'conc'* of Paris, at which appeared all the stars of the day, including Buffalo Bill. Madame Rasimi had become its manager for the second time in 1910; she was known for her skill and taste in costuming.

Colette was continuing to follow Abel Gance's career. After *Mater Dolorosa* (see above), she now refers to his *Dixième Symphonie* (1918), which Delluc similarly praised and criticized: "It's a *work*. It has a character, an idea, an existence . . . I know his fault. But I know that it will become a quality, perhaps the primordial quality of Gance. Here it is: He is not simple. He is always ready to emphasize." Henry-Roussell's *L'Ame du Bronze* (*Soul of Bronze*, 1917–18) received stunning praise from Delluc in *Le Film* (January 1918) for its dazzling photography, but it is otherwise abominable patriotic melodrama: jealous engineer pushing his rival into molten steel; soul of the victim, at the end of the film, rising from the cannon forged from the murderous metal to forgive his assassin, dying on the field of battle . . . If Colette and Delluc could say that such a film was not in the least a progaganda work, one imagines with horror what real propaganda works must have been. *L'Ame du Bronze* starred Harry Baur, Lilian Greuze, and Gaston Rieffler.

We once more see Colette's passion for documentary films, especially those about animals or plants. Her enthusiasm was exceptional and far in advance of its time; the remarkable scientific films of Jean Painlevé would not appear until the 1930s. Henri Fabre (1823–1915), to whom she refers, was one of the foremost entomologists of his time.

The manager or the owner of a popular "movie house" in Paris said recently, refusing a very good film:

"That one isn't the sort for my house. There's too much outdoors and nobody in evening clothes."

The story made people laugh and shrug their shoulders. When I was told it, I laughed before thinking. I didn't understand or defend it until later, when I had found in it something other than the expression of an ignorant snobbery and the contempt, still honorable among certain sorts of Parisians, for everything having to do with outdoors or sport.

I was at first tempted to treat my movie-house owner as he seemed to merit. I would have liked to say to him: "Are you the one who educates mass taste by using the cinema? Or are you the one who leads the public toward paperback thrillers in pictures, toward criminals in white ties, and torture chambers made out of painted cardboard? You're the one, aren't you, who demands desperate countesses and bloody marquesses, and high-society adultery in Art Nouveau decors? You're the one . . . you're the one . . ." But I didn't say anything at all to him, and it wouldn't take much to make me apologize to this teacher of souls, whose speech is earthy because he can command no better words.

At a time when ramparts of committees, societies, and cinematic leagues are forming to protect a threatened industry, a threatened national art, and are drawing—with what effort— French cinema toward more luminous heights, my manager will bring down on himself curses from the specialists and the technicians. But what is he asking for? People in evening clothes, and not so much outdoors. He ought to have added, in his popular language, "Me, I want a thing to be nice-looking, and the audience likes a little *luggsury*."

He is not only right in some obscure way, but he has reasons he would be incapable of expressing. He wants *luggsury*.

And the longer the war lasts, the more we lack sugar and bread and gasoline, the more he will ask, on behalf of his audience in worn-out jackets and spongy, broken-down shoes, for *luggsury* and still more *luggsury*. I won't try to explain this need simply by the thirst for superfluity that torments human beings deprived of necessities. The source of it must be found in the progressive impoverishment of the theaters and the music halls. For three years we have lived in an increasing shadow. Artificial light, dimmer every day, no longer inundates the stages or our private homes. By a law of mimicry, bright colors are disappearing from our clothes, in which shades of sand, earth, and troubled water are replacing all the others, and mourning, alas!, we have no lack of, nor of the dark violets and the mauves of half-mourning . . . A music hall on the rue Blanche, if it had had in its favor only material splendor, would have attracted to its lobby of colors and lights a crowd made anemic by the dark; but the spectacle on stage had no match in the season, or the year. Madame Rasimi can no longer transport from Ba-Ta-Clan to Montrouge and from Montrouge to Grenelle troupes clothed in velvet, glittering with paste jewels; and what is attempted currently in the local café-concerts leaves spectators no illusion about the novelty or the freshness of the refurbished costumes . . . What is left for the public? Where can it bathe itself in decorative illusion, adventure and romance, high life, society, inexhaustible splendor? At the cinema. Only the cinema spends, wastes, destroys or miraculously builds, mobilizes hordes of extras, rips embroidered cloth, spatters with blood or ink thousand-franc dresses; only there will you see a gentleman in a white tie not giving an instant's thought to his three-hundred-franc evening clothes when he grapples with a bandit—and triumphs, in rags.

So the vote of a public that is worried, tired, badly heated, dimly lighted, suffering in body and tormented in heart, goes first, and logically, and childishly, to the most concrete and tangible *luggsury*: evening dress and the drawing room, which my movie-house manager was demanding for them. And yet apart from *The Cheat* and a few others, the finest flower of the cinema is not the high-society dramatic film . . .

Never mind. In France, should one ever despair? At this awkward moment, we are working again in France at shots taken in the sunlight. I have seen, in one week, films like the *Tenth Symphony*, overflowing with qualities and defects, with new discoveries and errors, films like *L'Ame du Bronze*, in which the means of moving the audience operate through their very discretion, and which gained for Henry-Roussell this piquant compliment: "You'll never make this into a propaganda film—it's not boring!" I have seen "documentaries" in which the hatching of an insect, the unfolding of a butterfly outside its chrysalis, set the fairytale quality of stage illusion before our eyes and, thanks to photographic enlargement, open to us the forever-mysterious world where Fabre lived . . . Oh, that is the thing itself, luxury, magnificence, fantasy! The feathery and irised material of a butterfly's wing, the palpitations of a minuscule bird, the vibrating bee and its tiny hooked feet, a fly's eye, the flower whose image has been captured on the other side of the world, unknown waters, and also human gestures, human looks brought to us from an unknown world—that is it, that is the thing, inexhaustible luxury! Patience: it will be known at last.

A SHORT MANUAL FOR THE ASPIRING SCENARIO WRITER*

These four *chroniques* in dialogue were first printed in *Excelsior* under the title "Colette's Diary" and given the general title "Short Manual for the Aspiring Scenario Writer." This general title disappeared in *Film* and *Filma*, where the four, reprinted word for word from *Excelsior*, had only their individual titles; the series appeared in *Film* in 1918 and in *Filma* in 1918–1919. Colette thus got the maximum from her spirited dialogues.

The dialogues are full of allusions to contemporary cinema, among which the alert reader will spot Pina Menichelli's owl headdress and the black velvet mask of Feuillade's serials. The black cape and the velvet mask had first appeared in *Fantomas* (1913–14), but were not "old-fashioned"; in the *Judex* serials (1917–18) Feuillade was still filming an Avenger who wore a black cape with silver clasps and a large-brimmed black hat. The dimensions of the huge Italian filmic rooms are now, on the average, nine meters by fifteen—even larger than Colette had remembered them the year before in her review of *The Shadow*. Her attack on the director in "Luxury" shows that she had not quite forgotten or forgiven her Italian experiences while filming *The Vagabond*.

I. The Femme Fatale

Question: What is a sensational film?
Answer: A sensational film—with the exception of American films—is one that does not deal with actual events. For

---

* Translated by Stanley Hochman. Portions of this "manual" appeared in *Women and the Cinema*, edited by Karyn Kay and Gerald Peary (Dutton, 1977).

example, almost no French film has attempted to portray real or imagined incidents of the war.

Q.: How do you explain this?

A.: I wouldn't think of explaining it, because I am a peaceful soul who shies away from pugilistics.

Q.: What is the very first sign that a movie is destined to be sensational?

A.: The lighting. If, for example, you notice that in the first hundred feet of the reel a director has already used silvery-pink tones for a factory office, Rembrandt blacks and golds in honor of a supernumerary slipping into his coat in the vestibule, and close-ups of a head against black velvet to emphasize the indecision of a gentleman trying to make up his mind between a canter on horseback or an automobile ride, then there is a good chance that the film will be a sensational one. Oh yes, I was forgetting—a sensational film owes the public a "presentation," in enormous close-ups, of its principal actors.

Q.: Tell us a little something about this presentation.

A.: The presentation of the sympathetic heroine has few specific characteristics. On the other hand, that of the femme fatale is a shattering revelation, and from the very first minute we know what we can expect from her.

Q.: Why?

A.: Because 1) the femme fatale is almost always in décolleté; 2), she is often armed with a hypodermic or with a flacon of ether; 3) she sinuously turns her serpent's neck toward the spectator; 4) and—more rarely—having first revealed enormously wide eyes, she slowly veils them with soft lids, and before disappearing in the mist of a fade-out risks the most daring gesture that can be shown on the screen . . .

Q.: Easy, now . . . !

A.: . . . What I mean to say is that she slowly and guiltily bites her lower lip.

Q.: You had me worried there. . . . Is that all she does?

A.: That's all, but it's enough.

Q.: You don't mean to imply that the characterization of the femme fatale in a sensational film is limited to that?

A.: Unfortunately not. She also uses other weapons—I have already mentioned poison and drugs—such as the dagger, the revolver, the anonymous letter, and finally, elegance.

Q.: Elegance?

A.: I mean by elegance that which the woman who treads

on hearts and devours brains can in no way do without: 1) a clinging black velvet dress; 2) a dressing gown of the type known as "exotic" on which one often sees embroidery and designs of seaweed, insects, reptiles, and a death's head; 3) a floral display that she tears at cruelly.

Q.: What does the evil woman do when she is alone on the screen?

A.: She lights a cigarette and stretches out on the divan. Or else she slyly busies herself writing. Or she rereads letters and "documents" that she withdraws from an unsuspected hiding place—the base of a lamp, a parrot's cage, or the sixth square of the parquet. Or she goes to the window, draws aside the curtain, and raising her arm sends forth some mysterious signal.

Q.: And what happens to the femme fatale at the end of the sensational film?

A.: She dies. Preferably on three steps, covered by a rug.

Q.: And between the apotheosis and the fall of the femme fatale, isn't there room on the screen for numerous passionate gestures?

A.: Numerous, to say the least. The two principal ones involve the hat and the rising gorge.

Q.: Pretend that I've never seen them.

A.: The femme fatale's hat spares her the necessity, at the absolute apex of her wicked career, of having to expend herself in pantomime. When the spectator sees the evil woman coiffing herself with a spread-winged owl, the head of a stuffed jaguar, a bifid aigrette, or a hairy spider, he no longer has any doubts; he knows just what she is capable of.

Q.: And the rising gorge?

A.: The rising gorge is the imposing and ultimate means by which the evil woman informs the audience that she is about to weep, that she is hesitating on the brink of crime, that she is struggling against steely necessity, or that the police have gotten their hands on the letter.

Q.: What letter?

A.: *The* letter.

Q.: Is there no other way she can express such different emotions?

A.: It's not the custom. The rising gorge is the thing. . . . The heart thumps. The flanks swell. The staring eyes seem about to pop out of their orbits. The stricken wretch suddenly swallows a flow of saliva. And the handkerchief also rises, from her waist to her lips, and . . .

Q.: Enough, enough! I'll give you a good grade for this all-too-faithful evocation, but other examinations are scheduled: the Society Woman and the Leading Man.

II. The Leading Man

Q.: What do you mean by a Leading Man in the movies?

A.: A Leading Man is the character of indeterminate age—but always a bachelor or divorced—who is responsible for the fate of the young girl, widow, or divorced woman who will be confided to his care at the end of three or four thousand feet of film.

Q.: Tell us about the general characteristics of the Leading Man.

A.: Before the advent of American films, the Leading Man was required to have a pleasing face, an elegant air, a much too well fitting cutaway with mohair braid, and a fur-collared cape.

Q.: And has this panoply—if I may use that word—undergone modifications since our friends and allies have begun making movies?

A.: The word "modifications" is totally inadequate: what we are dealing with is a veritable revolution in the *habitus corporis* of the Leading Man. The horse of the Far West, occasionally without saddle or bridle, has replaced the mohair-embroidered cutaway; the elegant air is demonstrated in the use of fists; and the great train robbery has replaced the garden party.

Q.: Does this new state of things create any problems for the Leading Man?

A.: No, if by problems you mean the need to be enormously proficient in horsemanship, swimming, jiujitsu, boxing, marksmanship, and tightrope walking.

Q.: But what if the Leading Man doesn't care for these various sports?

A.: He still has a few ways of not sinking to the level of the Second Lead. The best of these consists of becoming an Avenger or—what amounts to the same thing—the Mastermind of a Secret Association of Criminals. In this way he can substitute, in the first case, majesty for acrobatics, and, in the second case, cold cynicism or wild fury for aptitude in sports.

Q.: Haven't you just said, somewhat paradoxically, that the roles of Avenger and of Criminal Mastermind are the same thing?

A.: I said it, but not by way of paradox. Any Leading Man will tell you that there is no appreciable difference between the role of the Avenger and that of the Principal Bandit. Whoever plays one can easily play the other; even the costumes are almost the same. The black cape of the Avenger fits the Bandit beautifully, and the leggings or velvet mask detract nothing from the righter of wrongs.

Q.: Did you say cape? And velvet mask? Are you joking when you mention such old-fashioned accessories?

A.: On the contrary. I'm perfectly serious—although somewhat sad—and quite respectful of the usages imposed by the most modern films on their important Leading Men. A child of six knows that any Bandit worthy of the name signals his role to the public by his sombrero, his cape, his mask, his checkered neckerchief, his boots . . .

Q.: Enough, enough! Do you know of any Leading Men who busy themselves with anything other than extravagant philanthropy or outrages against the law?

A.: Yes, of course. There are Leading Men who are exclusively fashionable and sentimental, though the type seems to be on the wane. Thank God, however, we still have rich, young, orphaned marquises bored with life, and illegitimate sons of the best society.

Q.: And what does the rich, young, and orphaned marquis do when he is bored?

A.: He stretches out on a lion skin.

Q.: And then?

A.: Isn't that enough?

Q.: But nevertheless . . .

A.: He smokes Turkish tobacco, and with a wicked gesture tosses away his cigarette before going off to steal his best friend's fiancée. In this latter case he wears at-home attire—incestuous offspring of the pajama and the quilted robe—and an unstarched shirt open at the neck to the very limit, the collar folded under. The same shirt, when worn by a Leading Man playing a musician of genius or a temperamental sculptor, is no longer a symbol of evil but merely signifies the noble independence of the artist free of middle-class prejudices.

Q.: How does the Leading Man behave when the woman he loves or desires comes to visit him?

A.: He slides open the door hangings so that she can come in.

Q.: You mean the door, don't you?

A.: No. The door hangings. Never the door. Then he kisses her hand and gestures imperiously to his valet, saying "Leave us!"

Q.: Why does he gesture imperiously?

A.: Because he is a Leading Man and he is acting in a serious film. In a comic film the imperious gesture is not necessary: one can merely behave as in real life.

Q.: What happens then?

A.: A series of "extreme close-ups."

Q.: And then?

A.: The silhouette, against a bright window, of a couple embracing, their lips joined.

Q.: And then?

A.: The disappearance of this same couple, who are replaced on the screen—and this is a recent invention—by a symbol.

Q.: What symbol?

A.: That depends on the nature of the protagonists. A grimacing and Asiatic objet d'art is suitable for the perverse young Leading Man; an enigmatic Renaissance bust stands in, during the embrace, for the femme fatale. If the Leading Man is taking advantage of abused innocence, a fluttering dove held captive in a cruel hand is called for.

Q.: What do you think of the introduction of symbols on the screen?

A.: I think that though it may give us some piquant insights into the taste of the scenario writer, it may also induce some regrettable errors in the spectator and falsify his conception of the leading actor.

Q.: For example?

A.: Example: "You see," cried a young woman in a darkened movie theater, "you see—the duke's not as bad as you said! He only wanted to frighten the young girl by making her believe he had a gun. But it isn't a gun, it was just a little pigeon."

III. The Society Woman

Q.: How can the Society Woman be recognized on the screen without any help from the script?

A.: By the fact that she is less well dressed than the woman who is not accepted in society, and by her excessive use of black taffeta. Other signs also prevent any possible error—for example, the bunch of daisies and the victoria drawn by two unprepossessing horses.

Q.: But the Society Woman isn't guaranteed exclusive use of daisies or the victoria, is she?

A.: No, but by a subtle convention the demi-mondaine and the adventuress more often prefer orchids and a limousine.

Q.: What is the usual facial expression of the Society Woman on the screen?

A.: She scarcely has any choice but between boredom or pain, both of a very distinguished variety. In the movies, a true Society Woman suffers: 1) from a brutal, jealous, and alcoholic husband; or 2) from a youthful error—actually quite honorable —the fruit of which she conceals in a distant province.

Q.: What are the consequences of these two sets of circumstances?

A.: There is only one: as soon as the other characters turn their attention from her, or she finds herself alone on the screen, the Society Woman is constrained to raise her eyes to the heavens and sigh.

Q.: Is that all?

A.: And what more would you do in her place?

Q.: You're not here to ask questions but to answer them . . . Doesn't that sign foreshadow sad events?

A.: Sad indeed, and not long in coming. Before 600 feet of film have been unreeled, the Society Woman receives a letter, sometimes anonymous, in which the spectator may note a completely unrestrained orthography, the trace of a hasty and literal translation if the film is a foreign one, and—finally—an absolutely revolutionary syntax.

Q.: What happens next?

A.: Several cases of nervous prostration in the audience.

Q.: Why is that?

A.: Because from the first appearance of The Letter, projected *in extenso* in an enormous close-up, the knowledgeable spectator abandons all hope. He knows that the Society Woman, whose fate is linked to that of the letter, will soon reread the letter, which will tremble—still in an enormous close-up—between two hands that are as big or bigger than either of us and that sport black fingernails . . .

Q.: Black fingernails? You must be losing your mind! A Society Woman!

A.: . . . black, I say, because the manicurist has colored them red. This Letter, already twice offered as food for our anxiety, resumes its normal size, and the Society Woman, horrified, first hides it in her bosom and then in a piece of furniture that has a secret compartment . . . Alas, it is only so a servant, dismissed or suborned, a thief, a suspicious husband, an innocent son, or a detective can employ violence to get at it some 150 feet of film farther on. He looks for it—he finds it—he reads it—horrors, he makes us read it, still *in extenso* in an enormous close-up! At this point the Society Woman can choose between a swoon, if she is the fragile type, and a revolver, if she wants to save the honor of her name. But we, the public, we have absolutely no choice. Whether the husband brandishes it under her nose or the stricken son sobs over the fatal paper, we the public will not escape the projection—in an enormous close-up—of The Letter . . .

Q.: I see . . . Would you mind talking about something else for a while? I'm beginning to feel somewhat upset . . .

A.: Impossible. The Society Woman and The Letter, The Letter and the Society Woman, the one hiding the other, the other chastising the one, will go hand in hand till the very end of the film. We will witness the preparations for bed—oh, very discreetly, to be sure: a Society Woman never undresses on the screen—of the Society Woman who, having scarcely dozed off, awakes with a start, or else sinks into a nightmare, a nightmare which . . . a nightmare whose . . .

Q.: What nightmare?

A.: I was hoping you would ask that question. The nightmare of The Letter. In a velvet-ringed fade-in, in a "medallion" in the left corner of the screen, there once more implacably appears, in the handwriting of an ambitious illiterate, The Letter . . .

Q.: Yes, yes . . . But can't we get back to the Society Woman?

A.: Have we left her for so much as an instant? Not a moment of respite! Now it will be necessary for the eternally damned traitor to flee with The Letter, to put it in a "safe place" —in the movies that means a place from which someone will fish it out moments later. It will be necessary for the Society Woman, dressed in black taffeta and coiffed with a tiny hat with a flowing veil (she can still be recognized by the fact that she rarely wears a tailored suit or traveling clothes, reserved to the femme fatale or "the American woman"), to race after The Letter . . . We will read The Letter in the hands of the traitor, we will read The Letter snagged against a cliff and flapping in the wind, we will read The Letter sealed in a bottle and floating on the ocean, The Letter recopied, The Letter forged, The Letter sold, then The Letter repurchased, The Letter damp with tears, and finally The Letter crushed between the fingers of a dead woman, a saint, a veritable martyr—between the fingers of the Society Woman.

Q.: Oof!

A.: Where are you off to, sir? Are you forgetting that the unconscionable persecutor of the Society Woman, now prostrated by grief and remorse, will piously pry open the clutching fingers of his victim, smooth out the paper, and read you THE LETTER?

IV.   Luxury in the Movies

Q.: What is luxury in the movies?

A.: That depends.

Q.: You won't be able to get out of it by an ambiguous comment and a knowing smile. Be specific.

A.: At least let me know what kind of luxury you mean. In the movies we have the luxury of wardrobe, the luxury of furniture and decoration, and the luxury that consists of immolating—in order to assure the conjugal happiness of a delicate young woman—disemboweled horses, capsized automobiles, edifices, boats, planes, Ninevite and Babylonian palaces . . .

Q.: For the moment, restrict yourself to telling us what you know of luxury in the most usual sense of the word—luxury limited to the setting and costumes of romantic comedies and sophisticated dramas.

A.: I understand: that intelligent luxury, that "tasteful" elegance, which signals to the admiration of foreigners, films whose scenarios, editing, intertitles, and general arrangement of properties are the work . . .

Q.: . . . of one of our most beloved authors?

A.: What have *those* people got to do with the movies? The work, of course, of a director.

Q.: But . . .

A.: Who at present devotes himself to the development of the film's script? The director. Who dissects the scenario into images with the masterliness of a surgeon? The director. Who looks after the commercial fate of the film? The director. Who edits into lapidary sentences the text being photographed? The director. The director, I tell you.

Q.: That's true. Glory be to the director!

A.: I agree with you. And I will even add that his natural instinct for luxury, his familiarity with a highminded and sophisticated life, the perfect knowledge he acquires by living among the great of this world, generally so form him that his peremptory genius can create—without reference to anyone or anything—visions of American billionaires, reigning princes, adventuresses blooming in Oriental opulence.

Q.: I don't really care for the tone of irony I detect. Keep to the topic.

A.: But I haven't really left it. You asked what luxury is. The Italian cinema replies: "It is abundance, it is quantity. Just look at my 30x40-foot boudoirs afloat with a dozen sidechairs and as many armchairs—all of them gilt. Look at my grand pianos, my Renaissance chests, my dozens of consoles and thousands of electric candelabra. All I need now are a few life-sized statues, and I'm ready to give you a 'small' salon—with, of course, a divan in the center." That's the answer of the Italian cinema.

Q.: A divan in the center?

A.: In the center, and covered with animal skins, naturally. In the center—I absolutely insist on this point! The luxury specialists in the movies, whether they come from Italy or elsewhere, have so decided. Casually tossed in among the crush of side tables and easy chairs, far from any wall, window, or corner—the divan!

Q.: How do you explain this bizarre state of affairs?

A.: Only one explanation seems possible: respect for the principle of least effort. It is easier to be assassinated, to embrace a mistress, to fall into a swoon or melt into tears—all events that are as proper to a divan as a vine to an elm tree—on a centrally located piece of furniture than on a couch pushed up against a wall.

There is always a moment in the long and discouraging cinematographic day in which the proud maxim "Be opulent and inventive" gives way to "This will have to do." It is at that fatal moment that the requisite but unfortunately far-off historic chateau is replaced by a handy suburban villa, the high-backed throne by a rocking chair, and fine crystal by cheap café glassware. It is at that same moment, after having promised he will treat you "to a high-society evening à la Rothschild" that the director's pride, innovative and combative intelligence, and growling stomach all weaken simultaneously: suddenly he is willing to have his leading lady—absolute queen of elegance— invite to her receptions nobody but salesgirls adorned in the démodé dresses worn to graduation exercises, and "gentlemen" gotten up like morticians. He accepts it all because in the final analysis he is only human—in the other words an easy prey to lassitude, bitterness, and temporary fits of "to hell with it." He accepts—but rest assured that it pains him, and that as soon as he finds the occasion, he will appropriately or inappropriately satisfy his thirst for luxury by sending the wife of a shipping clerk to darn socks on the terrace of a white Monacan palace, or by generously allowing a Bohemian painter to throw a studio party in one of those Italian gardens whose peerless porticos, statues and fountains, cascading roses, and trailing wisteria seem to have been loaned by the caretaker to some brazen stranger.

BEL-GAZOU AND THE CINEMA

This dialogue first appeared in *Excelsior* on December 4, 1917, as part of "Colette's Diary," and was later collected in *La Chambre Eclairée* (Paris: Edouard Joseph, 1920). "Bel-Gazou," Colette's daughter, Colette de Jouvenel, was a little more than four years old in 1917.

"What're we going to see after the soldiers, Mummy?"
"*The Daughter of the Forest.*"
"Is that a film from Merica?"
"I think so. . . . Would you like that, Bel-Gazou?"
"Yes. I like Merican films."
"Why?"
"Cause when the man sits down in the basket of eggs, everybody laughs. Mummy, why didn't you laugh when I sat

down in the basket of eggs in the kitchen, and then later on
when I turned on the faucet like he did?"

"Hush! Not so loud!"

"Will there be kids?"

"I don't know. Maybe . . ."

"I like it lots when there are kids. Cause when they climb
over the wall, and they go into the hen-house of the man who
lives next door, and then when they make the hens fight, and
then they tie them up in handkerchiefs and kidnap them, everybody laughs. Mummy, why didn't you laugh when I kidnapped
the black hen, and then when I—"

"Shush! You talk too much."

"And then the music, Mummy, you'll read me the writing
on the blackboard, won't you, Mummy? Cause I can read just
like anybody, but sometimes the letters are bigger than my
eyes and they can't get in."

"Quiet, Bel-Gazou, it's starting."

"Yes . . . Ooh! Look at the pretty little house, made out of
trees going sideways."

"That's the trapper's house."

"The trapper, is that the man that trappers birds?"

"The word is 'traps.' "

"Then did the movie make a mistake? Is that the trapser's
house?"

"No, it's . . . Shush, now. Look at the cute little baby in its
cradle."

"What's the baby's mother doing? Is she picking the baby
up?"

"No, she's taking it away."

"Where?"

"A long, long way, with that man who's waiting for her in
the carriage, do you see him?"

"Is the man her husband?"

"No, her husband is the one with the long beard, the
trapper."

"So she's going away with the trapper?"

"No, she's going to leave with the man in the carriage."

"Why?"

"Because . . . Don't you ever stop asking questions?"

"Oh, look, Mummy—she isn't going away with the man in
the carriage, cause the trapser's coming and he took back the

cute little baby. She's going to come back with her baby. No, she's leaving it—Why is that?"

"Because . . . She's saying that she wants to live her own life."

"Livernlife, does that mean leaving her little baby?"

"No . . . yes . . . almost . . . Look at the trapper, doesn't he look angry!"

"What's he saying to the lady, Mummy?"

"He's telling her she's behaving like a—No, he's saying— He's saying that she shouldn't take the little baby out so late. So . . . she's going out for a walk alone."

"With the man."

"Shush! You shouldn't say things like that."

"Isn't he a man?"

"Yes, he is . . . You talk too much, you really do, you're giving me a headache. Look at the poor trapper."

"Oh, is he poor?"

"No, he's unhappy. You see, he's crying. He's all alone."

"All alone with the little baby that its mummy livernlifed! Is that the end of the story?"

"No, it's only the first part. Look, it's beginning again."

"Oh, yes, there's the pretty house. What's that lady?"

"That isn't a lady, that's a little girl. She is the little baby we saw just a moment ago, but grown up. And this is her father, the trapper."

"Has he grown up?"

"No, of course not!"

"Don't trappers grow up?"

"Not any more than other grown-up persons. Bel-Gazou . . . if you can't keep quiet for *one minute . . .*"

(*Silence. Things happen on the screen. Bel-Gazou explodes:*)

"There it is! There it is! Mummy, it's coming!"

"What?"

"The basket of eggs! The little girl's starting to break the plates and the bottles and the chairs . . . Ooh, Mummy, they're going to bring the basket of eggs!" (*She applauds.*)

"Will you keep quiet! It isn't a film to laugh at. The little girl is breaking everything . . ."

"Why?"

"To show that she's a savage girl, that she doesn't want to be anything but a savage girl, that she isn't going to go away to the big city like her mother, that she's going to keep on being the trapper's daughter . . ."

"Are they going to spank her, Mummy?"

"No. The bad people wanted to take her to the city, but she escaped, do you see? So she's showing them how strong and wild she is; she's saying to them, 'I dare you to catch me, I'm the trapper's daughter! Look how I can break these chairs, these plates, the benches, everything! That's how a trapper's daughter behaves!' "

"And they're not going to spank her?"

"No, not at all."

(*Long silence from Bel-Gazou.*)

"Bel-Gazou, are you asleep? Are you bored?"

"No, I'm thinking."

"Of what?"

"Is it hard to become a trapper?"

"Why? Would you like to be a trapper?"

"No . . ." (*Dreamily*) "I was thinking about it for Papa. . . ."

CINEMA

From *Aventures Quotidiennes* (Paris: Flammarion, 1920).

No automobiles were parked in front of the entrance to the Musée Galliera last Thursday; we might have believed that the theater reserved for "Art in the French Cinema" would be empty. Quite the contrary; it was packed to the doors with a silent public that included children and adolescents. This good, humble audience—come patiently through the stormy weather by slow and inconvenient means of transportation and now squeezed onto benches in a stifling hall hung provisionally with black curtains—received its just reward. With them, I watched what we can never see on our movie-theater screens, on which the glories of America have no other rivals but *Didi découche* (*Didi's Night Out*) and *Patochard cherche sa belle-mère* (*Patochard Looks for his Mother-in-Law*). Two magic words had attracted me; I know that it is useless to look for spectacle, marvels, incontestable miracles in the cinema elsewhere than in what is called the "educational film."

A part of the presentation took us on a tour of France, over the tops of rolling hills, along rivers choked by their flat and narrow valleys; the weary voice of a professor explained that the form of these hills, this body of water, these trees, depended on an invisible stratum underneath the soil, a chalky layer, or a silicate clay. A small farm of the Perche region showed proud Percherons, their dappled satin coats gleaming over the play of their muscles. In a granite quarry, stonecutters raised blocks, cut out columns with their pickaxes . . . Schoolchildren, you will never be able to forget the joyful light, like the light of a soapbubble, that glided over the flanks of these horses with their Roman muzzles, or the strange many-toothed form of a black tool that bit the white stone; your memory couldn't possibly fail to retain the gesture of the two hands of a quarryman, gigantic, black, breaking before your eyes a friable block, striated with pure white, in order to teach you that kaolin hides itself like truffles, and that like truffles it clothes itself with a thick clay! From the top of a mobile chute, schoolchildren, you have seen wheat streaming like lava into Marseilles, a stream so dense that we seemed to hear it murmuring like rain . . . Schoolchildren, stand up for your rights against those who still protest, in the name of imagination, against teaching by moving images. It is not the ignorant or foolish people who say: "To feed the child's imagination with precise images is to straiten and impoverish it. Teaching by films makes the child a mere storehouse of images and encourages the atrophy of every sense except the visual."

At first glance, the objection does not seem negligible. Our civilized senses lose no opportunity to impoverish themselves. I am told that without music, movie houses would become public dormitories; I am also told that faced with a film, a child hardly thinks. Perhaps, in fact, he thinks very little while watching a complicated action in which human movement counts for a great deal. The beating of his heart, the shifting of his eyes, replace thinking during those moments when the protagonists of a kidnapping or a murder chase one another across the screen and revolvers explode in puffs of cotton-batting. The interruptions for subtitles leave the child gasping as though from a respiratory arrest, and, I am inclined to think, his mind finds in them no opportunity to rest itself, to turn fruitfully inward. Exciting films, rapid races, and all those sports whose speed exceeds the normal rhythm of our heart and lungs, eliminate all thoughts that are not of self-preservation or of painful pleasure.

But if the child and the adult are given cinematic spectacles preserved from novelistic adventure, neither will stint their expressions of surprise, the quality and vivacity of their joy or their interest. I remember that during the film *Way Down East*, the audience, every evening, like a single person, gave a long murmur of admiration at an incomparable landscape rich with the rising sun, weeping willows, a wide river, all wet with the morning dew. In spite of the courage and the talent of Lillian Gish, the moment of real emotion found its expression here, in a sigh, a relaxation, a regret.

In the same fashion, last Thursday at the Musée Galliera, there were two moments when all the young hands clapped, when the mouths exhaled and then immediately cut short their "Ahs" of respectful ecstasy. In the first one, a "slow motion" shot rose from the ground, immobilized itself in the air, then held on a sea gull suspended on a breeze. The undulation and the flexing of the wings, the mechanism of guiding and direction in the tail, the whole secret of flight, the whole simple mystery of aviation, revealed in an instant, dazzled everyone's eyes. A bit later, a "fast motion" documented the germination of a bean, the birth of its tunneling radicelles, the avid yawning of the cotyledons from which sprung up, throwing its serpent's-head like a spear, the first sprout . . . At the revelation of the intentional and intelligent movement of the plant, I saw children get up, imitate the extraordinary ascent of a plant climbing in a spiral, avoiding an obstacle, groping over its trellis: "It's looking for something! It's looking!" cried a little boy, profoundly affected. He dreamed of the plant that night, and so did I. These spectacles are never forgotten and give us the thirst for further knowledge. We want, for ourselves and our children, not an indigent imagination, but the extravagance of reality, the unbridled fantasy of nature; we want the fairy tale of the germination of peas, the Arabian night's tale of the metamorphoses of a dragonfly, and the explosion, the formidable distention, of the budding lily, half-opening in long flat mandibles over a dark agitation of stamens—a gluttonous and powerful labor of flowering in front of which a little girl said, in a very low, somewhat frightened voice: "Oh! A crocodile!"

MAE WEST

The first of the following two selections is an excerpt from "Les Cinéacteurs," a piece written in 1934 and collected in *La Jumelle Noire* (*Black Opera Glasses*). From the same collection comes a 1938 piece on the apparent decline of Miss West.

I

...I hope that we are not too quick to dismiss the astonishing actress who has only to appear in order to convince us, to gain our vote by means as sure as they are unexpected—I mean Mae West. "And do you know, she's like that in real life!" If that is so, we could rely almost solely on her private life, her authorial independence, her impetuosity—like a wholehearted cavalry charge—even her greediness, to keep her for us just as we see her in *She Done Him Wrong*. However, I'm dubious; in *I'm No Angel* her mastery already seems a bit mechanical. She has not been sufficiently on her guard against the scenario, which lacks bite; the scene with the lions leaves us unmoved. Happily, the beautiful blonde she-devil spirits away all the weaknesses of the film with a sway of her hips, a glance that undermines morals, and a damnable little "hu . . . hum" on two notes.

But I feel that she is being pulled in different directions. And moreover—an unforgivable detail, a violation of principle —she is a little thinner.

II

What's wrong? She's thinner. Nevertheless the film critics, who don't mince their words, reproach her with both the mediocrity of her latest film and her corpulence. One speaks of "fat haunches," another calls her "the adipose beauty," a third makes fun of her age, and the fourth is indignant at her cynicism.

I wanted to see this film, which isn't good, in which Mae West is said to "kill" nobody, though she was so "killing" in *She Done Him Wrong*. But Mae West, ever since *She Done Him Wrong*, has been worth going someplace to see. She alone, out of an enormous and dull catalogue of heroines, does not get married at the end of the film, does not die, does not take the road to exile, does not gaze sadly at her declining youth in a silver-framed mirror in the worst possible taste; and she alone does not experience the bitterness of the abandoned "older woman." She alone has no parents, no children, no husband. This impudent woman is, in her style, as solitary as Chaplin used to be.

Impudence is rare in the cinema. In every country, to ensure its survival it finds itself obliged to borrow the mask of simple grossness and a joviality that dishonors the dialogue. By means of such concessions, it remains an exclusively virile virtue.

If some pretty young American tries to use it for her own ends, the result is desolating. The star has only two ways, both blameworthy, of adopting impudence: to resemble a bad supporting actress in a tragedy, or to have the air of a drunken woman. When we went to see *She Done Him Wrong*, we perceived that Mae West had invented something in the acting art. Since then she has continued, with the nonchalance of a woman of wit and the obstinacy of a trader.

To enlighten my judgment, I would have liked America to send us a great deal of Mae West, since she is the *auteur* and the principal interpreter of her films. It would have interested me to know how, by being insisted upon, the best discoveries spoil, and what is the process that ankyloses and discolors a character so rich, so hardy, so un-American: the woman without scruples, the female rival of the male débauché, the brave enemy of the male, valorous enough to use the same weapons as he. Balzac, who was quick to see things, knew and showed these women warriors. Except for Madame Marneffe, he places them, as is his right and his preference, in the highest ranks of the French peerage.

For Mae West, the age of vice is not 1900 but 1907 or '08: the era of giant hats made popular by Lantelme, the clinging dresses of Margaine-Lacroix, the straight corsets that enclosed the female body from under the arm to the knee—corsets for the sake of which Germaine Gallois stipulated in her contracts that she would not have to sit down on stage. In comparison with such rigors, 1900 was easy, and Mae West's instinct was true when it led her to barricade herself in 1907. Just think of the kind of low drama she acts almost without gestures, except for the local undulations of her backside. Think of the murdered woman, camouflaged by a great head of hair that Mae West combs as she says in her nasal voice to the man calling to her: "Wait a minute, I'm doing something I've never done before." And can you honestly name another artist, male or female, in the cinema whose comic acting equals that of this ample blonde who undulates in little waves, who is ornamented with her real diamonds, whose eye is pale and hard, whose throat swells with the coos of a professional dove?

The only trouble is that since then, due to a major *maladresse*, she is thinner. I am looking at stills of *She Done Him Wrong*. During the short and restrained hand-to-hand struggle between the two women, two breasts, white, powerful, strongly attached to her torso, all but spring nude out of Mae West's bodice. She has the short neck, the round cheek of a young blonde butcher. Her arms are athletic, the cloth of the clinging dress creases, rides up from the well-fleshed thighs onto authentic buttocks.

Through lack of inspiration or good counsel, she has rejected these "advantages" of former days, reduced them all too visibly. In her latest film she is falsely fleshy. Her princess-style dresses don't cling to her living flesh but to immobile padding. The short arms have lost their character of compelling force. The essential signification of sensuality and animality abandons the shrunken body, the face barricaded behind make-up and fearing every moment. Thus the dimples in the cheeks, thus the cruel and generous smile she once had, no longer charmingly and infallibly contradict her hard eyes. This implacable gaze, the expression of utter lack of clemency of a Mae West turned to stone—I hardly expected it to remind me, by a resemblance more of inner nature than form, of Castiglione's paralyzed Countess, who, threatened less by mankind than by time, saw her approaching death.

BLACK AND WHITE

A 1935 piece, "Noir et Blanc" was collected in *La Jumelle Noire*.

Let them not come too soon, those colors for which cinema is looking and which it calls the colors of life.

We wait for them without impatience, not yet resigned, after the latest experiments, to the indiscreet clarity, the flat springtime, and the monotony they throw over the deep domain of black and white.

Black, white, their combinations, their infinite contrasts, demonstrate to us every day that they adapt very well to the arbitrary, that is, the intervention of human art. What will become of cinema if it is again reduced to the photographic verisimilitude by which it was dominated until it was able to free itself?

What will happen to the gripping contrast of shadow and light, psychological commentaries of incomparable eloquence? The technique of the color film will not rediscover them except by forcing, by playing tricks with, the colors of nature, which rarely superabounds with polychrome excesses. We already see the necessity of creating a cinematographic palette, which is a betrayal of the natural colors that the laboratories are so avidly seeking . . . Before I have even lost this black and white, my premature regrets and my apprehensions are aroused by the film I saw yesterday.

Max Reinhardt's *Midsummer Night's Dream* unrolled its virgin reels, its kilometers of film, for five or six pairs of eyes. It was a spectacle that for me was not without melancholy. Only two years ago Reinhardt planned to put on *The Dream* at the Théâtre Pigalle and asked me to do a French adaptation of the text. We lacked only backers. Bizarre, delicious evening on which we celebrated our agreement! Over our cooling lobster we exchanged ideas with the aid of the kind interpreter whom our rapid talk kept dinnerless. I admired how the director of *Die Fledermaus* was already able to draw in the air the size of Bottom's ass's-head and to replace Titania with a spiral of smoke . . .

"Yes, yes," he said, "we'll keep Mendelssohn . . . Shakespeare, Mendelssohn, they've been together such a long time . . . After fifty years of living together, there are no bad marriages . . ."

The spiral of smoke that symbolized Titania I saw again last night. Around a gigantic tree, the veteran of a clearing, it rose, serving as a highway for all the creatures born of our dreaming when it is at its sweetest and most fruitful, when it turns toward childhood and, enchanted, creates. Reinhardt's imagination, a cinematic technique that admits no obstacles, a luxury that consists in taking time, in beginning again, again, and still again, and a conjunction of diverse efforts have all given birth to a translucent people, elfs in spun glass, a Titania through which one can see, as through arborized agate, ferns and little branches of heath. The white of pearls, the white of milk, the whitish-blue of the full moon, the whited gold of the rising sun . . . Tiny white children, pathetic, with hair of frost; white lightning-bolts like a thousand fires, scattered by the somber Oberon; white of fog that swallows up graceful, imponderable bodies, fleshy petal-white of tuberoses on the body of the last adorable daughter of Night . . . They are too rare, in the cinema, these moments when we are touched simply by the perfect and sufficient harmony of lines, of lights, of the opportunity for silence, movement, and immobility.

It is not my function to make premature criticisms of the troupe of actors to whom Reinhardt has entrusted Shakespeare's text. But my astonishment at the actor playing Puck is my excuse for breaking with the usual conventions. He is a child of twelve, perhaps a little younger. Having seen it yesterday and only briefly, I forget his name, which tomorrow will be famous.* Of course, all children are remarkable screen actors.

Hollywood is a kindergarten of prodigies, where the blessed parents take their ease while their progeny, between three and seven years old, assume the responsibility for assuring the family's future. Tiny little France has Robert Lynen, Gaby Triquet, Paulette Elambert . . . But now I'm stupefied to learn that Puck really exists. No mechanical training, no hard schooling, could have taught this faun-child the art of enunciating his words, of understanding the difficult old English, of ennobling its phrases. A miracle of rhythm animates him, sets aflame his small body, his masterless and malicious face, which seems unaware that we are spying on him.

His voice will doubtless sound around the world. It is the true voice of Oberon's forest messenger, a voice that has never battered itself against the walls of human habitation, a voice as raucous as a peacock's call, strong and many-toned. But above all one must hear it as it drones out onomatopoeias that the child has perhaps invented for himself, snuffles of a little boar, chattering of a squirrel, and especially a rising laugh, victorious, impossible to describe, and more savage than all his other sounds.

* Mickey Rooney.

BACKSTAGE AT THE STUDIO

"L'Envers du Cinema" is composed of two parts, the first and longer of which was written in 1917, the other in 1935. Before being collected in the posthumous *Paysages et Portraits*, the first part was published successively in *Femina* (September 1917), *Le Film* (October 8, 1917), and *Filma* (December 15–31, 1917). The first part concerns the 1917 filming of *The Vagabond* in Rome; the second, that of *Divine* by Max Ophuls in 1935.

I

Outside, it's Roman spring: a sapless azure in which swallows' wings scythe, a day of clouds hardly moved by a feeble warm breeze, and of roses in the gardens, lilacs, acacias, whitethorn, wisteria, that a single day of heat fades and that exchange above the Via Nomentana their perfume of vanilla fritters and orange flowers.

Inside, under the skylights of a studio without walls, it is already—and will be until the cool September breezes—a furnace. The arid air offends the throat and the bronchi—"but," as one of the apprentices of the Società Cinematografica says, indicating the thermometer, "it doesn't often go above 120°."

The midday cannon has boomed above Rome. From the caretaker's shack the odor of hot oil and fried fish, followed by the sizzle of onions, has crossed the glass theater. Several minutes later the air wafts the smell of coffee and orange peel. Twelve-thirty—one o'clock—two—and no supple Italian actor, no huge-eyed extra, has yet rushed, first toward the dressing rooms and then to the *trattoria*: this world guarded by transparent gates, ruled by the motion of sun and clouds, has broken with the customs of millennia.

The star will eat her lunch toward 4 P.M.; more fortunate, an actor in a small role stealthily polishes off a *frittata* between two slices of the national bread, mealy and compact. I am hungry. Five hundred yards from here I could find a *fiacre*, an ageless horse, a worm-eaten coachman full of shadowy ill-will . . . It is not my work that keeps me here, it is the work of others. I am only the witness, the meddler, the lazybones: the author of the scenario they are "shooting." Never mind, I stay.

I am present at this spectacle I have seen a hundred times, that has renewed itself for me a hundred times. The program for the day includes several attractions: a fistfight between two rivals, in a set of a shabby music hall; the discovery of a letter, setting the scene for a goodbye . . . For the moment, the delay prolongs itself, and the stoutest hearts waver. A white and blonde matron, enormously fat, engaged at so much the pound to play the role of the Fat Lady, pants in her sequined tight jacket; one thinks of the sparkling death-agony of a fish in faraway seas.

Stoic, in pearl-gray trousers, the young male lead rests standing up. He has slipped a folded handkerchief between his collar and his neck, and fans himself with a newspaper. He doesn't speak, he doesn't complain; his bull-like face, that of a handsome man of the people, expresses only one thought: "I may die standing up and suffocated, but let there live after me the crease in these pearl-gray trousers, the crease that in a moment will be bent, one time only, for the action of kneeling in front of this dazzling young woman . . ."

Dazzling, in fact. There is nothing whiter than her white, powdered face, unless it is her naked arms, her bare neck, the white of her eyes. Every time I look at her eyes my memory whispers to me the phrase of Charles-Louis Philippe: "She had eyes of a great expanse . . ." Black, her hair; black, her eyelashes; her dark mouth is open over her white teeth—she is already just like her cinematic image, and the professionals of Italy and France will compliment her to you in a manner that admits of no reply: "Anything more photogenic than her you couldn't find!"

This veteran young beauty defies the crushing light. She has trained herself—with what pain!—to have eyelids that don't blink, a motionless forehead; my eyes tear on seeing her lift her statuelike gaze toward the midday sun . . . She sweats only slightly at the roots of her carefully waved hair, and sometimes, without a muscle of her face twitching, a round tear, the fruit of her wounded eyes and tense eyelids, falls from her lashes and runs down her cheek.

This young woman, the star, has been cooking under the glass roof since nine in the morning. Yesterday she made eleven changes of clothes, stockings, shoes, hats, hairstyles. The day before, half-naked in the gardens, she shivered under lilacs dripping with rain. Tomorrow, at 7 A.M. an automobile will carry her to the still snowy mountains, twenty-five miles there, twenty-five back, nowhere to stop in between. Last December, with the temperature at 27° F., she went swimming in the ocean. For a detective film she was thrown under a train, from which she emerged blackened and slightly burned with cinders, and then was seated on the fender of a moving car . . .

A strange destiny, one to think about. Hard work under austere conditions, deprived of the recompense which triumphs over fatigue every evening at the theater: the applause, the warm contact with the public, the comfort of being looked at and being envied . . . Is it only the hunger for making money that sustains the principal actors and actresses of the cinema and makes them take daily risks? I can't believe it . . .

"Rrrrrrrrrr . . ." The continuous purring of the camera alerts me that the work is beginning again. The thermometer registers 91°, but from the swaying of the clusters of wisteria against the burnt wall, from the sudden flight of rose petals, I know that the *ponentino*, the west wind, has risen, spreading its cool wings over the city, presaging the setting of the sun and the clement Roman night . . .

"Andiamo!" cries the director, and he adds an *"Allons-y! Let's go!"* which is understood by everyone, since—we should blush for it!—managers of the X-Company speak rapid and easy French, and so does the director, and so do the actors; the Fat Lady coos in French like a great fat pigeon, and the diminutive bit-part player whom I asked—in what mangled Italian!—to animate his mimed song a little, replied:

"I no make more the acting with the hands, I'm *romanzero*."

"*Ro*—?"

"I don't sing except the stories, at the cafés. The *romanzero*, he don't make the acting with the hands."

They film. They film "fillers," "transitions," those comings and goings, shots of open and closed doors, corridors, which, placed like ingenious sutures between the important scenes, will give the audience the illusion of truth, of real life, of ubiquity . . .

Attentive to the director's instructions, the beautiful black-and-white young woman sways into the magnificent light of 3 P.M.

"You come in here, you go out there, in between you stop a moment and listen uneasily to see if your husband's following you."

She listens, reflects, poses this Sibylline question:

"How much?"

"Six feet, maybe seven . . ."

A hermetic dialogue, in which the initiated can understand that this "transition" must be acted at a pace that will allow it to be captured on at most seven feet of film. This filmic argot is spoken in Paris just as it is here, and I would often forget where we were, the distance from the borders, if I were not reminded of it by the languor of the air and the unusually calm attitude toward a job which among us infallibly excites nerves and crying jags. "Here," Renan wrote, "the rhythm of life is a degree slower . . ." A bit too much serenity enfeebles the passion of the great lover, and I give up trying to understand why we used to reproach the Italian actors for excessive movement and expression. How gentle they are, even that one, playing the role of an acerbic comedian—yes, that one, who just now raises to the cameraman his worldly-wise face, creased by an internal grin, and his eyes blanketed under their heavy eyelids . . .

"*Presto, presto*, Ecce Homo!"

Ecce Homo? It's actually him. It's the man—the man who played *Christus* and is no more than justly proud of it. But his wife, to whom I am praising this easygoing deity, glows with pride.

"Don't you think he was handsome as Christ? Do you think he looked well on the cross? Didn't they have luck finding somebody with a fallen diaphragm! Isn't that right, Your Holiness?"

The irreverent blonde who is speaking like this—without a trace of accent—calls out in passing to a sumptuous footman, laden with years and gold braid, who is bearing a platter on which well-curled fennel sets off leg of lamb and whipped potatoes. He turns toward us an admirable Italian face, long, embellished with noble wrinkles, crowned with silver.

"Your Holiness, come and be introduced . . . He was the one who did the pope in that movie, you know, the one that was so well done that everyone thought they'd filmed the real pope . . . He's seventy-eight years old."

His Holiness smiles, balances his platter on his trembling left hand, and raising the right, grants us, on the run, the papal benediction . . .

Let us leave these profane jokes; the so-photogenic young

lady is going to "shoot" an important scene of my scenario, for which no one has either asked my advice or consulted me; if they had, I would have given them to understand, reinforcing my advice with diplomatic periphrasis, that pyjamas on a woman, even accompanied by a Hindu turban, go better with vaudeville than drama.

The series of rites unfolds itself in an atmosphere of general sweatiness. In a set representing an actress's dressing room, a three-sided mirror is pulled back, then brought forward, then taken away, then returned; the dressing table waltzes from one side of the set to the other. An old touring trunk is given the honor of being placed in the foreground, until the moment when the director notices that it carries, among some twenty hotel stickers, the very legible words "Dresden," "Munich," etc. Exile of the trunk, to the sound of kicking. In prances that strange animal, six-legged and caparisoned in black, made up of the camera and cameraman. Groans from a portion of the animal. Redistribution, in an immobile group, of the photogenic young woman, a frail gentleman, another robust gentleman, the Fat Lady—you can hear her breathing from the other end of the studio!—a white Pierrot, an eccentric fashion-plate of a girl—sixteen years old, the sweetest possible virginal face—and a Calabrian peasant. A shout:

"*Gira!*"

And the purr of the motor: the whole group animates itself without a sound; the frail gentleman holds by the wrists the young woman in pyjamas and mouths silent curses at her. She struggles, twists her slender wrists, opens her mouth for a great groan which we hardly hear, and whispers into the face of her tormentor, her face the mask of a woman screaming: "I forbid you . . . I forbid you to treat me this way . . . Coward . . . miserable villain . . ."

The robust gentleman says nothing; he restrains himself and clutches at his cane. His whole left leg is thinking of the crease in the pearl-gray trousers . . . The other actors, in the background, murmur and move about in place like a screen of trees blown by a sudden wind . . . A shout:

"*Basta!*"

And the collective expression of the group falls away; the shoulders sag, the eyes lose their momentary fire, the knees relax . . .

"Basta per oggi! È finito!"

È finito! Nevertheless, as the adolescent cries of joy of the released resound, the director detains the photogenic young woman, who is listening to the program for tomorrow:

"Tomorrow, little one, we're filming at Nemi and the car leaves at 8 A.M. Bring the costume for the flight, the dress for the garden, the evening dress with the coat, all the accessories. Don't forget anything, all right? Nemi isn't just around the corner . . ."

She listens in hopeless submission, nods "yes, yes," and recites in a low voice the litany of her baggage:

"The pink dress, the gray stockings, the doeskin slippers, the black tulle robe, the violet coat, the white gloves, the diadem, the kimono, the furred mules, the blue suit . . ."

And as if until this minute, by an effort of will, she had been in command of nature, she suddenly begins to sweat freely and goes off toward her dressing room reciting her psalms:

"The violet coat, the blue suit, the furred mules, the diadem, the gray stockings . . ."

My eye follows this slim silhouette, this body only a moment ago tensed and now soft and swaying in the silk pyjamas, and I ask myself again: "The thirst for gain, success on the screen, the love of a daily flirtation with danger—could they be enough to draw a young woman to this existence for year after year? There is love of the craft, I know, and also the spirit of rivalry. But what else?"

A snatch of dialogue between two young cinema actresses comes back to me:

"It isn't as good as the theater, and it's back-breaking work," said the first.

"Maybe," said the other. "But in the movies, you can see yourself . . ."

Perhaps this delicate narcissism should also be noted in the way certain stars of the cinema commonly think and express themselves. One of the most notorious and beautiful of the Italian *prima donnas* criticizes, curses, or admires herself on the screen as if she were talking about another person, with a sort of hallucinated candor:

"Did you see *La Piccola Fonte*?" she said to me. "Didn't you think it was good? In the garden, when *she* drags herself along the wall and the door, *she* has a way of holding herself, a way of moving her arms, that's lovely . . ."

Among the women who consecrate their youth and the perishable flowers of their faces to the screens, might there not be a sort of lovers' fanaticism toward those mysterious "doubles" in black and white, detached from them by some cinematic miracle, eternally free, complete, surprising, more full of life than they themselves—"doubles" whose existence they contemplate as humble creators, sometimes delighted, often astonished, and feeling always toward them a certain lack of responsibility?

II

The more I see them, cloistered in their work, the more I admire cinema actors. For two months I have been seeing a great deal of them—not enough to suit me. I am ready to ask myself once more where they get their energy. The bitter epigram of one of them does not enlighten me, because it is redolent with a kind of perverse pride, a surly modesty.

Worn out, I was leaving the studio at the end of one of those interminable work days that begin at daybreak under false sunlight, fail to take into account lunch and dinner hours, have only contempt for the limits of human endurance, and often end—since the theaters claim their personnel at eight—only to begin again after midnight . . . I was telling X, an actor in both the theater and the cinema, about the diverse feelings toward cinema actors inspired in me by my own weariness and their courage: "Bah!" he said to me, "you're never exhausted when you're well paid."

He affected bravura under his makeup, which had been done over twice since noon, and posed as the avid businessman. But I am no dupe. Although they greatly exceed the honoraria available in the theater, the profits of cinema do not justify the actors' heroism. I am only now beginning to study—reproaching myself for leaving it until so late in the cinematic day—what a cinematic vocation might be, its true essence, its goal and its reward when this goal and this reward become differentiated from rapacity.

Because, for people of my generation, film will always be surrounded by a sort of aura, defensive and not easily penetrable. At twenty-one, my daughter is already a director, fervent, impatient to show what she can do. She gnaws at her leash of "assistant" and is an example of humility. For four years she has been *inside* the cinema. So long a novitiate has made her unable to comprehend my reasons for astonishment. She shares the impassibility of the screen actors; like them she "rests" bolt upright, and like them she maintains a lengthy silence because only one man has the right to storm.

She is capable of discussing subtly the afflictions, the infantilism, the wonders of the cinema; but she will not enlighten me about the basic cause, the emotional source, of such a marvelous equanimity in the face of work and silence . . .

One day during the coldest week in February, I was at the Billancourt studios, where fifty young women, half-naked, were filming music-hall scenes. For seven consecutive hours, sheltered under the heavy special makeup, they underwent the temperature extremes of a cloth-covered courtyard, iced by the east wind and then briefly overheated by a catastrophe of Klieg lights. Following Max Ophuls' quick commands, they climbed up and down the raw wood steps unprotected by guard rails, running and turning with inexhaustible grace. A terrible arrow of light pierced in passing Simone Berriau's golden eyes and Gina Manès' phosphorus-blue ones. Phillippe Hériat, nude and chromed, shuddered with cold and refused the robe that would have tarnished his metallic makeup. No starving extra permitted herself to faint. At a cry from Ophuls—"We can hear the feet on the stairs! Take off your shoes!"—fifty young women, Simone Berriau among them, took off their shoes without a word and ran barefoot over the unfinished wood, among serpentining cables, metal shavings, rubble, and nails.

This was the same day on which the hands of an animal trainer were to drape over Simone Berriau's shoulders a live python, almost as heavy as a man . . .

"What will he do?" I asked the serpent's trainer shortly before this happened.

He shrugged his shoulders, uncertain.

"You can't tell . . . He's young, you see, and intelligent . . . Not bad-tempered, you understand, but he doesn't know the lady . . . The best thing is to let him alone. If there's any trouble, I always have this . . ."

He showed me, very naturally, a heavy, double-edged knife. Then, from a valise that was keeping warm on a radiator, he took three yards of python, draped it around his neck, and taught me to gently scratch "Joseph's" chin, which was richly marbled, here and there almost pink.

When he laid this formidable silent actor on the shoulders of "Divine," dressed as a dancing girl, she sagged a moment, then straightened up. Then she was left entirely alone with "Joseph," and both were covered with pitiless Klieg lights. At first the serpent was at the level of her hips. It circled her waist solidly and sent off its agile head in the direction of her neck and bosom. It explored her whole bust, which it touched gently with its long bifidal tongue. A sort of grin of anguish flitted over the dancing girl's face, cracked open her mouth to show her gleaming teeth. The serpent's head disappeared behind her shoulder, drawing the body after it in indescribable ophidian progression, and I thought that the ordeal was nearing its end . . . But at the top of her gilded headdress, the python's head reappeared, raised itself like a rattler's. A moment more, and it flowed down the temple, stopped at the corner of the eyebrow, licked her cheek . . . Simone Berriau's large eyelids fluttered downward, hid her eyes, and Ophuls allowed her to be rescued . . . But I think that he was more moved than she, who was already shaking off the evil spell and inquiring:

"Did it work? Were we all right, Joseph and me?"

Vocation, vocation—a need to touch the emotions of the mass, to appeal to the common judgment . . .

M. CHARLES BOYER, OF HOLLYWOOD

First published in *Paris-Soir*, May 1, 1939, this piece came to light only recently and was not included in *Colette au Cinéma*. In 1979 it was re-published in *Cahiers Colette Numero 2* by the *Société des Amis de Colette*. It is included in the present volume by the special permission of Mme Colette de Jouvenel, the novelist's daughter.

Whether we wished it or not, whether or not our taste takes us once a week to the cinema, they are our familiars, the actors whose vogue imposes on the screen their dimensionless elegance, their almost monochrome beauty. Soon, no doubt, some discovery will lift the interdict that still lies over the use of color, and the human face will free itself from toned blacks, diverse whites; landscape will emerge, in the green of its leaves, the blue of mist and sea, the red of sand, from the last photographic malediction that has kept it a prisoner of inanimate tones.

Living photographs have been a habit with us for too long for us to break with them without unease. In a film made last year, we did not care to like Marlene Dietrich in color. Faced with the candied pink on her cynical lip, the anemic gold of her hairstyle, the hesitant azure of her look, we hung fire, because we are only rarely able to love at first sight. Even while wishing that the cinema will become a complete miracle, the youngest, the most enthusiastic of its fans are strongly attached to tall female deities whose bosoms are amber-colored or pearl-gray, whose magnified mouths are the color of chocolate, who have in their eyes a transparency varying from speckled slate-gray to the black of anthracite. The same for heroes with handsome teeth and ebony hair. And the same for the clever children, for the animals and the flowers . . . All that will pass. The arbitrariness of color will replace arbitrary black and white. The varicolored screen and its stars will hold no more nor less place in our daily life, which they have conquered, than black and white once did.

We forget the name and the face of flesh-and-blood people we have met many times, we testify distractedly to the changes and the destruction time brings; but with regard to its stars the cinema robs us of the least hope of uncertainty. Plastered to the walls, forcing her way through the window, arrogating the front page of movie weeklies, blown out of all proportion, endowed with violet eyes and marbled on pestiferous slabs at cinema doors—in two weeks the so-called "discovery of the year" engraves her name and her features on your memory. The equally monomaniacal newspapers repeat *ad nauseam* that she has just reached her obligatory sixteenth year and that only a miraculous stroke of luck led her to the seventh art. She sometimes has a great deal of grace, enough to triumph over these punishing proceedings. This is the moment when she must adopt a design for her mouth—which her makeup will superimpose on her authentic young lips—and efface the often delicious arc of her upper lip.

The debut of a chosen young man, a star-to-be, doesn't show the same explosion of forced blooming. Male material is less exploitable, deprived as it is of great agglutinate eyelashes, hair teased into feathers or rolled into curls. Even nude and

muscular, he does not—at least in France—so immediately
"rise" to the vertical conquest of the city. Only the American
studios reserve for their wards the surprise of falling asleep
as supporting players and waking up stars. But America has
enormous powers at her disposal, including that of the liberty to
fool herself. Serviceable, Errol Flynn passes for a leading player
until the day when Hollywood decrees that he has little eyes,
that his thighs are too long, and that he doesn't "make a good
couple" with anybody.

"Make a good couple" . . . These screen marriages, which
set Jean Gabin and Simone Simon side by side, link William
Powell and Myrna Loy, and keep an airborne Ginger Rogers in
the arms of Fred Astaire, are important enough almost to double
the costs of a film, and its profits as well. They become so
important as to make us question the success of either one of
the protagonists alone, so much so as to make us think that
some law of psychology may govern what the laws of technique
and photogenic qualities thought could be decided solely by
themselves. "Two of us, finally!" cry the heroes of a banal love
story; because, for a long time our celebrated screen effigies
behaved a bit like Sarah Bernhardt on tour, that is—dare I write
it?—as if in a desert populated by inferior beings . . . Now
finally two—and sometimes three—alone together. Everybody's
happy, except when some mysterious repudiation separates
lovers brought together by their contracts. Then the universal
witness, the public, adds its voice, and perhaps it is the one to
decide. Possibly its criticism lights first on the physique of the
couple. "That baby-face of hers, do you really think it goes with
his bullet head? In that role I'd rather have seen . . ." Everyone
passes the divorce decree on the celebrated couple and re-
marries them as he or she pleases. Even a success leaves the
universal witness somewhat discontented. *Mayerling*, which
could congratulate itself on pairing the young talent of Danielle
Darrieux with His Solidity Charles Boyer, didn't blind me so
thoroughly that I didn't regret seeing in Him and Her an identical
penchant for the long fixed stare with eyeballs almost bulging.
He used it magisterially, according to the needs of the film; she
slightly abused it, according to the exigencies of the close-up.

Is this not worth mentioning? Excuse me, but in movie
making everything counts. Our children are even more demanding than us—why, unfortunately, isn't their intransigence di-

rected against those stomach-turning scenarios? Thanks to the cinema our children have developed the instincts of woodsmen. The other day, an actress on the screen looked at her wrist and remarked, "Five o'clock already!"

"Listen to her!" cried a disillusioned child from a seat near mine. "Five o'clock! Look at the shadows the trees cast!"

This week, She and He, united on walls, on sliding panels, on the hoardings of construction sites, and in the pages of movie magazines, are called Irene Dunne and Charles Boyer.* Where Marlene Dietrich, one of the ideal spouses of our great leading man, failed, Irene Dunne succeeds wholly. I need no further proof than my own satisfaction and the exceptional indulgence that these two actors, inspired by each other, make me feel for a scenario consisting of carefully measured parts of ocean liners, Madeira seen through Santa Monica, a chapel and a Catholic grandmother, and "Plaisir d'amour" swollen to the proportions of a public menace. Two better-than-good actors have fine sport with these syrupy traps, and the neatness, the airy tangibility of Irene Dunne allows one to love Charles Boyer's indelible air of being in a waking dream. I am very far from pitying the fortunate fate of this expatriate-by-contract. But I am afraid that, having chosen, he will change, because life in Hollywood is cruel to the artist who won't or can't change, who senses his own well-defined nature, experiences the outrage of a personality and a conscience, has what is known as a bulldog temperament. Maurice Chevalier is coming back (he didn't exactly hurry that decision, you will say); Simone Simon is throwing it all over and coming back; Mireille Balin sobs, and comes back. Annabella and Charles Boyer have settled down on the shores of the Pacific. I don't believe that it's too difficult for the gentle Annabella to offer her face and heart—both equally unmarked—to a new country, a new life. But I have just seen on the screen an American Charles Boyer just like the Charles Boyer I knew in former times in Paris, with his velvet, suspicious, Arabian eye, his habit of falling silent in the middle of a sentence, his nonchalance, his unexpected decisiveness. Under the shade of the lovely trees of California, in the sunny luxury of his house there, that Charles Boyer sometimes must think, as the burnt man thinks of water, of the old nights in a darkened

* *Love Affair* (1939).

theater, the ecstatic public near enough to touch him, and the huge sofa on which playwright Henri Bernstein's "Gabriel" furiously rolled back and forth, holding in his arms the long slippery body of Yvonne de Bray.

Colette herself did the scenario for La Flamme Cachée *(1918), "a four-part drama" starring her friend Musidora, who is shown above accepting the benediction of her poor lover (Maurice Lagrenée) when she decides to marry a wealthy suitor (Jean Yonnel).*

Photo courtesy Cinémathèque Française

Members of the romantic triangle in La Flamme Cachée, *starring Lagrenée, Musidora, and Yonnel—later one of the leading actors of the Comédie Française—are shown during their earlier student days in a location scene shot before the facade of the Sorbonne.*

Photo courtesy Cinémathèque Française

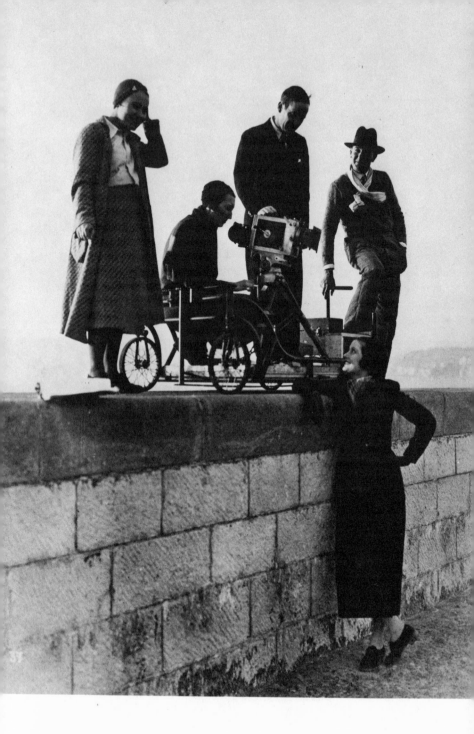

The 1931 sound version of La Vagabonde *came fourteen years after the silent version which inspired Colette's bitting "A Short Manual for an Aspiring Scenario Writer." Shown on location (l to r) are the novelist's daughter, Colette de Jouvenel, assistant director; Solange Bussi, director; Rudolf Maté and Louis Née, cameramen; and Marcelle Chantal, actress.*

Solange Térac Collection

Chéri was adapted for the screen in 1950 by Pierre Laroche but featured dialogue by Colette. Directed by Pierre Billon, it starred Jean Desailly in the title role and Marcelle Chantal as Léa.

Below are Yvonne de Bray as Mamita and Danièle Delorme as Gigi in the 1948 adaptation of one of Colette's most popular novels. The novelist herself did the dialogue for this version. On the right, Leslie Caron in the musical film version directed by Vincente Minnelli in 1958. The all-star cast featured Maurice Chevalier, Louis Jourdan, Hermione Gingold, and Eva Gabor.

Photo courtesy Cinémathèque Française

Danièle Delorme and Jean Tissier are shown below in Jacqueline Audry's film Minne, L'Ingénue Libertine *(1950). A silent film based on the same novel was shot in Paris in 1916 but apparently never finished, or at least never distributed. It starred Musidora, who also directed.*

Jacqueline Audry Collection

In 1956 actress Danièle Delorme and director Jacqueline Audry joined forces again in Mitsou, *their third film adaptation of a novel by Colette. Right, Danièle Delorme, François Guérin, and Claude Rich.*

Jacqueline Audry Collection

Claude Autant-Lara's film version of Le Blé en Herbe *featured Edwige Feuillère as an older woman who takes an adolescent, Pierre-Michel Beck, as her lover. The director joined the prestigious writing team of Jean Aurenche and Pierre Bost in doing the scenario.*

DIALOGUE AND SCENARIO BY COLETTE

LAC-AUX-DAMES

"We still search in vain," wrote Maurice Goudeket in *Près de Colette* (1956), "for the scenario of *Lac-aux-Dames*, and every chance of recovering it appears exhausted." Without the manuscript, the next best thing was to secure the working script of the film which contained the dialogue precisely as written by Colette. Marc Allégret, the director of the film, had kept this script, and it is thanks to him that we have been able to recover Colette's "lost" dialogue, which, according to Philippe de Rothschild, "contributed to the world-wide success of the film."

Rothschild's money was behind the enterprise. He had recently finished a three-year association with the Théâtre Pigalle and was now turning toward the cinema, which was still in the very early sound era. Rothschild's project was to make a film for the most part in exteriors, not in the studio. With this in mind, he chose a book by Vicki Baum, *Hell in Frauensee*, which had appeared in 1932, and he asked Colette, whom he had known for several years, if she would do the dialogue. She agreed and signed a contract with his "Société Parisienne de Production" on June 15, 1933.

The idea of asking her to do a film about the outdoors and nature made sense in terms of Colette's long-standing denunciation, in her criticism and *chroniques*, of studio artifice. However, if one is to believe her correspondence, the actual task did not inspire her with delirious enthusiasm. She writes to Hélène Picard: "I'm caught in a piece of stupid work like a cog in a machine, writing a scenario based on a book that isn't mine. And the hours of work—sometimes collective—are so capricious I don't know how to get away" (June 1933). And to Mrs. Léopold Marchand: "Arrived here a week ago, exhausted. Worked nine or eleven hours a day with Philippe de Rothschild and his henchmen. The *day after* I arrived, Marc Allégret came by airplane to work four hours with me! It's hard to earn money." Colette had the habit of these picturesque recriminations, we know; "to live without writing, oh, what a miracle!" was her heartfelt cry. But she wasn't the only one to complain. Asked the same year, 1933, by the same Philippe de Rothschild to adapt Zola's *La Bête Humaine*, which was to have been directed by Marc Allégret but was not made, Roger Martin du Gard evokes in his letters to Gide the furious working pace he had to maintain.

It is not inappropriate to mention André Gide. Because, surprising as it may seem, Gide seems also to have been involved in *Lac-aux-Dames*. A letter from Gide to Martin du Gard reports that after the filming, he was brought in to rework some of the dialogue of the film; Marc Allégret confirms the point. In the dialogue that you will read, though the essential is by Colette, several passages are Gide's.

Certainly, Gide's role should not be overestimated. He was called on for a few finishing touches because he was on the scene* and because Colette had stayed in France. Perhaps her fatigue and her other projects—she was getting ready to take over as drama critic for the *Journal*—made her decide that it was enough to have her daughter, Colette de Jouvenel, on the set: she writes to Hélène Picard in August 1933: "My daughter is in Austria with a film crew; she is the second assistant director of a film for which I wrote the dialogue. She worked hard for three weeks in Paris during the worst of the heat. But the film is being made in the Austrian Tyrol, in a country of lakes and mountains; she's thrilled."

Shot in 1933, the film did not come out in Paris until August 1934. It rapidly became a huge success, in great measure due to the actors, principally to Simone Simon, who played Puck. Colette had received her and her leading man, Jean-Pierre Aumont, at La Treille Muscate (an indication that Colette's role was not merely to write the dialogues but

* The film was shot in the Austrian mountains.

also to take part in the conception and elaboration of the film). Simone Simon remembers that Colette said, seeing her, "This is my Vinca!"— the name of the heroine of *Le Blé en Herbe* (*The Ripening Seed*), which had appeared in 1923. It is tempting, as Marc Allégret suggests, to connect the novelistic character, Vinca, with the cinematic character, Puck: there is the same mixture of manifest purity and innocent provocation. The comparison suggests, in any case, that Colette put much of herself into this work, in spite of her complaints and maledictions.

Reading the dialogue, one is struck to discover the extent to which *Lac-aux-Dames* blends harmoniously into Colette's other work, the extent to which it by right belongs to her. Doubtless this is due in large part to the principal character, Eric Heller, who is so closely related to Fred Peloux, Colette's Chéri. Eric appears to be a simple variation on Chéri; like him, he beautifully illustrates the idea of the man as object in Colette's works (for which see Marcelle Biolley-Godino's recent book, *L'Homme-objet chez Colette* [1973]) ; like Chéri, Eric does not exist except through the medium of women. Without them, he literally drowns, he is paralyzed, he returns to nothingness. One woman succeeds another with him—someone to save him from drowning, someone to nourish him, someone to save him from a false step, someone to assure him a rosy future, everyone to protect him and adore him like a child. Of course, one thinks also of Bel-Ami, but Maupassant's hero creates his destiny, from woman to woman, as a thinking man, organized and cynical, while the antihero of *Lac-aux-Dames* is constantly buffeted like a straw on the ocean waves, constantly overwhelmed by unforeseeable accidents which he could never survive if someone did not run to his assistance. The man-object: though the conception of the character obviously belongs to Vicki Baum's novel and clearly exists before Colette's intervention, one must admire the sureness with which Colette has integrated him into her own universe and her mythology.

This is accomplished through a subtle transmutation in which the passivity of the character is condemned and underlined. Under Colette's pen, Eric becomes a man systematically acted upon by women; desired, harassed, and protected by them, he is placed in a situation of total dependence on them. It is a dependence that is reflected by his total subservience to the author's whim. It is the author who guides him with assurance among several possible loves toward the most useful passion, toward a happy marriage with the daughter of the rich captain of industry. She takes him in hand like an attentive mother, careful to assure her runt the most brilliant possible future.

This schema brings to the foreground all the mediocrity of Vicki Baum's original, which is followed closely by the film. Colette changes the names of only two characters; Urbain Hell becomes Eric Heller, and May become Dolly. The one notable difference is that Baum's hero endures, among others, the assaults of "la Bojan," a celebrated actress who is Puck's mother. The suppression of this disturbing woman, mature and avid for young flesh, has the effect of erasing a possible resemblance between this and the universe of *Chéri* (Camilla Bojan would have been too much like Léa), and of throwing the adolescent Puck into higher poetic relief. The antithesis between the two shores of the lake, between nature and "the world," is greatly reinforced—an antithesis dear to Colette, which we will rediscover later in *Divine*. The character did a great deal for the success of the film. He was inserted into a milieu designed to contrast with that of the summer visitors and the tourists: "crazy" family, philosophical father, exotic cabana, enormous dog— all this picturesque detail a bit external, seemingly borrowed from American comedies in the style of Frank Capra, in which charming bohemian families are opposed to traditional bourgeois ones. Colette's dialogue, on the other hand, suggests from moment to moment, and almost involuntarily, certain direct preoccupations of the era: brief allusions to the economic crisis, to the innumerable unemployed, and even—through a character named Meyer, an enigmatic person wrongly suspected of swindling—to a few overtones of a still discreet anti-Semitism; need we mention that the film was made the year Hitler came to power in Germany?

What should one think today of *Lac-aux-Dames*? The reputation of its director and its scenarist, and the excitement on its first release, raise expectations that the film may not fulfill. Certain elements have evidently aged—above all, probably, the story of the "official" love and its conventional ending. The film is balanced between two poles, the two shores of the lake; the poetic shore (Puck) has almost certainly held up better than the worldly shore (the official fiancé). The reader must judge.

In order to make Colette's dialogue intelligible, it was necessary to take from the working script phrases describing the sets, the development of the characters, and of course the silent scenes. We have reduced these phrases to the essential. However, it seemed to us that Colette's role was most likely not confined to writing the dialogue; with Jean-Georges Auriol, she probably played an important part in the initial adaptation of the book. By Colette's own admission, the final product was "a collective work" in which it was difficult to distinguish her contribution from that of other collaborators on the film. For this reason, every time that the description goes further than simple indications of time and place, we have placed in quotes those phrases tending to define an atmosphere, a state of mind, or a character. These are certainly not all Colette's, but one may imagine that she contributed to their inspiration. Note also that the film, at least as reconstituted today and presented on television, does not contain all the scenes that can be read here; some were cut in the editing, were not filmed, or could not be found. This is the case, for instance, with the scene in which there finally appears, as a veritable *deus ex machina*, the character named Meyer, and with several short scenes beside the swimming pool. However, this shortened version of the working script is the closest approximation that can now be made to what Colette actually wrote. Our thanks go to Marc Allégret, without whose consent and help this work could never have been recovered.

Aerial shot of the Salzkammergut region (many lakes). Shot of the Sankt-Wolfgang lake, where a small paddle-wheeler moves forward through a setting of mountains covered with forests. Shot of a village bordering the lake. Terrace of the Weisse Hirsch (White Stag) Hotel. A couple, the Count and Countess Stereny, are having tea. Gypsy orchestra. The count signals to the orchestra leader, who approaches.

Leader: Monsieur le Comte?
Count: Ask Madame.
Anika: Play . . . (*She gives him a Hungarian title.*)
Leader: Very good, Madame la Comtesse. (*He plays several bars on his violin.*)
Anika: Yes, that's the one.

As the leader goes back to his orchestra and raises his arms to give the signal, a thunderous march bursts forth. It's a fanfare from the firemen's band seated in the stern of the old steamboat, which has just docked.

*Arrival of the boat. Twelve hotel porters wait on the pier.
The paddle wheels slow in the water. Several travelers disembark. A crowd.*

*Hotel terrace. Anika looks absentmindedly at the new
arrivals, then turns quickly toward her companion.*

Anika: Give me my hat. (*He obeys; she hides her face.*)
Count: Why?
Anika: Shh. Someone I know.
Count: And?
Anika: I mean . . . somebody who knows me.
Count: Ah, I see! Which one?
Anika: That tall blond boy with a suitcase and a ball.

*The new arrival, carrying a valise and a medicine ball,
wearing a gray city suit, very plain and very worn, looks around
him to get his bearings.*

Count: Who is he?
Anika (*looks at him covertly*): A very sweet boy.
Count: And?
Anika: Very intelligent.
Count: Ah . . . (*Smile and little gesture expressing how little
the count thinks of that quality.*)
Anika: He's an engineer . . . or a professor. He invented something in chemistry. In any case, he's honest . . . (*The count
gazes at Eric—that is the young man's name—narrowing his
eyes almost in contempt.*)

*The pier. Eric looks unhurriedly around him. He hears a call
—Hey!—turns his head, and discovers a little boy; it's Matz.*

"*Eric smiles at him, asking with that pleasant but amplified
tone that grown-ups feel obliged to take toward children:*"

Eric: What do you want?
Matz (*not at all impressed, squints and outstares Eric*): Are
you the swimming instructor?
Eric (*not taking him seriously*): Not yet. I've only just got here.
Matz (*who is not going to be imposed on*): I'm the person sent
to meet you. My name is Matz.

Eric (*listening to him with a serious air, clicks his heels to-gether and parodies a salute*): I'm glad to meet you. Eric Heller. (*They shake hands; Matz takes the luggage.*)
Matz: If you'd kindly step this way . . .

Hotel terrace. Anika still with her face hidden. The count looks after the retreating Eric.

Count (*softly*): This young man . . . does he have money?
Anika (*small smile to herself*): Sometimes.
Count ("*seems irritated by this simultaneously logical and stupid reply*"): Money, for god's sake . . . I mean *money* . . . enough to pay a hotel bill? (*Anika purses her lips doubt-fully.*) Enough to pay the florist bill, at least? (*Anika makes another moue; "irritated, the count drops his sights still further."*) Enough to pay the parking attendant?
Anika ("*smiles at the memory of her liaison with Heller, charming but hardly impressive*"): Perhaps he could pay for the newspapers. (*The count shrugs.*)

Village street. Eric and Matz walking. From habit, Matz is giving a sales pitch.

Matz: Do you know this area?
Eric: No.
Matz: Lac-aux-Dames, the Ladies' Lake, so-called for the twenty-four virgins who perished to a man here, drowned while attempting to escape the gallant attentions of a party of knights in the Middle Ages. Its ideal climate brings to-gether swimmers from all parts of the world from April to October. Across the lake, on the Isle of Swans, you will see the famed manor-house of the noble family of Dobbersberg, which our local architects have no hesitation in saying dates from the twelfth century. (*He pauses, out of breath.*)
Eric (*amused*): Bravo. You're a guide?
Matz: Sometimes. I also carry letters. I do errands. Odds and ends. (*Stops in front of a vending machine and turns toward Eric.*) I've left my money at home. You wouldn't have two sous?
Eric: My poor Matz, you're out of luck; I'm broke.

Matz (*shakes the handle of the vending machine; a bar of chocolate drops out*): Hey, did you see that? (*Eric laughs, but Matz exclaims.*) Oh!

    The ball, put down while they have stopped, has started off all on its own and is bounding down the slope; it disappears at the corner, down another street that leads to the lake. They run after it.
    Edge of the lake. The ball falls into the water. Matz and Eric arrive at a run. Matz wants to dive for it.

Eric (*stopping him*): Wait!

    He lies down on the ground and vainly stretches his arm out toward the ball. But a young woman swims toward it rapidly, seizes it, and throws it to him. He catches the wet ball in his arms and stands there nonplussed. Dolly, emerging from the water, looks at him, laughing. A second young woman, Carla, a bit younger, bobs up out of the water "and also stares at Eric, but with more admiration, it seems, than her sister, who is still laughing."

Carla: Finally, a good-looking man!
Dolly: Let's hope he plays tennis . . .
Carla: Shall I ask him?
Dolly: We're scaring him. Look, he's blushing.
Carla: Blonds blush so easily!
Eric (*squints "exaggeratedly in the sunlight to give his face something to do"; the two sisters burst out laughing and dive into the lake "like naiads"; he asks Matz*): What are they laughing about?
Matz (*tugs him away by the sleeve*): Come on, come on; Brindel's waiting for us. Business first.

    Swimming pool. Brindel, a big man with a long pipe, walks up and down the row of cabanas. Matz accosts him.

Brindel (*brusquely*): You finally got here, kid?
Matz (*important, indicates Eric*): Here's your man.
Brindel (*looks Eric up and down disdainfully, puffs on his pipe, and finishes by deciding*): Good-looker.
Eric (*his hackles rising*): Excuse me?

Brindel: I haven't said anything yet; it's your move. You came about the job?

Eric: I can, during the summer, fill the position of a swimming instructor.

Brindel ("ready to discuss, to bargain"): And "culture"?

Eric: What culture?

Brindel (air of a connoisseur): Physical culture!

Eric (pulls out papers while Matz begins imitating Brindel): Ah! . . . Here are my certificates of study, to show you what I can do.

"Old man Brindel looks at him circumspectly, like an old peasant. When Eric gets out his precious diplomas, we can see one from the School of Engineering of some École Centrale. He's about to give it to Brindel, but folds it up again and gives him the other, on which we read his title of swimming champion."

Eric: Excuse me, it's this one.

Brindel (raises his eyebrows to read and says unenthusiastically): Champion . . . Look, as far as I'm concerned, I'm not looking for a champion. I want a swimming instructor for ladies, gentlemen, and children, and a professor of culture. *(He adds with elaborate casualness):* You know the conditions?

Eric (brusquely): No.

Brindel (takes Eric by the arm; draws him along; cordially): Here, we're all one big family.

Eric: What does that mean?

Brindel (stops and looks at him): It means that there's no such thing as a regular salary.

Eric (unenthusiastically): Oh?

Brindel (more amiable, from time to time taking hold of the lapel of his jacket): But you'll make it up very well, because of your percentage on *all* the lessons that you give: thirty groschen a lesson! At the end of the season, it all adds up . . .

Eric ("tired of this volubility; feebly"): Yes, yes . . .

Brindel ("as if Eric had said 'No, no' "): I know what I'm talking about; I filled in four days for my last swimming instructor

. . . I couldn't do it anymore. Too many girls and women going through your hands . . . My wife made some scenes! (*Rests his elbow on the balustrade; Eric looks at his stomach.*) But thirty groschen per lesson! You can see the advantages from here!

Eric (*looking at the swimming pool*): I see. (*Matz imitates Brindel's gestures.*)

Brindel (*draws Eric along again*): And that isn't everything. Your lodging is free.

Eric (*waking up a little*): You provide the room?

Brindel (*expansive gesture*): I provide it!

Eric: Does it have a few conveniences? Running water?

Brindel: Running water just down the way. (*He stops "as if in front of the eighth wonder of the world" and shows "the last cabana in the line, a cabana just like the others."*) Here we are! (*They enter; a cabana "as denuded and unprepossessing inside as outside." Dark dividing walls between it and the other cabanas, a stool, a narrow camp-bed. Silence from Eric.*) Now, if this isn't enough for you, I wouldn't stop you from lodging elsewhere, at your own expense . . . I'm a reasonable man. (*He observes Eric.*) Is it yes or no?

Eric ("*gives a feeble nod of his head and lets fall*"): It's yes.

Swimming pool. Eric comes out of the cabin, the door of which closes badly. He looks unhappy.

Matz (*appears*): Monsieur Heller! Monsieur Heller! A letter for you already!

Eric (*lights up*): From America?

Matz (*looks at the envelope*): No, from Vienna! (*Eric looks disappointed.*) Is your girlfriend in America?

Eric ("*thinking out loud*"): No, I'm waiting for a letter, a very important letter that will make me rich right away.

Matz ("*looks incredulous; joking*"): No kidding?

Eric (*obstinate*): I'm not kidding in the slightest. (*He explains, after having glanced at the letter and thrown it aside.*) Listen. I'm going to tell you a big secret . . . I've made an important discovery. Very soon I'm going to be managing an immense, immense factory.

Matz: In America?

Eric: No, but the news is going to come from America . . . Would you like to be my friend?

Matz: And how!

Eric: All right, then go to the post office every day . . . see if the letter has come.

Matz (goes on): Do you know Vefi's inn? She's really nice, Vefi. I'll take you there. If it's me who brings you, she'll do you right.

Eric: Thanks, you're very kind, but I've already eaten.

Matz (astonished): Where?

Eric (gestures): Here.

Matz: Ah! (*Gives him some fruit.*) Here! They're for you, your dessert.

Eric (the fruit isn't ripe): You picked them a little early.

Matz: You can't always choose your time.

Eric (suspicious): Matz, did you by any chance . . . ? Look at me. Do you know what that's called? Tell me what that's called.

Matz: It's called being hungry.

Hall of the Petermann Hof. The porter, Eggenhofer, is putting up a little placard with Eric's photo and the inscription: "Swimming Lessons for Children and Adults."

Brindel (in charge of the whole operation): It's not straight . . . It's leaning too much toward the other side. Good-looking kid, huh? Image of me when I was his age. ("*Eggenhofer measures him with his eyes, wordlessly.*") And ready to handle anything: swimming, diving board, Australian crawl, the whole works. A sportsman, a real sportsman. And even better than that: a gentleman. A *real* gentleman. They don't always go together. This 'un's an exception. That comes from his being an engineer. (*They go toward the front door; "Eggenhofer is looking at Brindel incredulously."*) He's a professor, he does engineering, he does experiments. And, I forgot, he doesn't do anything now, he's out of work, which is why he's got himself a job as a swimming coach for the summer! Not a red cent! But proud—so proud he wouldn't take dinner at our place last night even though he hadn't eaten anything but thin air. (*Incredulous and contemptuous smile from the porter, who sits down; Brindel tries to convince him, pounding his hands on the counter.)* I'm telling you. And when he cleaned up the beach this morning, I— and I'm an honest man, and a tactful man—*(The porter looks at him over his bifocals.)* Well, I offered him a little tip . . . *(Porter smiles again, skeptically.)* The look he gave me! What do you think of a guy like that?

Porter *(simply)*: I think he's crazy.

Brindel *(offended)*: Crazy! You should say, a real sport!

Another part of the hall. Coming from their rooms, two of the hotel clients, Mme Mayreder and Mme Ritter; as they pass, they glance mechanically at the notices and go toward the door, then think again "and, impelled, turn back to look at the photo of Eric."

Mme Ritter: Isn't he handsome!

Mme Mayreder *(sighs in turn)*: Ach!—yes, isn't he handsome!

Mme Ritter *("little caressing gesture with one finger in front of the photo")*: His back, do you see the slope of his back?

Mme Mayreder *(sighs again)*: Ach! . . . Yes, I saw it. And look at his pectorals!

Mme Ritter *(a shade malicious, voice slightly lower)*: Is he more handsome than your husband?

Mme Mayreder *(sighs yet again)*: My husband doesn't have pectorals.

Mme Ritter *(toward the photo)*: And the legs—look at the legs . . .

Mme Mayreder *(absentmindedly, melancholy)*: My husband doesn't have legs.

Mme Ritter *(convulses)*: Your husband doesn't have legs?

Mme Mayreder *(still distracted, her gaze far away)*: Not that you'd notice.

The two mature ladies exit as Dolly arrives; she casts a glance toward what they were looking at, then recognizes Eric and approaches the photograph in her turn; she contemplates it, "one might say, as a connoisseur, as the future mother of a family." Meanwhile Brindel continues his commentary in front of the porter.

Brindel: And the other day at the Golden Lion I said to Vefi, the waitress: Give him a big helping, he hasn't had anything in his stomach for two days. He refused it . . . What do you say to that?

Stopping in front of a nearby mirror, Dolly listens without seeming to. The porter's skeptical air incenses Brindel.

Brindel (raising his voice): You have to see that form when he takes off from the side. And regular in his training! He's a man of steel. A man of chromed steel. This very moment, you know what he's doing? Swimming the lake from end to end . . . I ask you! At seven in the evening!

Dolly (suddenly interrupts, and the two men respectfully get to their feet to listen to her): What? The swimming instructor is going to go across the lake?

Brindel (obsequious): Yes, Mademoiselle Lyssenhop.

Dolly: Swimming? And alone?

Brindel: Yes, Mademoiselle Lyssenhop.

Dolly: But that's terribly dangerous!

Brindel: Yes, Mademoiselle Lyssenhop.

Dolly: But he's going to drown!

Brindel ("eager to please Dolly"): Yes, Mademoiselle Lyssenhop. *(Shriek from Dolly; he recovers himself.)* I mean . . . no, Mademoiselle Lyssenhop, impossible!

Dolly (no longer listening to him, turns toward Eggenhofer): Porter, give me three schillings in change, please.

Porter (opens his drawer): At your service, mademoiselle.

Hotel terrace. Carla is looking interestedly through the telescope. Dolly, her sister, arrives at a run, visibly eager to take her place.

Dolly: What are you looking at? *(Carla doesn't answer, screwing up her face and closing one eye to see better.)* Carla! . . . You're a fine sight . . . If you could see the faces you're making . . .

Carla: What?

Dolly (wants to get at the telescope): Let me see.

Carla (resists): Let me alone.

Shot through the telescope: Eric swimming in the middle of the lake; a rowboat follows him, Matz rowing with all his might. But the picture goes dark and an inscription appears: "Ten groschen for two minutes." Carla turns jealously on Dolly, who is suddenly calmer.

Carla: That's mean . . . Quick, Dolly, give me some change!
Dolly ("innocently and regretfully," hiding her change behind her back): I don't have any. If you want some, go ask Papa.

Carla goes away resentfully. Dolly takes her place at the telescope and selects a coin from a handful of change.

Hotel salon. In one of the armchairs, a book in his hand, Monsieur Lyssenhop. "He's an industrial magnate who, twenty years ago, was no more than a simple foreman. His elegance is a bit flashy. He is amusing himself with the book like a monkey who is pretending to read." Actually he is examining the Countess Anika, who is stretched out on a chaise longue, almost opposite him, and seems to be bored with the pile of magazines beside her. Byplay from Anika as she does not succeed in lighting her cigarette. Lyssenhop hesitates to rise. He finally decides on it, lighter in hand, when Anika exhibits in her turn a lighter set with diamonds.

Lyssenhop: Allow me, madame . . .
Anika (after having pretended not to notice him, has ended by lighting her cigarette, "very nonchalant, very grande dame"): Thank you.
Lyssenhop (clears his throat, indicates his lighter): These charming toys are a bit capricious.
Anika (smiling): My lighter was working well this morning, but it's almost empty! I smoke so much!
Lyssenhop (insinuating, a trailing-away voice): Is it a passion?
Anika (vague and pathetic): No, it's ennui . . . Loneliness . . . A woman who falls prey to ennui always ends by doing something foolish . . .
Lyssenhop: When she doesn't have devoted, unselfish friends to save her.
Anika (disenchanted): Oh, I know all about men's unselfishness . . .

Lyssenhop: There are still men, heaven be praised, who have retained respect for Woman, admiration of Woman . . . worship of Woman . . .

Anika (*sighs*): Oh! If my husband could hear you!

Lyssenhop (*suspicious at this evocation of a husband and acting patriarchal*): That's the problem with the younger generation. Your husband . . .

Anika: Count Stereny. (*Carla appears in the background and looks at them, amused.*)

Lyssenhop: Thank you. Count Stereny—is doubtless a very young man.

Anika (*lowers her eyes*): Oh! to look at him . . .

Carla (*approaches*): Papa! Quick, Papa . . . (*Breaking off, as if surprised.*) Oh, *excuse* me!

Lyssenhop (*raises his voice*): What do you want now?

Carla (*as if Anika weren't there*): Money, Papa! Dolly and I are completely broke! (*Seizes the bill that her father hands her after having smiled graciously at Anika, as if to excuse herself.*) Thank you, Papa! Au revoir, Papa! (She runs off.)

Lyssenhop (*little bow*): Let me introduce myself: Oscar Lyssenhop. I'm in the construction profession.

Anika (*very woman-of-the-world*): What a lucky father! Such a charming daughter!

Lyssenhop: Two. (*Anika, who hasn't understood, "turns toward him with a silly smile. He goes into detail, holding up two fingers."*) Two daughters. (*She smiles; he continues in a sugary voice.*) No doubt I will have the great good fortune of making Count Stereny's acquaintance?

Anika (*feigns apprehension*): My husband? He's out at the moment, fortunately . . . He's so dreadfully jealous!

A window bangs. Lyssenhop jumps. Just the wind. He recovers.

Hall of the hotel. The Count enters, sees Anika and Lyssenhop, approaches the porter.

Count (*detached air*): If the garage telephones again, say that I intend to buy the car.

Sound of wind. A paper rises into the air. A door closes by itself. Another window bangs shut; a pane breaks. On the lake, the storm gathers force; "Eric, tired, rests for a moment on his back." The wind sweeps the terrace of the hotel. A parasol turns itself inside out. Hats are blown away. The two sisters' dresses flutter.

Hotel terrace. Carla, running, reaches Dolly's telescope.

Dolly (straightens up and cries to her): Give me ten groschen . . .

Carla (taking revenge): It's my turn now . . . You go and ask Papa for money.

She takes the telescope from her helpless sister. Everyone has taken refuge in the hotel. They are almost alone. Carla seems to be scanning the lake vainly for Eric.

Dolly (impatient and anxious): What's he doing? (*She takes the place of her sister, who makes a gesture of surrender.*)

Lake. Eric is swimming, making a strong effort to struggle against the waves. He treads water to cry out for help, hands making a megaphone: Yoo-hoo! Matz's response reaches him faintly. Matz is rowing in mist and peering anxiously around him. The shore they are aiming for is still a good hundred yards away. On the terrace, Dolly remains alone at the telescope, soaked with rain. Eric is fighting, but masses of water are striking him. He makes a great effort. The shore is closer. A wave submerges him. He comes up exhausted. In the fog, he has lost his direction. Above the water there appears a flickering light. Gradually we distinguish the shape of a dinghy, a lantern at its bow, at its stern a silhouette, steering, enveloped in a Tyrolean cape. "Eric calls on what remains of his strength to reach this unexpected help." He nears the dark hull of the boat and raises his eyes toward a voice that calls to him.

Voice: Give me your hand, I'll pull you up.

"But Eric does not take the hand offered him. He begins to swim again, animated by a desperate courage. He even finds strength to call out."

Eric: Is it still far?
Voice: Thirty yards . . .

"*Eric keeps swimming. The waves begin to diminish in violence and height.*"

Beside him the boat protects him, the steering oar helps him on.

Voice: Hold out! We're almost there . . .

Boathouse. Eric reaches it, swimming beside the dinghy, and hangs on to the float. Puck throws aside her cape and comes to help him out of the water. He falls on the boards, half unconscious. Puck rapidly beaches the canoe, then returns and kneels beside him; "looking like a peasant girl, she is wearing short elastic-sided boots, a cotton dress with a tight-fitted bodice and a wide skirt, a thin short-sleeved blouse. Everything is soaked and sticking to her body."

Puck: Do you feel bad? (*Silence.*) Shall I help you breathe?

Out of breath and exhausted, he doesn't answer. Puck begins to rub his body vigorously. He tries to talk.

Puck (*puts her hand on his heart, then raises his arms above his head*): No, shush. (*Pause.*) Don't try to speak. (*Pause; she continues to rub.*) You don't know this lake! What on earth made you do such a foolish thing? If I were your mother . . . Just think, without me, you'd never have made it . . .

Eric (*forces his eyes open and replies proudly*): I would—!

Puck (*laughs at him*): What a mule you are! Without me, you'd have been drowned! and even then . . . If you think it was easy to row through this fog . . . (*She begins to hum.*)

Eric: Where are we?

Puck: On the Isle of Swans, of course.

Eric (*raises himself painfully on his elbows, with a smile of hope*): Then I crossed the lake? We're really on the other side?

Puck: Isn't that what I said?

Eric (*happy, lets himself fall back*): Thank you! You're a good kid.

Puck (*bursts out laughing*): I am not a good kid. (*She hangs up her oars, murmuring a song.*)

Without me,
Who would have got drowned?
Without me,
Who would never be found?
Soaked and exhausted, battered, spent,
Who got his punishment?

Eric (*in a tired voice*): All the same . . . you're a strange little girl!

Puck (*gathers up her cloak and throws it over Eric*): Come on . . . You can't stay here, you're completely naked! Give me your hands. No, not like that . . . like this . . . that's it . . . I'll help you to my cabin.

She helps Eric to get up and supports him to the back of the boathouse, toward a door, which she opens. "Staggering and supporting him, she should look like an ant dragging a mountain." Their progress allows us to see a part of the chateau, brilliantly lit; a landau draws up on the carriage drive, a lackey opens the door of the vehicle, and two guests in full evening dress get out.

Interior of Puck's cabin, looking a bit like an Oriental dwelling, thanks to the furnishings and doodads. Eric falls on the bed with relief.

Puck (*goes to him; he is shaking and draws the cape around him*): First, take that off. Come on, quick! . . . (*He resists a bit, then surrenders.*) Good! I'm going to find you some pants. (*Eric, in his bathing suit, follows her with his eyes; she opens the door of her wardrobe and uses it as a screen.*) I'm soaked too! (*Searches in closet.*) What can I find to give you? There, put those on . . . (*She throws him a pair of silken Chinese pants, then takes off her soaked clothing, dries herself; we see an arm, a bare shoulder.*) Are you all right?

Eric (*has put on the enormous pantaloons, but doesn't know how to keep them up*): I think I've put them on backward.

Puck: There is no backward.

Eric: I don't know how to fasten them.

Puck: You don't fasten them. You wind them around your body. (*He obeys; she reappears in an exotic costume, wringing her wet hair.*) And now, what on earth can we do

with you? I can't take you to the chateau. There are crowds
of people, a reception . . . That's why I'm out here . . .

Eric (*stretched out again on the bed*): But who are you?

Puck: I'm Puck.

Eric: Puck . . . That's not a name.

Puck (laughs and sits down on the bed): Why not? Do you
want to know my whole name? I'm Mademoiselle de Dobbersberg, but everyone here calls me Puck.

Eric: That's a theater name.

Puck: Of course; my mother is Camilla Bojan.

Eric (*raises himself up on his elbow, astonished and incredulous*): What? Do you mean you're La Bojan's daughter?
La Bojan of the Vienna Opera? And I took . . . I mean, I took
you for a peasant girl.*

Puck (*smiles maliciously and begins to knead his feet to warm
them*): But I am a peasant girl. I live here all year round.
What else! Mama has other things to do . . . always parties
. . . receptions . . . But fortunately I have Papa! Papa is a
scholar. A philosopher. He's very nice . . . a little weird . . .
so am I. And you? (*Eric laughs, enchanted; she looks at his
feet.*) In any case, you're a good fellow . . .

Eric: How do you know that?

Puck: You have handsome feet. Papa says that good people
have handsome feet. (*Eric, exhausted, lets himself fall
back; she leans over him.*) Eh? You're not going to faint,
are you? What's the matter?

Eric: I'm hungry.

Puck: What luck! So am I . . . Wait a second. (*She goes to the
telephone.*) Hello . . . Give me the kitchen. Is that you,
Lenitchka? I'm down in my cabin. I want dinner . . . No, I
don't want to come up. What can you bring me? (*Eric
listens.*) Yes, bring everything . . . and for two! I have a
guest. What? There's a pie? Terrific! (*She hangs up and
comes back to Eric, who is smiling.*) Are you getting warm?

Eric: Thank you, Puck! (*A scratching at the door.*)

Puck: Come in! Don't you know how to open a door anymore?
(*The door opens by itself; Tiger enters majestically and goes*

* Here Eric briefly switches from friendly *tu* to formal *vous*.

to Puck, who shows the dog to Eric.) This is Tiger. Tell him
what your name is, so he'll recognize you.

Eric (*holds out his hand, Tiger puts his paw in it*): How do you
do, Tiger. My name is Eric.

Puck: You like him, don't you? Me too. (*Door opens again; they
look toward it.*)

Lenitchka (*appears with a tray heavy with food, plates, silver-
ware*): Good evening, everyone. (*Eric sits up, already feeling better.*)

Puck: Ah, here's Lenitchka! My dear, old, fat, round, good,
sweet nurse Lenitchka! What a long time you took.

Lenitchka (*goes to set the table; pleasant smile*): Monsieur is
making a tour of the countryside?

Puck (*pushes her aside*): Come, set it all down here!

Lenitchka: Monsieur has not had favorable weather!

Eric: Actually, I haven't—with this storm—I very nearly
didn't . . .

Puck (*has set out the plates and shoos Lenitchka off*): Go 'way,
leave us! You, eat, don't talk.

*Eric dives in; Puck gnaws at some corn on the cob, all the
while watching her protégé. Shriek of a siren in the distance.*

Eric (*looks at Puck*): Do you hear that? (*Siren closer.*)

Puck (*goes to the door, followed by Tiger*): Stay here! I'll be
back.

*Shore. A strong arc-light gropes across, then comes to rest
on Tiger and Puck. The motor of the boat shuts down; we see
several silhouettes.*

Puck (*shouts*): What do you want?

Skipper (*from the boat*): You haven't seen a swimmer around
here? A man who tried to swim across during the storm?

Dolly (*we see her on the boat*): A tall blond man, very handsome. You haven't seen him, by any chance, madame?

Puck (*under the light, her corn in her hand, coldly*): He is
quite safe, madame.

Dolly (*affectedly*): Where, madame?

Puck (*chin high*): With me, madame.

Dolly (*irritated*): Who are you? Where is he?

Puck (*proudly*): I am the daughter of the Baron de Dobbers-berg.

The motor stars up again and after a farewell wave from the skipper to Puck, the boat moves off; she watches it disappear, grimaces, throws her corncob away and goes off with Tiger.

Interior of the cabin. Empty plates. Tiger stretched out. Puck seated cross-legged on the bed, Eric lying down next to her, his head on her knees, eyes closed.

Eric (*nearly asleep*): Tell me . . . that boat?

Puck: What boat?

Eric: The siren, just a while ago . . .

Puck: It wasn't anything. (*Pause.*) You wouldn't like to tell us, would you, Tiger and me, where you come from? Tiger would be so pleased. (*Silence; Eric is resting.*) Listen; I'm going to ask you questions. What is your mother like?

Eric (*smiles gently in a half sleep*): Mama . . . she's a very little mother, tiny, like this . . . and so good . . . she's helped me . . . she sacrificed herself . . . But listen, Puck, it's a secret . . . I'm going to be rich . . . *very* rich.

Puck (*completely natural voice, not at all astonished*): That's good.

Eric: Because I've invented, all by myself . . . a really extraordinary thing . . .

Puck (*leaning over him, attentive*): Yes.

Eric: And very soon I'll be managing an enormous, enormous factory. Don't you believe me? (*He sits up suddenly.*)

Puck (*just as natural, but a bit more grave*): Me? Of course I do . . . yes, I do . . . Why not? And a fiancée, do you have a fiancée?

Eric (*at peace again*): No.

Puck (*seems to think*): But you will have one?

Eric: Probably, when I fall in love.

"*Suddenly, with a motion that nothing has prepared us for, she carries Eric's hand to her mouth and bites it on the thumb, like a little animal. Eric utters a faint cry and sits up.*"

Eric: Ah! (*Looks at the mark on his hand.*) Why, Puck?

Puck (pushes Eric away, then holds him; he lies back in the hollow of her lap; she turns her face away.) I don't know . . . It was stronger than me. Go away! No, don't go . . . I don't know what I want anymore.

Tiger goes to the door and gives a muffled bark.

Dobbersberg: Are you in there, Puck? *(He pushes open the door and enters.)* Oh, excuse me . . . you have company!
Puck (losing none of her naturalness): Come in, Papa! Let me introduce my castaway.

Eric sits up suddenly.

Dobbersberg (calm and slightly ironic): A pleasure, monsieur.
Eric (nods slightly to the baron and clicks his heels together): Eric Heller.
Dobbersberg (with his own heel-click): Baron de Dobbersberg.
Eric (bows politely): The storm took me by surprise. Without your daughter, I don't know if I'd . . .
Dobbersberg ("calmly, without astonishment or protective indulgence"): It doesn't surprise me. This child has a mania for rescuing things. The number of persons, and especially animals, that owe their lives to her is incalculable. Rescuing is in her nature.
Eric: That's very admirable.
Dobbersberg: It's a little childish . . . *(Pause.)* I saw that someone was looking for you just now, monsieur. As soon as you feel yourself sufficiently recovered, I hardly need say to you that my boat is at your disposal.
Eric: Monsieur, I'm embarrassed . . .
Dobbersberg: Not at all, not at all. *(Measures Eric's height with his eyes.)* I would be glad to lend you some clothing, but . . .
Eric: Naturally. *(Follows the baron toward the door.)*
Puck: You'll come back?
Eric (turns): Yes.
Puck (sweetly): Often?
Eric (at the door, with the baron who is smiling at his daughter): Yes.

Boathouse. Calm water. Cloudless sky. The baron lights a lantern.

Eric: I didn't expect the return trip to be so calm.

Dobbersberg: The lake is treacherous . . . It has sudden angers, like miniature tropical tornadoes.

Eric: Have you been to the tropics, monsieur?

Dobbersberg: Yes. I wish I had never come back from the tropics. It was the memory and longing for them that made me raise this child as I have . . . (*He gathers up the mooring rope of the dinghy; as if to himself.*) Yes; she's strange . . . isn't she?

Eric: She's full of surprises.

Dobbersberg: That's the word: she surprises. A fit product of solitude, freedom, and instinct. A pure being . . . free from lies. What miracles are reserved for her, or what catastrophes? (*He seems lost in thought, then slowly unmoors the dinghy.*) I'm waiting for them . . . She's waiting too. But she's only waiting for the miracle; she doesn't know about the catastrophes. (*He smiles and points out the boat to Eric.*) I hope, monsieur, to see you both again tomorrow.

Eric (*getting into the boat, astonished*): Both of us?

Dobbersberg: You and the boat, which you will have the kindness to return.

Eric: With pleasure, monsieur.

Dobbersberg (*pushes the boat out into the lake, then straightens up*): Shush!

Eric: What is it?

Dobbersberg: Listen . . . That's Puck singing. She's singing about your meeting this evening . . . She sings like children and savages sing . . . Monsieur, I owe this song to you.

The boat moves out on the lake. The baron follows it with his eyes, then turns away. In the distance, Puck's song.

Swimming pool. Image of a jar with a frog at the top of a little ladder. Morning sun. A woman is mopping; Brindel is repainting something; an inflatable rubber horse drifts across the pool; colored streamers flutter at the top of the flagpoles. Dressed in his swimming instructor's costume, Eric kneels, takes the water temperature, and then writes a number on a blackboard: sixteen degrees.

Brindel (*joins Eric*): How much?

Eric: Sixteen.

Brindel: Sixteen? You must be kidding! In the middle of August!
(*Takes the blackboard, erases Eric's number, and inscribes 19.*)

Eric (*little gesture of protest*): But—?

Brindel (*laughs*): You're just starting in this business.

Ticket window of the pool. On a placard: "Swimming lessons. Book of 20 lessons: 15 schillings." At the window, M. and Mme Mayreder, both in pocketless black bathing suits. She had just bought from Brindel a book of tickets, which she is holding out to her husband.

Mme Mayreder: Here, you keep it.

M. Mayreder (*without taking it*): Where do you want me to put it?

Mme Mayreder: In your pocket. (*Her husband pantomimes: no pockets. She is impatient.*) In the cabana, wherever you want . . . (*She forces it into his hand.*)

M. Mayreder: Then this joke is serious?

Mme Mayreder: If it's serious, it's not a joke. I want to become athletic. And besides (*she looks at Eric, far away, with a sigh*) bathing might put *you* in shape, too. (*Pitying smile for her husband.*)

M. Mayreder: I've already tried it.

Mme Mayreder: Where?

M. Mayreder: In my tub.

Mme Mayreder (*superior*): There's no comparison.

M. Mayreder: It's the same water.

Swimming pool. Eric finishes giving a lesson to a little girl; he lifts her out of the water and unbuckles her safety belt.

Eric: Who's next?

Another little girl (*bouncing forward with a timid coquetry*): Me, M. Heller, but please don't make me swallow too much water.

Diving board; dives; horseplay and laughter; Lyssenhop, in Tyrolean costume, leaves his daughters, who are sunbathing. A young girl is stretched out on the edge of the swimming pool.

Another girl (approaching): Aren't you going in the water?
First girl: I don't much feel like it. I'm getting warm . . .
   (*The other girl pushes her into the water, laughing.*)

   *Child riding the rubber horse. Swimmer traversing the pool
in an Australian crawl. Faultless dive from the board. Another
diver prepares himself. Eric follows him for a moment with his
eyes, but hears his pupil shrieking as she swallows a mouthful
of water; he energetically jerks up the pole that supports her.*
   "*Several atmosphere closeups to be chosen on the spot:
floats with flags; intertwined legs; two girls combing their hair;
card players; lovers; fingers letting sand flow through them;
people taking photographs.*"
   *Eric is now busy with Mme Mayreder, who fearfully enters
the water; her husband is watching uneasily.*
M. Mayreder (calling to her): Josephine! Be careful! Don't forget your grandfather died of a stroke.

   *But eager to make a good impression on Eric, Mme
   Mayreder, very carefully, has entered the pool.*

Eric (begins the lesson): We will start today with the movement of the legs. First stretch out the legs . . . then bring
   the knees up as far as the stomach . . .
*M. Mayreder ("follows this lesson with an uneasy eye, con-
   fused and critical; mentally taking part in all his wife's
   difficulties. He can't stop himself from coming to Eric's
   assistance in his own way, imitating his wife's movements
   in miniature and calling out"):* Pay attention, Josephine,
   bring up your stomach as far as your knees!
*Eric (raps out the beat for Mme. Mayreder as he walks. She is
   doing her best):* One—two—one—two—

   *Beach by the swimming pool. Dolly and Carla stretched out
on the sand. Dolly looks in front of her.*

Carla (pokes her with her elbow): Are you interested in Mme
   Mayreder? (*Dolly shrugs; Carla insists.*) Or do you want to
   learn to dog paddle?
Dolly (ill-tempered): Leave me alone.
Carla: What's the matter?

Dolly: Look and you'll see. It's beginning again, like yesterday.

"*Matz, on the diving board, looks toward the other shore with enormous binoculars.*"

Dolly (looking in the same direction): Don't you understand?
Carla (doesn't understand very well): What's he looking for?
Dolly (irritated sigh): That little idiot across the lake.

"*We see what Matz is looking at: Puck, on the other shore, in a bathing suit, makes signs of pleasure and welcome and runs toward a flagpole, to which she attaches several fantastic banners she has prepared in advance: stockings, pantaloons, pyjamas, a blouse.*" She runs them up the pole.

Eric (to Matz, still giving the lesson): One—two—one—two—
     What does she say? One—two—one—two—
Matz (on the board): Just a minute. I'm looking at the code-
     book . . .

Matz's hand is holding a notebook the cover of which bears the title SIGNAL CODE. A page turns and we read:

Stockings	Are you coming?
Pantaloons, pyjamas	When?
Blouse	OK, understood.
Crocodile	Impossible
Bowl	Kisses
Casserole	Signal tomorrow.

Matz (leans down and yells): She asks if you're coming this
     evening. What shall I say?
Eric (still giving the lesson): That I'm coming this evening.

Matz attaches a white flag with three red spots to the flag-pole and hoists it. "Puck, on the other bank, hand shading her eyes, sees it and makes joyous hand-signals."

*Eric (smiles at the sight of the banner, then goes back to his
     pupil):* One—two—(*but his path up and down the float is
     blocked and he calls out gently but firmly*): Messieurs,
     Mesdames, please clear the float. Please clear . . .

They do, except for Dolly, leaning on her elbows on the rail-ing, and M. Mayreder who is observing his wife.

Eric (*watching his pupil*): Stretch your legs . . . (*He bumps up against M. Mayreder, whom he hasn't seen, and says to him loudly*): Please clear the float!

Dolly, to "clear," ducks under the railing and involuntarily jostles M. Mayreder.

M. Mayreder (*cries out*): My pince-nez! (*Eric turns around, sees them falling into the water and plunges after them.*) My pince-nez! There they go . . .
Mme Mayreder (*abandoned, frightened, sinks, swallows water, struggles to the surface again, howls*): I've had enough, I want to get out!
M. Mayreder (*half-blind and unthinking*): Then get out!
Mme Mayreder (*thrashing*): I can't, because of the safety belt! Help me!
M. Mayreder (*blinded*): I can't because of the pince-nez!
Mme Mayreder: What pince-nez?
M. Mayreder: Mine! They fell in the water.
Mme Mayreder: I told you so!
M. Mayreder: What?
Mme Mayreder: I told you to wear glasses!
M. Mayreder: I don't want to, they make me look old!

Other side of the swimming pool. Dolly reaches the ladder and climbs out of the water. Eric emerges behind her, the pince-nez in his hand, and ascends in his turn, watching her covertly. "As soon as he is out of the water, as soon as he has no other movement to perform, he is embarrassed, can't speak, can't do anything but leave."

Dolly (*nonchalantly begins a conversation without looking at Eric*): How annoying, I always hit the water too flat when I dive.
Eric ("*squints at the sun to hide a timid smile*"): Did you hurt yourself?
Dolly ("*pretends to take an interest in the drops of water running down her arm*"): Hurt, no, I'm so used to diving . . . But I'm not happy with the way I dive.
Eric ("*his look caresses Dolly's silhouette from head to*

heels"): It's only because of the way you take off. You're built just right for swimming.

Dolly (*flattered by his appreciation, sneaks a furtive look at him*): I've swum ever since I was born . . .

Eric (*continues to speak "in a cool technical tone that gives him back his ease"*): Your whole musculature shows that. (*His brows knit, he minutely inspects Dolly's body and indicates with a hand on his own body the places he's discussing.*) The thighs are developed to take the greatest advantage of the knees, which only appear more delicate because of it. And the remarkable extension of the . . . thoracic cage emphasizes the . . . the firmness of the abdominal musculature. (*"But in the end, seeing Dolly smiling at him, he becomes confused and blushes"; their duet is interrupted.*)

Brindel (*suddenly appears, surly, jerking a thumb at the other float*): What about the job? Huh? Are you a tourist or the swimming coach?

Eric (*to Dolly, who thanks him with a charming smile*): Excuse me, mademoiselle. (*"But he has said too much before; he doesn't know where to go from here; he gives her a brief, gauche nod as she continues to smile at him, and ducks under the railing."*)

Village. Inn sign. Inside, Matz and Eric have just eaten. The waitress adds up the bill on a paper tablecloth; she is Vefi, "a pretty, solidly built peasant, dressed soberly and simply; but her bare arms are very close to Eric's face and as she leans toward us we can see a hint of breast down her décolleté."

Vefi (*straightening up*): That comes to one schilling twenty groschen.

Eric (*looks at the bill on the tablecloth and says nicely*): You've forgot the coffee, Mademoiselle Vefi.

Vefi (*regards Eric in ecstasy, serious, admiring, pleading*): Please, Monsieur Eric, no!

Eric (*doesn't understand*): Why not?

Vefi (*smiles*): The coffee's a present. For friendship. (*She gives him an eloquent look.*)

Eric (rises, pets her cheek with a friendly gesture; "she leans her cheek toward his hand like a turtle dove, then moves away"): Accepted, provided that I can do the same for you some time. Thank you, Mam'selle Vefi. See you tomorrow.

Village street. Eric and Matz are returning to the swimming pool. Eric stops suddenly, seeing Dolly, who, unaware of him, is leaving a shop with a handful of postcards, sticking stamps on them as she walks.

Eric (to Matz): Run to the pool. If Brindel asks for me, tell him I'm coming in a moment. (*Matz leaves, running.*)

Postoffice. Eric arrives on the run, goes up the steps, looks around the vicinity, sees Dolly, who is turning the corner of the street, quickly disappears into the post-office. Dolly reaches the letter box and mails her postcards. Eric, all innocence, comes out of the post-office and goes toward the letter box, which he reaches just as Dolly is about to leave; their paths cross. "He greets her amicably, without a word, and Dolly looks at him with immediate friendliness."

Dolly: Oh! Hello!
Eric (stops, delighted to start a conversation): Hello, mademoiselle!
Dolly (her face lights up): I didn't recognize you . . . because of your clothes. (*She blushes; he wants to slip away unobtrusively, but she detains him.*) Are you going back to the pool?
Eric: It's the end of my lunch hour. Until the fifteenth of September . . . that's my headquarters.
Dolly: Oh, you're only staying until the fifteenth of September! Will you be here again next year?
Eric: Probably not. I signed up only for the season.
Dolly (seemingly a bit disappointed): Ah!
Eric: I have to go back to my work . . .
Dolly: Your work?
Eric: I'm a chemical engineer.
Dolly (smiles, flatteringly): Ah!
Eric (adds quickly, humorously): An unemployed one.
Dolly: Oh!

Eric (*playing to the gallery*): Like so many others. A bad
   moment to get through. Next fall, I have high hopes of
   catching up.
Dolly: Ah!
Eric: Since I'm a chemical engineer . . .
Dolly (*a little malicious*): And unemployed . . .
Eric (*posing*): But more than that, an inventor.
Dolly: Ah!
Eric: But let's not talk about that.
Dolly: Why not?
Eric: I'm afraid I'd bore you.
Dolly: Not at all . . . On the contrary.

   *Village. A little cafe-restaurant with a garden, or an arbor,
or even open-air tables, where the patrons are not too exposed
to an indiscreet gaze. Anika is just leaving as Eric passes on
his way back to the swimming pool. Surprise on both sides.*

Eric (*stops short and exclaims*): Aniuschka!
Anika (*very elegant as always, looking left and right*): Shush!
   No, Boulli. You mustn't recognize me.
Eric (*laughing*): Then don't call me Boulli.
Anika: But it's such a lovely name! Here you must call me
   Madame la Comtesse.
Eric (*gently mocking*): Of course, if it gives you pleasure.
Anika (*offended*): Pleasure? I *am* Madame la Comtesse. I'm
   married, my sweet!
Eric (*smiles*): Again?
Anika: No, not "again." Look. (*She shows her wedding ring.*)
   Proof . . . (*She shows him a countess's coronet on her
   handbag.*) And that!
Eric (*small incredulous smile*): No need for so many pieces of
   evidence!
Anika (*looks down the street, then pulls Eric into the cafe*):
   Boulli, come with me . . . We mustn't be seen together.
   (*They sit at a table underneath the arbor. "Anika looks at
   him with a tender smile, as he sits beside her, and takes his
   hands."*)
Eric (*making fun of her*): Is this where Monsieur le Comte and
   Madame la Comtesse come to eat?

Anika (interrupts him): Shush! You mustn't say . . .

Waitress (comes to wipe the table): What'll it be, M'sieur, M'dame?

Eric (slight hesitation): Nothing for me; I'm going to swim.

Anika (to the waitress): Another coffee. (*"The waitress leaves without a word, very unenthused by this feeble order."*)

Eric (seriously): Anika, I have to explain to you why I'm here.

Anika: Never mind, Boulli, I know everything . . . You make me angry.

Eric (astonished): Why?

Anika: You're going about it all wrong. You can't chase two bunnies at once, sweet. The Dobbersberg girl isn't bad . . . But the Lyssenhop girl is ten times better.

Eric (naively; he thinks he's understood): Do you think she's pretty too?

Anika (a childish cynicism and the traditional rub of thumb against index finger: money, money . . .): Prettier? Be serious!

Eric (scandalized): Aniuschka! Do you know what you're saying?

Anika (shrugs, smiles): Oh, Boulli, you're useless for anything except making love . . . if you haven't forgotten that. (*Eric turns away; she become more tender and takes his hand.*) Boulli . . .

Eric: Shush. (*The waitress brings the coffee and leaves.*)

Anika (tenderly): Do you know that they're all mad about you?

Eric: Who?

Anika: Every one of them! They talk of nothing but you.

Eric: Who?

Anika: All of them! (*Gesture toward Eric's legs.*) And you walk about in a pair of pants like those! If the Lyssenhop girl saw you . . . (*With her finger she widens a rip in his pants.*) . . . in these pants?

Eric: But, Anika . . .

Anika (angry, irritated by Eric's timidity or his naivete): You need a fashionable pair of white pants! A pair like . . . that one! there, in the display window across the street, the white flannels . . . they're very good looking.

Shop window of a fashionable store. Display of assorted pairs of pants. Placard: "Unshrinkable Flannels." Greatly differing prices. Shot of the white flannel pants.

Eric: Supposing I just took the cotton pair. Cotton's cool, it's . . .

Anika: It's awful . . .

Eric: But . . . (*The saleswoman removes the flannel pair from the window.*)

Anika: But what? No, not the cotton. The flannel.

Eric: Twenty-eight schillings is twelve dinners. That's a lot of lessons.

Anika: One must know how to make sacrifices, Boulli.

They leave the shop. Eric has on the new pants and under his arm, a little package containing the old pair. They move off.

Night. The boathouse. Swans swim out of it, followed by the boat, which Puck is steering with her oar. A little lantern on the bow. Tiger is in the boat. Faraway song of Puck.

Puck (*sings*):
> On the other shore
> I sing . . . I wait
> The waves rock
> My dream, my boat . . .
> What will they bring me,
> Night and morning?
> Out there are kindled
> Fires and feasts . . .
> Here, in the dark
> Breaking the green waves,
> My oar streams
> With droplets of moon . . .

The lake at night. Another boat, with Dolly in the stern and Eric who has just stopped rowing. He bends over Dolly's hands and kisses them lingeringly. He raises his head, listening to the song. A kiss. But Puck's song troubles him and he turns his head away.

Dolly (*observes him without anger*): Do you hear? She's calling you. Will you go there this evening, as you did the other evenings? Listen to me. If you go back there again, you must stay there, Eric, because I don't want to be a summer flirtation.

Eric (*defends himself, convincingly*): Dolly, it's you I love, and I'm really a decent kind of man, not the sort who fools around.

Dolly (*shakes her head*): A decent kind of man can hurt a young girl terribly, Eric . . . Will you go there tonight?

Eric (*lying at Dolly's feet*): I won't go there again, not tonight, not ever, dear; I promise you.

"Dolly gravely receives this grave promise and caresses his hair." Their boat recedes in the distance.

Puck (*in her boat, continues to sing*):
> From the other shore
> He came to me!
> Beautiful boy
> Born from the lake
> Battered by wind
> Wet by the rain!
> Blond son of day
> Whom the night threw
> Into my boat . . .
> Here in the dark
> Your body streams
> With droplets of moon.

Hotel. Night. Bedroom of Dolly and Carla. Dolly enters and lets herself fall dreamily onto one of the beds. From the bathroom Carla enters in a nightdress, brushing her hair.

Carla (*goes to the window and looks into the garden*): Come look! (*Dolly gets up and leans out the window with Carla to see.*)

Garden of the hotel. Lyssenhop flirts with Anika, who is stretched out on a deck chair; he is seated, leaning toward her, listening to her in raptures.

Anika (*"the great lady, full of noble feelings"*): The moon loves diamonds. They say she makes them more beautiful.

Lyssenhop (*taking Anika's hand in his own*): Who says that?
Anika (*very lyrical*): A legend of my beautiful country.

Back to the window with the two sisters, who struggle not to burst out laughing, then speak in muffled voices.

Dolly: Poor Papa! He has his secrets too . . .
Carla (*closes the window*): He doesn't keep them half as well as you do. Where were you?
Dolly: With *him*, of course!
Carla: I thought so. (*She sits by her sister, who begins to undress, stretches, smiles.*) Did he kiss you?
Dolly (*with abandon, letting herself fall back on the bed*): All the time!
Carla (*more and more curious*): How did he kiss you? (*Silence.*) Does he kiss well? (*Dolly, dreaming, says nothing; Carla, enthusiastic, looks for the best possible praise.*) Anyway, how he dances! . . . How he dances! . . . He'd make an amazing professional ballroom dancer.
Dolly (*sits up, indignant*): Him, a ballroom dancer! You're crazy! What's a mere ballroom dancer? (*Still indignant, she takes off her shoes and noisily drops them.*)
Carla (*maliciously*): What's a swimming instructor?
Dolly: He isn't a swimming instructor. He's an engineer, as you very well know!
Carla (*scratches her shoulder*): Anyway, it's not enormously important, unless you were thinking of marrying him . . .
Dolly (*defiance*): We'll see about that, too! (*She slams the bathroom door.*)
Carla (*thunderstruck*): Dolly! (*She goes over to the door, opens it; in a softer voice.*) Dolly!
Dolly (*taking off her slip*): Exactly. As poor as he is.
Carla: Is he poor, do you think?
Dolly (*putting on her nightdress*): Poor as Job.
Carla (*curiously*): What makes you think so?
Dolly ("*standing, motionless, seeming to weigh her words*"): A lot of things . . . The kind of . . . respect he inspires in me. He doesn't have a father-director, like us, or an uncle-administrator, or shoes made to measure, or a well-cut jacket, or anything . . . He's alone . . . That's beautiful, it's . . .

Carla (*being practical*): It's not fun.

Dolly (*decisively, ardently*): I'll be poor with him if I have to! I'll give up everything! We'll only have a little auto, and a tiny apartment, five or six rooms . . . (*She unmakes the bed, pounds her pillow.*) I don't care, I love him! And I want to marry him! And that's enough! And next Saturday I'm going to introduce him to Papa! (*She mimes.*) Monsieur Eric Heller, engineer! How's that?

Carla: And you think that'll be enough to impress Papa?

Dolly: Why not? Besides, on Saturday, Eric will be in a tux.

Carla (*smiles, mockingly*): Oh, then, that'll take care of everything.

Lobby of the hotel. On the bulletin board, a new poster announces a dance for Saturday night. The porter tacks a notice to the bottom of the poster: "Evening Dress Obligatory."

Eric's shack. Matz, on the stool, elbows on the table, is reading an invitation to the dance. Eric, seated on the bed, is mending a pair of pyjamas.

Matz (*reading*): "Grand Petermann. Grand Celebration of Youth. Supper. Paffle . . ."

Eric ("*his needle is too long; he pricks himself*"): What?

Matz: That's what it says . . . Oh, no: "Raffle, two orchestras, special attractions. Evening dress obligatory."

Eric (*lifts his head*): Let me see that. (*He looks at the card and, disappointed, reads the final line.*)

Matz (*wanting to look knowledgeable*): Will you appear in full evening dress or a tuxedo?

Eric: A tuxedo. I haven't got full evening dress.

Matz: But you don't have a tuxedo either.

Eric: Yes, I do.

Matz: Where?

Eric (*motions with his head*): In the drawer.

Matz (*unconvinced*): No kidding? (*Looks in the drawer, pulls out papers.*)

Eric (*riffles through them*): Here's my watch . . . Here's my bicycle . . . Now, where's that tuxedo? Here we are . . . (*It's a receipt from a pawnshop.*) To get it, I need sixty-two schillings for my "uncle."

Matz: And you have them?

Eric: No.
Matz: So?
Eric: I'll find them.

    Pool. Brindel glaring at Eric furiously.

Brindel (*brusquely turns his back*): Sixty-two schillings? Are you trying to kid me?

    Village. Jeweler's. Eric at the counter in front of the jeweler, who is biting a medal.

Eric: I won it in the interscholastic championship. It's the silver medal.
Jeweler ("*smiles pityingly and throws the medal down on the counter; it makes a dull sound*"): Friend, it's the lead medal.

    Village. Cafe. Eric and Anika at a table. Anika looking desolated. "She empties her purse on the table; cosmetics, loose change, which she pushes around with a finger."

Anika: My poor Boulli, I'm as poor as you.

    The other side of the lake. Puck, sitting in the kitchen garden, is greedily eating gooseberries. Suddenly she sees Eric, who is bending down to look under the leaves. She grasps his hand as he passes by her and breaks into a fresh, unspoiled laugh, calling to him.

Puck (*laughing*): Yoo-hoo!
Eric (*kneels beside her*): What are you laughing about?
Puck: Because you're looking under all the leaves for me, as if I were a grasshopper or a snail.
Eric: And why are you hiding?
Puck: I'm not, I'm picking gooseberries. The best are underneath. Do you like them? (*She makes him eat one.*)
Eric (*little grimace*): They're bitter, Puck!
Puck (*picks gooseberries*): Here, in the mountains, things ripen so late . . . Do you want more? (*Eric shakes his head.*) Would you like me to bring you some tender little artichokes? (*Shakes his head again.*) Don't you want anything? Why have you come so late? (*Eric lowers his eyes.*) Are you bored with me?

Director Marc Allégret supervises a scene from Lac-aux-Dames *(1935)
an adaptation of a Vicki Baum novel for which Colette wrote the
dialogue. Simone Simon played the tomboyish Puck; Jean-Pierre
Aumont was Eric, the penniless swimming instructor.*

Photo courtesy Cinémathèque Française

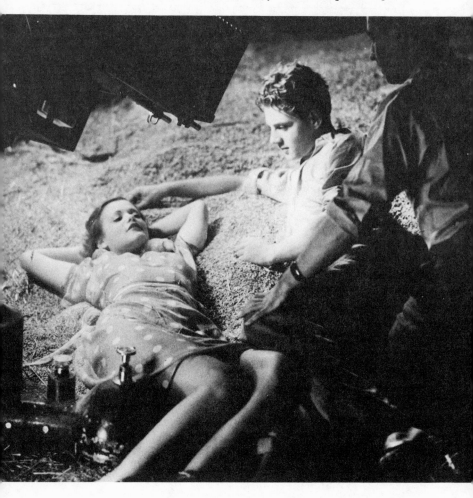

A page from the shooting script of Lac-aux-Dames. *The addition of the word "petite" is in Colette's handwriting. The other additions are by novelist André Gide and were made during actual shooting in Austria. Colette had remained in France.*

From Marc Allégret's shooting script

Eric: What a question, Puck! I'm worried, not bored.

Puck: Worries! Why haven't you told me about them?

Eric: Just give me time! Maybe that's why I'm here.

Puck (filling his mouth with gooseberries): Tell me, then.

Eric: How can I when you keep stuffing my mouth with gooseberries! . . . Puck, wait, listen . . . Oh . . .

Puck ("unhappy at seeing him getting into a tangle, she looks at him with great seriousness and reproaches him"): Eric, are we really friends?

Eric: My little Puck, you're my best friend!

Puck: Then we shouldn't be so polite with each other. What's your trouble? What do you need?

Eric (impulsively): What I need—(*Then he stops, drawn in two directions.*) Listen, Puck, don't make fun of me. I need, I need terribly—

Puck: What? Go on!

Eric: A tuxedo!

Puck (*astonished, bursts out laughing and jumps up*): And what are you going to do with a tuxedo, Seigneur?

Eric (*ready to get angry, stands in turn*): What one usually does with a tuxedo. I want to wear it.

Puck ("*looks him up and down, then laughs*"): You, in a tuxedo? How funny . . . But that's not what you need. Giving swimming lessons in a tuxedo!

Eric ("*his mood darkened by this childish gaiety, he turns away, moves a step away from her, kicks the ground with his foot*"): I don't think that's funny. There was a time when I put on a tuxedo every evening . . .

Puck ("*comes to stand by him, puts her arm around him, suddenly sad to see her friend melancholy*"): I didn't mean to hurt you, my darling. You want a tuxedo? Something like that ought to be easy to find.

Eric: You think so?

Puck: But . . . Is it so important, not having a tuxedo?

Eric (*nods*): Very . . . I can't explain to you . . . It's *very* important.

Puck (*has an inspiration*): Would you like Papa's?

Eric: I'd rather have mine . . .

Puck: Where is it?

Eric: Very far away . . . Sixty-two schillings from here.

Puck: Sixty-two . . . Oh, I understand! You don't have the sixty-two schillings.

Eric: That's right.

Puck ("*laughs; she turns out the two little pockets of her outfit, and gathers up nuts, a small handkerchief, shells, a half-eaten fruit, a pocketknife, and a two-sou piece*"): Wait for me; I'll go make up the difference.

Eric (*wants to hold her back; constrained*): Please . . . I don't want to . . .

Puck (*looks at him without embarrassment*): What? Are we friends or aren't we friends? (*She runs quickly across the kitchen garden, jumping over bushes.*)

Interior court of the chateau. "The baron is walking about slowly. In his left hand he holds a book, and his right hand is resting on a little wheeled standing desk, on which he is taking notes." The servants pass by silently, so as not to disturb him. Puck enters. He raises his head and smiles at her. Her expression is slightly unhappy.

Dobbersberg: Trouble again?
Puck (*silent at first, she looks at the coats of arms on the wall of the chateau and finally asks*): Papa, do I have a dowry?
Dobbersberg: Yes, why?
Puck: When I get married, will I have my dowry?
Dobbersberg: Of course, Puck.
Puck ("*begging prettily*"): Could I have a little bit of dowry now?
Dobbersberg: A little bit? How much?
Puck (*hesitates, looks at her feet, confesses*): Sixty-two schillings.
Dobbersberg: How much?
Puck (*raises her head*): Sixty-two schillings, Papa.
Dobbersberg ("*feigns concern*"): That's a lot of money, Puck.
Puck ("*conspiratorial air*"): I know, Papa.
Dobbersberg: Well, this one time . . . (*He takes out his wallet, plucking from it notes of 50, 10, and 5 schillings, which he gives to Puck.*)

Eric's shack. An insert has let us see the postal order form addressed to Mme Heller: 62 schillings. In front of the shack, the mailman is giving him a postal notice.

Mailman: A package for you at the station, Monsieur Heller.

Station. Eric is waiting in front of the freight office.

Employee: Monsieur Heller?
Eric: Yes?
Employee: A package, sixty-four pounds, from Vienna.
Eric (*stupefied, sees the employee wheel out a bicycle and makes no move to take it*): But . . . ?
Employee (*surprised*): Isn't it yours?
Eric: Yes, obviously, but . . .
Employee (*indicates a baggage tag on the handlebars*): Look, there's your name spelled out right there . . .

It isn't a tag, but a letter, that Eric detaches from the handlebars and opens. Shot of the letter from Mme Heller to her son: "My dear boy, Thank you very much for the 62 schillings. I am sorry but the tuxedo has been sold, because you hadn't paid the interest. With the 62 schillings I have redeemed your bicycle, which will be more useful to you. Have a good time, don't catch cold. Don't drink ice water. Love and kisses. Mama."

Brightly lit hotel, the evening of the ball. Faraway dance music. Through the windows, we see couples "gaily whirling, and, in silhouette, a frieze of heads, the seated parents." The orchestra has been installed on a balcony; the gypsy fiddlers play with expansive lyricism. "The couples, all very young, dance Viennese waltzes without getting dizzy." The parents watch them tenderly. "Byplay: silent chatter, murmuring into ears . . ." In her partner's arms, Carla stops in front of the chair of Dolly, who, restless and nervous, is keeping watch over the entrance door. End of the dance.

Carla (*sits down near her sister*): Oh, don't look like that! He'll come! Really. (*Curious and excited.*) Oh, look . . .
Dolly: Is it Eric? Where?
Carla: No, it's Papa!

Another corner of the ballroom. Anika and Lyssenhop are seated at a table.

Anika (*affected air*): You look at me too much.
Lyssenhop (*gallant*): I'm only doing what everybody else is doing. You're the belle of the ball!
Anika: Be serious!
Lyssenhop: I've been serious all my life! You've made me a young man! *I* wouldn't be capable of spending an evening like this playing cards . . .

Little salon with card tables. Count Stereny is playing bridge. Someone addresses him:

Partner: Stereny, it's your bid.
Count: I pass.

Dolly and Carla's table. "Two men ask the two sisters to dance. Carla gets up immediately. Dolly refuses with a world-weary air." Carla dances off.

Eric's shack. "He is standing in the doorway, listening to the music coming from the hotel. After a moment, irritated, he suddenly slams the door, turns away, and lies down with a despairing air."

The other shore. "Puck is seated on the bank, knees under her chin. She is looking into the distance. Tiger is beside her. She suddenly stands to see better." She sees, far away, the lighted window of Eric's shack. She again sits down.

Puck (*softly lays her hand on Tiger's head*): You see, he isn't with the other one either. He's at home.

Hotel. Dolly and Carla leaving the ballroom. Carla seems very agitated and annoyed by her sister's tormented attitude.

Carla: You're not really tired.
Dolly: Of course not. But I can't bear it anymore. I've been waiting for him an hour, a whole hour. He must have stayed away on purpose.
Carla: No, listen. You say yourself he's shy. I bet that he didn't dare come.
Dolly (*in front of the entrance*): He's gone to see the little baroness again.
Carla (*stops her*): No, he hasn't, you're crazy! (*Tries to lead her back to the ballroom.*) Come on, come and dance. It'll make the time go by.
Dolly (*determined to leave*): No, I'm suffocating here.

As they leave, two police inspectors enter—one in a tuxedo, the other in a business suit—and fixedly stare at them.

First inspector: Excuse me, mesdames. (*The other consults a photo.*)

Dolly: Thank you, but I'm not dancing. (*She leaves abruptly, followed by Carla who has thrown a curious glance at the two men.*)
First inspector (*to his colleague who has shown him the photo*): That's not the one.
Second inspector (*photo in hand; we recognize Anika*): She must be at the dance. Let's go.

Manager (*halts the two men at the entrance*): Pardon, messieurs . . . Your cards?

First inspector: Of course. (*Shows his police identification and then enters the ballroom.*)

Manager (*bows and excuses himself, then, in a low voice, to the second inspector, who has remained behind to guard the door*): Excuse me, Inspector . . . Is it a serious matter?

Second inspector: A little thing . . . We won't disturb anyone. (*Shows the Manager the photo.*) Do you know this woman?

Corner of the ballroom. Lyssenhop and Anika still at their table.

Anika: You make me blush. You don't think of anything but—

Lyssenhop: And you, you don't think of it enough. You don't talk about anything but this childhood friend of yours, Boulli, Boulli. I'm sick and tired of your Boulli!

Anika: But he so much wants to meet you.

Lyssenhop: Oh, for—

Anika (*not discouraged*): Why not?

Lyssenhop (*trying to add a note of gallantry to the conversation*): Because I'm jealous.

Anika: But he isn't one of my lovers! He's a manufacturer—

Lyssenhop: Manufacturers can fall in love—I know.

Anika: Now, be nice to him.

Lyssenhop: I will be nice.

Anika: Will you let me bring him around?

Lyssenhop: Bring him . . . I'll make him welcome.

Anika: Oh, thank you, very much!

The inspector in the tuxedo advances awkwardly through the crowd of dancers, approaches Lyssenhop and Anika's table, and stops. Lyssenhop half-rises and greets him cordially.

Lyssenhop: Ah! Monsieur, good evening . . . Madame has just mentioned that you were coming.

First inspector (*stupefied*): Is that right? She's really got guts.

Lyssenhop (*to Anika*): Guts? Do you have "guts," my dear?

First inspector: I'd advise you not to use that tone.

Lyssenhop: What? What? What?

First inspector (*indicates the exit with his thumb*): Come along with me.

Anika (*cries out, jumps up, and rushes away*): Ach!

Lyssenhop (*holds back the policeman, who wants to pursue her:* Do you mind . . . I forbid you to lay a hand on that lady!

First inspector (*amused, defers his pursuit for a moment to seize Lyssenhop*): That's a lady?

Lyssenhop: Help! This man's a criminal! Will you take your hands off me! I'm going to call the police!

   Brouhaha. Scandalized cries. A crowd gathers. The orchestra stops playing. Anika, hidden behind a curtain, pokes her head out, sees that everyone is occupied with Lyssenhop, and makes her escape through the window.

First inspector: Not so much noise . . .

Lyssenhop: This is an outrage!

   Cardroom. All the players are standing and craning to see. Someone has climbed up on a chair. "Only Count Stereny is still seated, calm as ever."

Count (*uninvolved air*): We're not continuing, messieurs?

Cardplayer: In a moment, if you like, but I want to see the arrest.

Another player: No one's been arrested here since 1885. (*Brouhaha, cries.*)

   Stereny rises, goes to look out the door, exits into the hall, then, as discreetly as possible, heads for the staircase.

   Hall. Two inspectors drag Lyssenhop toward the exit and handcuff him.

Lyssenhop (*struggles, shouts*): It's unheard-of, unheard-of! Unprecedented! Where is the countess?

Manager (*demands an explanation from the inspector in a suit*): Yes, yes . . . but that doesn't explain why you've arrested Monsieur Lyssenhop! (*The orchestra strikes up.*)

Second inspector: Lyssenhop?

Manager: Yes.

Second inspector: I thought he had registered here as Stereny.

Manager (*thunderstruck*): Stereny . . . But you've made a mistake. That's Stereny. (*He points out the count, who is calmly mounting the stairs.*)

Second inspector: Hey! (*The count pauses with feigned astonishment.*) You, friend, come down here. I told you to come down. (*Stereny prepares to descend. Murmurs of astonishment.*)

Eric's shack. He is stretched out, reading the papers. Kerosene lamp. The door is open. Harmonica music in the background. Eric suddenly jumps up, hearing the splash of something falling into the water. Harmonica stops. Eric runs to the door. But Anika appears, soaking, "her evening dress clinging to her body." She pushes him inside and closes the door.

Eric: You?

Anika (*flings herself on his chest with a long childish wail*): Ooooh!

Eric (*takes her in his arms*): What's the trouble?

Anika (*groans, trembles, sobs*): Everything! (*Harmonica begins again.*)

Eric (*seats her on his bed*): Tell me. Look, Anika, tell . . .

Anika (*hides her eyes, then suddenly shouts*): They arrested him! If they find me, I'm done for!

Eric: Arrested? Who!

Anika: The count.

Eric: What count?

Anika: Mine.

Eric (*tries to understand*): But why—?

Anika (*fatalistic gesture*): Bad luck! He couldn't pay . . .

Eric: Pay? For what?

Anika: The auto he bought on credit.

Eric: He could have just given it back.

Anika: But he'd sold it.

Eric (*no longer sympathizes*): So?

Anika (*turns on her charm*): So I told him I wanted to leave him . . .

Eric: And you're leaving him?

Anika (*takes off her shoes and begins to remove her stockings*): Oh, no . . . Besides, I loved him too much! Then he borrowed from a guy . . .

Eric (*disarmed and terrified by her lack of conscience*): Good heavens! And then?

Anika (*holds out her stockings to Eric*): Here, Boulli, get these dry . . . Then he said one day, "Let's get out of here, it looks bad." And I didn't want to . . .

Eric (*draws away, a little embarrassed*): I don't believe this! . . . And after that?

Anika (*takes off her dress and explains candidly*): We went off to the country. But there wasn't any money. So he said to me, "Be a little nice to the men."

Eric: That's disgusting.

Anika: Oh, Boulli, it didn't go very far, you know.

Eric: Thank heavens!

Anika: Because then Ferdinand would come in and pretend to want to kill everybody . . . (*Practically nude underneath a silk slip.*) I'm cold, Boulli . . . Get this dry. (*She crosses her arms over her breasts, shivering, while, disturbed, he lays the robe over the back of a chair.*) Boulli, I'm cold.

Eric (*holds out his raincoat to her*): Here, put this on. And what happened today?

Anika (*sighs*): The cops!

Eric (*at the door*): Wait for me . . . They mustn't find you here.

Anika (*clasps him*): Don't leave me, Boulli, I beg you.

Eric: But I'm coming right away. (*He leaves; she starts to take off her underclothes.*)

Pool. Boardwalk by the cabanas. Matz, seated on the sill of one with an open door, is still playing the harmonica.

Eric (*approaches*): Matz?

Matz: Present.

Eric: You're not going to stir from this spot.

Matz: Never.

Eric: If anyone asks for me, you'll answer that I'm sick and in bed. Understand?

Matz: You're sick and in bed. Understood.

Eric: No matter who asks, you understand?

Matz (makes an "understood" sign): No matter who! (*He
   returns tranquilly to his harmonica. Eric goes back to his
   shack.*)

   *The shack. Anika's dress, stockings, and underwear are
hanging from a line. Partly hidden by the wash, Anika is nude
under Eric's transparent raincoat.*

Eric (regards all this with alarm): Oh, no.
Anika (has lighted the alcohol stove): No, what?
Eric: You can't stay like that!
Anika: You're right, Boulli, it's freezing. (*She throws the rain-
   coat at Eric, "then, naked, scrambles into bed, giving the
   little shrieks of a woman sensitive to cold, and pulls the
   covers up as far as her shoulders, leaving her arms outside
   the blankets."*)
Eric (appalled): You're getting into bed? . . . But you're not
   going to stay here?
Anika: No, Boulli, only until it's time for my train to leave.
   (*The harmonica music has stopped.*)
Eric (seats himself at the foot of the bed): Oh! . . . And when
   does your train leave?
Anika (nice and warm, makes herself inviting): At six
   tomorrow morning.
Eric: Good heavens! But you can't . . .
Anika: It won't be the first time I've slept in your bed, Boulli!
   (*The water boils over on the stove.*) Oh, the tea! Quick,
   Boulli . . .

   *Walk in front of the cabanas. Dolly and Carla in a discussion
with Matz, who hasn't bothered to get to his feet.*

Dolly (impatient): Then Eric isn't there?
Matz (stays calm): I'm filling in.
Dolly: I'm asking you *where he is*, you little idiot. (*Matz points
   his thumb at Eric's shack.*) Go tell him I'm here, and tell
   him now.
Matz (finger in front of his mouth): Shush!
Dolly: What?
Matz: He's sleeping.
Dolly: Then wake him up!

Matz: He's sleeping . . . with a lady!

Dolly (*angry, doesn't know what to say; tries to lead her sister away*): Oh! . . . Come, Carla!

Carla (*resists*): Wait a minute . . . Do you want me to speak to him?

Dolly: Are you crazy? Come on. (*They leave.*)

Matz (*alone, "summarizes the situation in an inspired tone"*): They're never satisfied.

Eric's shack. Seated near Anika, he is gently making her drink her tea.

Anika: That does me good. It's mint tea.

Eric: No, it's tea . . . in my toothbrush glass!

She drinks, but trembles because steps are approaching on the wooden walkway. Knock at the door. Fearful, Anika seizes Eric's arm, then wraps herself in the covers and envisions herself climbing up onto the roof of the cabin.

Eric (*getting ready to open the door*): Is that you, Dolly?

Carla: No, it's Carla.

Eric: Where's Dolly?

Carla: Home. She sent me . . .

Eric: To look for me?

Carla: Not exactly. She asks if it's true that you have a woman in there. (*Matz's head appears.*)

Eric: Yes, it's true, there's a woman in here.

Carla: Oh!

Eric (*getting angry at Matz, who slinks off*): You can get out, you good-for-nothing! I swear to you, Carla, I couldn't do anything else. It's Countess Stereny.

Carla (*"the comic turn of events not lost on her"*): Glory! . . . And here's Papa looking for her everywhere.

Eric: Could I have let them arrest her? She'll take the six o'clock train tomorrow morning.

Carla: The train—? But the police are watching the station . . .

Hotel. Lyssenhop's room. "He is pacing up and down like a lion in a cage. The Manager, bent almost double from bowing, follows him with a desolate air and tries to calm his fury, to get a word in edgewise."

Lyssenhop: No, not another hour. Not one more hour! Bring my
     bill and call my chauffeur.
Manager: Monsieur Lyssenhop, I assure you . . . We had noth-
     ing to do with this . . .
Lyssenhop: That would have been the last straw, wouldn't it?
     An outrage like that! Organized by the hotel! Perhaps to
     make the dance a little more exciting! Get out! I'm telling
     you to get out! (*"He opens the door of the closet, full of
     suits, and tries to force the horrified Manager to exit through
     it."*)

*Eric's shack. "Anika is finishing her toilette. Nose almost
touching the kerosene lamp, she is penciling in her eyebrows
with a match that she has just burned in the flame and is looking at herself in Eric's tiny mirror. She has again put on her
wrinkled dress and is covering it with the raincoat. She does not
stir as she hears Eric arrive." He has just got the boat ready.*

Eric: Come on, hurry up, we haven't any time to waste.

*Hotel. Lyssenhop's room. Dolly is there, putting on a
traveling coat. The chauffeur is strapping a suitcase. Lyssenhop
is still agitated.*

Lyssenhop: Where's your sister?
Dolly: I think she's over there.
Lyssenhop: Where is there?
Dolly: In our room.
Lyssenhop (*a knock at the door*): Don't come in!
Timid voice: It's the bill, monsieur.
Lyssenhop (*in a rage*): Slide it under the door. I don't want to
     see your face anymore.
Dolly: Papa, calm yourself, please.
Lyssenhop (*furious and contorted face*): I'm perfectly calm.
     (*A knock at the door.*) I said no. Don't come in.
Manager (*appears, looking as if he is just about to go over the
     edge; an air of defeat*): Monsieur, someone's stolen . . .
     stolen . . .
Lyssenhop (*first astonished by the intrusion, calms down a little
     and asks sardonically*): Someone's stolen something from
     you? It doesn't surprise me. In fact, I'm very happy!

Manager: But, monsieur . . . they've stolen your car. (*Dolly is stupefied.*)

Lyssenhop ("*controls himself, approaches the frightened Manager, who is expecting the worst, and gives him a nasty little smile*"): Go on, my friend. You can tell me anything you want, nothing will surprise me . . . Shall we set fire to the hotel?

Shore of the lake. Night. Eric's boat comes into view. Anika is shivering in a heap in the stern, almost numb. Eric helps her out. They climb the two yards of bank that lead to the road. Previously we have seen Lyssenhop's car, with Carla at the wheel, whirling through the countryside.
Eric (*looks toward the side of the road*): She won't be long.

Arrival of the car, which illuminates the two in its headlights. They run to it. "Anika rapidly dons a coat brought by Carla. They get in the car beside Carla, squeezing together on the seat. Carla turns toward Anika, delighted, and toward Eric, who has placed himself between the two women and put an arm around each to take up less place."

Carla: Shall we go?
Eric (*leans toward her*): This is marvelous, what you're doing.

Carla turns to look at him, smiles without saying a word, and puts the car in gear; they drive off.
The highway. The car passes by at top speed. A little train stops at a country station. The car arrives at the station. Eric jumps down with Anika, who, running toward the station, simultaneously waves back at Carla. She bursts onto the platform and jumps on to the steps of the train, then turns around and gets off in front of the horrified Eric.

Anika: Ah!
Eric: What?
Anika: I can't go.
Eric: What's wrong?
Anika (*hitches up her skirt and shows her bare leg*): I've got only one stocking.

Eric pushes her back into the train, which gives a lurch and moves off down the track; goodbye waves.

Exterior of the station. Eric rejoins Carla in the auto. "She looks at him with immense sympathy, looks for a glance, a word, or a kiss."

Carla: What do you say to the chauffeur?

Eric (smiles and gives her a warm handshake): Thank you, chauffeur.

Carla (for a moment keeps hold of the boy's hand): Kind chauffeur?

Eric: Very kind chauffeur. ("*He doesn't have the look of someone who has decided to say or do more; Carla decides after a moment to put the car in gear." It moves away.*)

Pool, Morning. Slanting, oblique light. Eric is stretched out on the diving board. Brindel is taking the water temperature; a maid is bringing out the chaise longues and other accessories. Dolly, in a swimming suit, comes out of a cabana.

Brindel: You're an early bird, Mademoiselle Lyssenhop!

Dolly: It's my last swim. We leave today.

Brindel: Would you like Monsieur Heller? (*He calls.*) Monsieur Heller!

Dolly (runs off): Thank you, but I know how to swim.

(*She climbs the ladder to the diving board and, surprised, discovers Eric, who looks at her without making a move. She hesitates, then advances to dive.*)

Eric: Dolly . . . (*She stops.*) My dear . . .

Dolly: I'm not your dear!

Eric: What are you?

Dolly: I'm the one you let go to the dance all alone.*

Eric (stops her as she prepares to jump again; she struggles; he makes her sit beside him): Darling . . .

Dolly: Why didn't you come? We would have danced together. Don't you think it means anything to me to dance with you?

---

* See Variant I at end of text.

Eric: If I hadn't had very good reasons . . .

Dolly (*stands, with an exasperated laugh*): Hah! hah! Blondes or brunettes, your very good reasons? It's always women with you!

Eric (*stands also, furious*): Always women with me! Dolly, I swear to you . . . If I hear you say things like that, I . . . I'll hit you!

Dolly (*elbows on the railing*): They're all after you! The little baroness, the countess . . . all of them . . .

Eric: There are times when you behave like a three-year-old. Dolly. You don't understand a thing!*

Dolly (*answers quickly, irritated*): Oh! Understand what? You're as impenetrable as a brick wall. What do I even know about you? That you're waiting for a letter . . . and that you go three times a day to the postoffice to see if THE LETTER has come! That's all I know! *(In a softer tone.)* And I know that you do the Australian crawl divinely . . . and that you're handsome.

Eric ("*vaguely shocked, or rather he regrets that this phrase should have been said at this moment*"): Dolly!

Dolly (*turns to look him over at her ease*): But as for your being handsome, the whole world can see that . . . ("*Melancholic and vindictive.*") I know as much about you as the first woman who sees you on the street.

Eric ("*ill at ease, disagreeable*"): I can't tell you everything, Dolly.

Dolly (*offended*): Really?

Eric (*explains quickly*): I have nothing bad to hide. But you're a little girl with not a care in the world . . . You have autos, silver shoes, dresses the color of moonlight . . . There's a whole world you don't know about, the world of the poor. There are men and women who are hungry, do you understand? They're hungry! hungry like animals! (*He laughs nervously.*)

Dolly ("*engrossed by these words*"): Why are you laughing? That's nothing to laugh about.

---

* See Variant II at end of text.

Eric: I know people—a hole in the soles of their shoes is a three-act play and a rip in their coat is a tragedy . . . People who don't have tuxedos or pearl buttons . . . Where would you learn about things like that? (*He laughs.*) People who can't go to a dance because . . . (*He stops, the words caught in his throat, and sits down on the railing.*)

Dolly (*vehemently*): You think I don't know anything about that world. I know more than you think. I know marvelous people who fight against their hunger, against their impatience . . . But they'll work it out, they'll succeed! And one day, you'll see, one day . . .

Eric (*overcome with the joy and the turbulence of his emotions, sits her down next to him and hugs her*): Dolly, Dolly dearest! I didn't think you'd understand so well . . . Did you understand?

Dolly ("*overwhelmed because he has her in his arms*"): Yes, but now I don't understand anything . . . Eric, take your arms away . . . ("*He untwines his arms; only her shoulder leans against him.*") Tell me, Eric, you aren't going to be terrible anymore? You're going to be very nice? (*He nods yes.*) Nice enough to talk to my father about your invention? Nice enough to . . . marry me?

Eric ("*becomes grave and stubborn again, beats his fist against the planks*"): When I receive the letter I'm waiting for. Not until then.

Dolly: What a stubborn mule you are! My poor dear, you're going to have to speak to my father all the same, and even ask him for my hand . . .

Eric (*anxiously*): Why?

Dolly: Because we're leaving, Eric.

Eric: It's impossible.

Dolly (*looks extremely sad*): Yes, it is, my father has had enough of Lac-aux-Dames . . . I must say he has good reasons. (*Silence.*) What have you chosen, Eric? (*Exchange of looks; she waits confidently.*) Eric? ("*His hands on her shoulders, he draws her slowly toward him; her heart leaps, but she contains herself and murmurs gravely.*") Forever?

Eric (*gravely*): Forever.

Dolly (leaps for joy, pulls him up): Come on, then! Our last
   dive! Together! (*"They look at each other, smiling, take the
   run and dive." Water splashes up.*)

   *Hotel. Lyssenhop's room. "He looks frazzled, full of haste and
   discontent. He is trying, in vain, to close a bulging trunk. He sits
   on it and pinches his finger. Furious, he gets up and kicks the
   trunk." Knock at the door.*

Lyssenhop (cries out): Who is it?
Dolly: Me, Papa.
Lyssenhop: Come in. (*She is dressed for traveling.*) Are you
   ready? Call the bellhop, then maybe *he* can close this damn
   trunk. Well, did you hear me?
Dolly (feet planted in front of him, not budging): Just a mo-
   ment, Papa. Monsieur Heller would like to speak with you.
Lyssenhop (grimaces): Who's that?
Dolly: Monsieur Heller.
*Lyssenhop ("another attack on the trunk, almost screaming in
   fury"):* He's chosen a fine time! What does he want, this
   . . . swimming instructor?
Dolly ("in her most natural voice"): To marry me, Papa.
*Lyssenhop ("falls to a sitting position on the trunk; his voice
   almost dies away"):* What? What did you say?
Dolly: To marry me, Papa.
Lyssenhop ("silent an instant, then, in a frigid tone"): That
   isn't funny.
Dolly: But I want to marry him, too.
*Lyssenhop ("understands, softens, seems almost ready to
   accept the situation; he is really very proud of his daugh-
   ter"):* It's very kind of you to let me know. You make fast
   decisions, daughter.
Dolly: You do too, Papa. You make sudden departures. We're
   in a hurry.
Lyssenhop: Oh, well, have him come in, your . . .
Dolly (being precise, going toward the door): Engineer, Papa,
   Monsieur Heller is an engineer. Remember that. (*"She opens
   the door and Eric appears, wearing his old, and only,
   jacket."*)
Eric: Bonjour, monsieur.

Lyssenhop (looks him up and down): Bonjour, Monsieur Heller. *(Indicates the trunk.)* Perhaps you would do me the kindness to close this trunk for me. *(Eric, astonished, looks at Dolly, then latches the trunk in an instant.)* Thank you! *(Eric doesn't know what to do.)* Well, then, Monsieur Heller; I'm listening. ("*Leaning against the door, Dolly impatiently twists the strap of her little pocketbook. Eric frowns. Lyssenhop is exaggeratedly amiable.*") I'm listening, Monsieur Heller.

Eric (explodes suddenly): All right, monsieur, I have to marry your daughter.

Lyssenhop: Have to? Well. And you, Dolly, do you have to marry Monsieur Heller?

Dolly (open): Absolutely, Papa.

Lyssenhop (examines his fingernails, changes his tone, becomes serious): Monsieur Heller, I'm neither a tyrant nor an idiot. Let me explain myself. Since I have only daughters, it's important to me to know the men that they will bring into my family and into my business affairs. So it's not enough for my son-in-law to have good looks and a nice manner. Am I saying all this correctly, Dolly?

Dolly (a delighted air): Terrific, Papa.

Lyssenhop (to Eric): So it's up to you, monsieur, to show me your good qualities and to make yourself known.

Eric (looks at his worn shoes): Monsieur, I have . . .

Lyssenhop ("trying to help Eric, makes him uncomfortable"): You have . . . ?

Eric: I have excellent health. I also have . . .

Lyssenhop: You have . . . ?

Eric: Excellent health, and a passion—yes, a passion—for work. And I also have . . . *(Dolly, in torment, moves from the door.)*

Lyssenhop: You have . . . ?

Eric (raises his voice): I have set the record for the 200-meter freestyle. I have my engineering degree.

Lyssenhop (benevolently): Ah!

Eric: And I've invented a . . . a little invention that . . . *(Again he looks down at his worn shoes and becomes confused.)*

Lyssenhop (comes to his aid): An invention?

Eric: Yes, monsieur; incombustible movie film.

Lyssenhop (*sits down in the overstuffed chair that Dolly, anxious, has pushed toward him, and indicates the trunk to Eric, who sits there*): But doesn't that exist?

Eric ("*on technical matters he will be able to defend himself better; he becomes animated*"): Not at the right price, monsieur! So far the cost is prohibitive.

Lyssenhop (*looks at his watch, seems to be thinking of something else, and says tranquilly, while Dolly turns gloomy*): Heller, I don't see why your invention shouldn't interest us. Submit it to our patent office and we'll look it over very carefully.

Eric ("*proudly answers, glowing*"): But I've done that, monsieur. I've given all the documents to someone who's taking care of it.

Lyssenhop (*astonished; "his disquiet becomes stronger as Eric's naiveté becomes apparent to him"*): Someone?

Eric: Yes. A consulting engineer.

Lyssenhop: You at least kept copies?

Eric: Oh, good heavens, no. Besides, it's all in my head.

Lyssenhop: And what news have you had of this engineer?

Eric: None, to tell you the truth, up to now.

Lyssenhop: How long?

Eric: A year, so far.

Lyssenhop (*choking*): A y—?

Eric (*completely natural*): Yes, well, one's got to have patience. Isn't that so? He's very nice. He took the documents to America. He's a smart fellow, you know.

Lyssenhop: So it seems . . . So you have confidence in him?

Eric (*calm, doesn't get emotional*): Complete confidence. We dined together several times in a little cafe. He's a splendid billiard player. We often played billiards together.

Lyssenhop: Billiards, billiards, that's interesting! And this consulting engineer, where's his office?

Eric: Well, you know, with this housing crisis . . .

Lyssenhop (*interrupts him*): Yes. And what is this man's name?

Eric: Meyer.

Lyssenhop ("*can't stand anymore; jumps up, exploding, turns toward the trembling Dolly*"): Dolly, are you trying to make a fool of me?

Dolly: Papa!

Lyssenhop (*"marches around the room vociferating"*): Or is this man actually a perfect idiot? He has an invention, and he confides it to . . . to . . . to the passing breezes! (*"Madly indignant."*) To someone named Meyer, who takes off with it! I can excuse anything, monsieur—but stupidity, when it gets to that stage, is a disease, monsieur, an incurable disease. (*Begins circling the room again.*) Go find your Meyer, if you can!

Dolly (*cries, desolated*): Papa, you aren't being fair!

Eric (*not losing assurance, holds Dolly back*): Let me, Dolly . . . (*Then addresses himself calmly to her father, who is still carrying on.*) Monsieur Lyssenhop, you're in a bad mood. Anyone in a bad mood, anyone can make a mistake. I'm not a businessman like you, but I have an instinct . . . an animal instinct. And I say that Meyer . . .

Lyssenhop (*repeats, irritated*): Meyer, Meyer . . .

Eric: . . . that Meyer is an honest man. Stereny is a man you can't count on. And we'll see who is right.

Lyssenhop (*shouts*): We won't see anything! Anything at all.

Dolly (*hurls herself at her father to intercede*): Papa, Papa . . .

Lyssenhop (*pushes his struggling daughter away*): Not a word, child! (*He looks at Eric with a bad-tempered air; we hear an automobile horn.*) A man without a penny can marry my daughter, monsieur, but an idiot, never! (*Horn.*) And to hell with this damned Lac-aux-Dames, its continual rain and its confidence men and its tarts and its imbeciles! (*"Storms out, pushing his daughter through the door. Eric stays in the middle of the room, appalled. Auto horn."*)

In the car, Carla, dressed for traveling, leans on the horn, looking toward the hotel; giving up, she collapses over the steering wheel.

Frogs in their bowl. The hotel barometer reads "Rain or Wind." Great clouds over the mountains. Rain. Rivulets and pools of water in the streets. Deserted and desolate hotel terrace. Drops falling from the wooden gingerbread trim of a roof, under the shelter of which are huddled some little birds. Water runneling from the sign of Vefi's inn. At the window, the innkeeper watches the rain fall. Inside, tables are set, ready for customers. Vefi is knitting.

Innkeeper (leaving the window): This weather, no one else is coming. *(She continues to knit without replying.)* You can put the table settings away.

Vefi (getting up): Perhaps Monsieur Heller will still come . . .

Inn keeper (bursts out immediately): I don't want to see that one here anymore . . . He's eaten here without paying, more than ten times. And what's more, it's your fault.

Vefi (frightened, begins to clear the tables, and asks timidly): My fault?

Innkeeper: You're so stupid . . . A chuck under the chin, an arm around the waist, and you let any gigolo get away without paying.

Lake. Rain. Pool without decorations or banners. Floorboards glistening with rain. Open door of Eric's shack. Inside, water drops from the ceiling, from cracks, into basins carefully placed underneath. Eric is trying to fix one corner of the partition, through which the water is seeping in, but the wood is rotten. He moves a photo of Dolly, swollen with humidity, and lies down on his bed.

Puck's cabana. With Tiger lying beside her, she is applying herself to writing a letter. "She makes Tiger sign it by pressing the dog's inky paw to the paper." The letter: "Why doesn't our friend come to see us anymore? We are very sad. At night, we cry. Puck de Dobbersberg and Tiger." Then she slides the letter into an envelope and turns toward Matz, who, at the other end of the room, is raptly contemplating a pretty seashell.

Puck: Do you want it? *(Matz nods his head, yes, and Puck gives it to him with the letter.)* But you promise not to linger on the way?

Matz: (going, seashell in hand): Merci, mademoiselle.

Pool. Matz runs barefoot on the soaking boards. Eric is in front of the door of his shack, carving a notch in it with his knife.

Matz: A letter.

Eric (*opens it immediately*): From Meyer?

Matz: No, from the lady at the chateau. (*He runs his finger over the notches in the wood.*) One, two, three, four, five. What's this?

Eric: The days it's been raining. Five days that I haven't given a lesson.

Matz hoists the white banner with three red spots, soaking and washed-out; it is still raining. "Then the clouds part to show the sun, which shines on the leaves, still covered with droplets."

The farmyard of the Dobbersberg chateau. Puck is coming out of a stable "with a charming little suckling-pig in her arms.

"Bright sunlight; she has a straw hat on her head. She smiles as she sees Tiger, who bounds all over her, and her face lights up as she welcomes Eric."

Puck: What a pleasure to see you!

Eric: I came because . . .

Puck (*joyfully*): Don't tell me why you've come. You've come, that's all.

Eric (*puts his hand on Puck's shoulder*): There are days when one's so alone, Puck . . .

Puck (*rapidly kisses Eric's hand, then shows him the piglet, which she is rocking in her arms like a newborn, closing her eyes*): Look . . . Isn't he sweet! . . . Pigs are lucky . . .

Eric: Why do you say that?

Puck: Look at all these babies: twelve at once.

Eric: What a strange little animal you are . . .

Puck ("*full of childish exaltation, hugs the little pig, then raises her head and sees the troubled face of Eric, looking at her*"): But what's the matter with you? You're all pale. Is there something wrong? What do you need?

Eric: What I need . . . (*Sound of a bell at the chateau.*)

Puck (*still in front of the barn; around the farmyard, a noon atmosphere*): Oh, it's lunchtime! Papa will come back through here . . . (*She puts down the piglet and returns.*) Let's hide ourselves, Eric!

Eric: Why hide?

Puck (*an air of authority*): I don't want people to disturb me when I'm with you.

Eric (*drawn along by her*): Where are we going?

Puck: Shush! (*"The hayloft. Scythes, a straw-chopper, dried grass. A gilded hill of mown hay. The half-light of a church. Crossed rafters holding up the roof."*)

Eric: But it's stifling here!

Puck: No, it's nice. You'll see. (*She begins to climb a ladder.*) Come on; it's my refuge.

Eric: What is there, up above?

Puck (*climbing, mysterious*): Cats, mice . . . birds that hunt at night and sleep in the day . . . Would you like to see their nests?

Eric (*"looks at Puck's legs emerging from her short skirt, stretched over her knee"; he shakes the ladder*): No, come down, the ladder's not steady!*

Puck (*plunges suddenly from the ladder and disappears in the pile of hay underneath*): Come find me, Eric!

"In one bound, Eric leaps into the hay, buries himself in it also, gropes with his two arms for Puck, finds one little hand, two little hands, pulls Puck to him; she goes limp and tumbles back into the bed of hay, pulling with her Eric, who falls full-length at her side. Eric is troubled; the girl, full of confident and sensual abandon. Eric gets hold of himself and rests Puck's head on his shoulder. She closes her eyes, seems to sleep a second, then speaks softly as if in a dream."

Puck: When I was little, I buried my dolls in the hay . . .

Eric: When was that? Last year?

Puck: Oh, no! I'm not little any longer, not in the least little . . . (*Inadvertently she touches Eric's arm, and he cries out.*) What's wrong? Did I hurt you?

Eric: No, it's nothing. (*"Puck turns her head, raises herself slightly; her mouth is very close to Eric's. It's she who embraces him, clumsily, precipitately. Eric returns her kiss in a much more voluptuous manner. She hides her face in the hollow of Eric's shoulder as he masters himself with difficulty." Tries to disengage himself; "he doesn't know if*

---

* Dialogue added in pencil: "Can you open the door? Here's the grain loft."

he is pleading with her to give herself to him or if he is trying to get her to behave.") Puck . . . Please . . . please . . .

Puck (*anguished, hushes him*): Don't say anything more, don't say anything! You're going to call me Dolly! ("*She bursts out crying, presses herself against Eric, who, overwhelmed, is perhaps about to prove to her that he won't call her Dolly* when a door suddenly opens and a ray of light passes over the young people. Surprised, but unable to move, Puck and Eric turn, not very promptly, toward the Baron de Dobbersberg, who has pushed open the carriage door. Eric sits up, frightened. Puck, not too disturbed, tosses back her hair from her forehead and remains seated in the hay. Embarrassment.*")

Dobbersberg (*approaches*): Puck, when will you finish playing with dolls? (*To Eric, who is getting out of the haystack and brushing off his clothes to keep himself in countenance.*) It's a childhood trick of hers, to bury her dolls in the hay . . . Excuse her for having treated you like one of her dolls . . .

Puck (*unhurriedly rises from the hay, takes Eric's hand and presses it against her cheek*): Feel how hot I am!

Dobbersberg (*to Puck, without the slightest severity*): They need you at the manor house, Puck. I'll accompany Monsieur Heller to his boat . . .

Puck (*uneasy*): But, Papa . . .

Dobbersberg (*does not raise his voice*): Go, my child. (*She leaves obediently.*)

Boathouse. The baron and Eric enter in silence. "The baron is very much master of himself; Eric seems terribly embarrassed."

Eric (*decides to say something*): This is the second time, monsieur, that you have discovered me behaving in an incorrect way . . .

Dobbersberg (*in an equable and natural voice*): It's true that in this region it might pass for incorrect behavior. Have you ever traveled to the land of the Eskimos, monsieur?

---

* Eric's line, Puck's and the beginning of these directions are crossed out in the continuity script; a MS correction merely gives Puck the lines: "No, no. Don't move. Let's not move anymore. Ah! How good the hay feels . . ."

("*Eric, disconcerted, has no time to reply; the Baron walks forward onto the float, continuing.*") Among the Eskimos, your behavior would seem quite natural. The Eskimos do a guest honor by offering him their daughters or their wives. What do you think of that code of behavior? I take it you don't find it unsympathetic. ("*He holds the boat by the end of its mooring rope so that Eric can embark.*")

Eric (*disconcerted, stammers before getting into the boat*): Good heavens, monsieur, I don't know, I . . .

Dobbersberg: It is true that we are not in Eskimo country and that I am not an Eskimo. I should therefore prefer not to conform to their conventions . . . ("*Eric takes his place in the boat and keeps himself in countenance by occupying himself with the oars.*") Shove further to the left, monsieur, to get your boat free . . . Nor, however, should I like to fail to follow the laws of hospitality . . . Therefore, Monsieur Heller . . . be careful of the pilings . . . therefore, Monsieur Heller, you must get me out of my difficulty . . . (*He throws the mooring rope into the boat.*) . . . by not visiting this shore of the lake again. Would you agree with me? ("*Eric makes a vague affirmative gesture.*") Good night, Monsieur Heller. ("*With a violent kick that reveals the extent of his irritation, he shoves the boat off and Eric rows away. Closeup of the Baron's disturbed face.*")

Notches on the door of Eric's shack: the five we have already seen and five more. Village. Eric stops in front of a bakery. "A baker's boy covered with flour brings from the shop a wicker tray covered with hot French rolls and puts it down on the sidewalk under Eric's nose." Elsewhere: a dog gnaws at a bone in front of him. Continuing his walk, "he stops in front of the vending machine, looks around to see that no one is watching him, and feels in the coin return, then beats on the side of the machine with his fist; it resounds loudly. Nothing comes out. Eric doesn't dare do it again; he goes off." In front of Vefi's inn, he looks through the window, hesitates, then walks back in the direction from which he came. Vefi appears in the doorway and runs after him.

Vefi (*catches up with him*): No luck, Monsieur Eric, the boss won't have it anymore.

Eric: Oh! I know that, Mam'selle Vefi. I wasn't coming in. Just passing by.

Vefi (*uneasy lest her boss show up*): Listen . . . (*She pulls him into the alleyway next to the inn.*) If you come in by the side door . . . (*She stands erect alongside Eric, nearly as tall as he is; he is leaning against the wall, emaciated and pale, his knees bent.*)

Eric: Why?

Vefi: Because I bet you haven't had anything to eat.

Eric (*vague*): That's true.

Vefi ("*humbly, pointing out with a look the door of her room, at the top of a narrow outside staircase*"): Run up to my room, at the top of the stairs. Wait for me. We'll have dinner together.

Eric (*begins to climb*): Thank you, Mam'selle Vefi.

Vefi (*happy, giving him her key and pushing him up the stairs; hurries off after having advised him*): But make sure no one sees you.

Vefi's room. Eric is lying across the bed, immobile, in shadow.

Eric (*speaks in delirium*): A consulting engineer . . . I tell you he's a consulting engineer . . . I have all of the documentation in my head . . .

Vefi ("*smiling, happy, appears; she is carrying a platter in one hand, some bread and beer under her arms; she has tucked an apple under her chin so that she can open the door*"): I'm sorry! I thought I'd never get through with work. ("*She puts down the platter and quickly sets out the dinner and a chair for Eric, whom she doesn't really look at but simply sees lying on the bed.*") There was a wedding downstairs; thirty people and a dinner with twelve courses . . . And then toasts! and speeches! You've really got to have patience in this line of work. And all the time, I thought of you waiting for me . . . (*Surprised at Eric's silence.*) Hey, what's the matter? You asleep? (*She comes a little closer, looks back* *and forth from the bed to the dinner standing all prepared, and as if deciding, drops her skirt and her blouse to the floor. She approaches the bed,* taps on Eric's shoulder, and shakes him.)* Are you asleep?

Eric (*delirious, tosses and turns in front of the horrified Vefi*): Forever, Dolly, forever . . . But will you look at that imbecile! He thinks that acid . . . He'll cause a fire . . . Will you let go my arm, Monsieur Lyssenhop! (*Calms himself a little, says as if it were a fact repeated until he is weary of it.*) I tell you Meyer is in America.

Vefi (*gets scared, cries out that Eric needs rest, touches his forehead, pulls open his shirt collar, takes his hand*): Monsieur Eric! Monsieur Eric! Wake up! You're frightening me . . . You've got a fever.

Eric (*half-opens his eyes, looks around with astonishment and almost with fear*): Matz! . . . Matz! . . . Oh! . . . Who shoved me into this . . . (*A little reassured.*) Oh, it's you, Mam'selle Vefi, I beg your pardon.

Vefi (*leans over him, kindly*): Monsieur Eric, you really must eat.

Eric (*looks at the food, shakes his head; he has beads of sweat on his forehead, stands with difficulty, feels ill.*) No, leave me alone, I want to go. ("*Swaying, he puts his feet over the side of the bed and gets ready to leave.*")

Vefi (*wants to detain him*): It's true you can't stay here if you're ill. I would have liked to nurse you . . . (*Motion to detain him.*) At least eat something, you're dreadfully weak.

"*He leaves and closes the door. Vefi remains seated on the edge of the bed; she looks for a moment toward the door, then takes her rosary in her hands and begins to pray.*"†

---

* Variant: Then, smiling to herself, she quickly takes off her laced-up vest and lets her skirt fall. In her peasant blouse and petticoat, she starts to slide carefully under the eiderdown, but she wakes Eric who groans in his half-sleep.

† Variant (first version): Vefi, stupefied, remains sitting on the side of the bed, stares for a moment at the closed door, rolls over on her side. We understand that, with her face hidden, she is crying . . .

Eric's shack. He is seated on his bed, leaning against the wall; he is in pain from his arm, which he is examining with a grimace of suffering. Matz is standing in front of him, leaning with his hands on his knees, looking at the arm.

Matz (*"nods his head with a knowing air"*): No, you can't stay like that. First, it's dirty, and second, it looks awful. And also I want to see what's underneath. Let me change that for you. You'll see . . . (*Takes a piece of cloth from a basin and some scissors.*) With this napkin . . . All right to cut this, huh? It'll hurt.

Eric (*exhausted; only the pain prevents him from falling asleep*): It hurts badly when it's touched. And I can't move it . . . No! Watch out.

Matz: It's sticking . . .

Eric: Not like that.

Matz: Let me wet it.

Eric: Oh! Gently . . .

Matz: Hey, look! You did that on a nail. I've already talked to Brindel about it. There are big rusty nails sticking out everywhere, and all of them covered with crud. (*He is changing the dressing with all the care he is capable of; he seems very impressed by the ugliness of the infected wound.*) You should put something on that. It's going to stick to the bandage again. I'm going to wind the napkin around it, in the meantime; but you know . . . if I were you . . .

Dobbersberg's chateau. Lighted windows. Shadows behind the windows. Dance music. Lackeys. The entrance brilliantly illuminated, as it was when Eric first arrived there.

Eric's shack. He is stretched out, completely dressed, his legs drawn up in the too-short bed. The kerosene lamp is smoking. Noise of rain. He is in a fever, tossing and turning. A knock. "He opens his eyes, thinks that the fever is making him hear things, closes them again." Another knock.

Eric (*clears his throat, raucously*): Who's there?

Puck: Me, Puck, open up.

Eric (*"gets up to a sitting position, stands swaying from side to side, and goes toward the door; he moves aside the chair that serves to lock it*"): Come in; it's open. (*He falls back onto his bed.*) You? At this hour?

Puck ("*rain running off her, under the hood of her cloak; her face seems smaller, pale, tired; she leans against the door, seems exhausted, nods yes*"): I came in the boat with Tiger. He's waiting for me.

Eric (*in bed, tries to smile*): And you choose this time of night to make visits to your male friends, Puck?

Puck (*takes off her cloak and sits down on the bed*): I didn't choose. I escaped. There's a big party at the chateau again tonight and Papa keeps a close watch on me since he told you not to come back . . . Is it true that he told you not to come back?

Eric: Yes.

Puck: And you didn't come back? (*Eric doesn't know what to reply; she regards him "with an air of mild reproach."*) I didn't tell you not to come . . .

Eric: You're speaking like a child, Puck.

Puck ("*defends herself gently*"): It's you who are speaking like a child. But I'm not a child anymore. That's what you refuse to understand, Eric. A child wouldn't suffer the way I do.

Eric (*with effort*): What do you want me to say, little Puck? You've come at a moment when I'm a bit . . . when I'm quite ill, I think.

Puck (*leans forward quickly, looks around her, bustles*): Are you sick? Have you caught a cold? This is such a bad place to live in . . . Would you like me to make you tea, or some grog?

Eric: No, let me alone . . . I only need sleep . . . oh, to sleep, above all, sleep . . . When will I be able to sleep?

Puck (*standing up, her eyes fixed on him*): Sleep . . . I don't either . . . I haven't slept since . . . for a long time . . .

Eric ("*rouses himself from his stupor*"): You don't look well either, my little Puck. What's the matter?

Puck (*turns her eyes away*): Don't you know? (*Then looks at him directly.*) Who would think it, Eric? It's your fault. You shouldn't have held me in your arms! Oh, Eric, what will I do? (*She lets herself fall onto his bed.*) Now I can't get along without you.

Eric (*"murmurs, smiling, to calm her"*): Now, little Puck, now then . . .

Puck (*quickly*): Yes, put your hand on my head. Again! Put your arm over my shoulder! . . . Eric, I feel as if I were dying of hunger . . .

Eric (*murmurs as if in a dream*): Dying of hunger . . . You too? (*He laughs to himself, nervously.*)

Puck (*Angry, then sad*): Don't laugh. Don't you have any pity for me? A little bit of pity? When you're not near me, I starve. My mouth, my eyes, my hands, Eric—everything in me starves for you. Tell me you love me a little, only a little . . .

Eric (*tries to calm her*): Shush, Puck. Don't speak so loudly. You're my little comrade, do you understand?

Puck (*continues, dreaming aloud*): Yes, a little comrade, that you don't love . . . Oh! Eric, if you didn't love me, why did you hold me in your arms? (*He is uneasy.*) It was wrong of you, Eric . . . What have you done, what have you done to me? In the barn, I felt as if I were—how can I say it to you?—as if I were an apple tree. All of me was so heavy, so sweet, so full of sap . . . I can't say it right . . . (*"Eric smoothes her head gently with his well hand; she takes his wounded arm to put it round her shoulders; he cries out from pain, and she jumps up, suddenly, frightened."*) Oh! Excuse me . . . I've hurt you.

Eric (*the pain bringing out the anger in him; in a low tone*): Don't touch me! What's the matter with you? What is it you want? (*"His delirium takes him again; he attacks Puck, cursing in her all the women around him who are not Dolly."*) What do you all want? Why don't you leave me alone? I've had enough . . . I've had it up to here! (*"Furious, feverish, delirious."*) I don't want you, any of you, whoever you are! You don't know when to keep your mouth closed . . . You don't give me a moment's peace. You run after a man even in his own house. Who do you think I am? (*"He begins to shout."*) I'm no gigolo! I'm an honest, respectable man, and I'll prove it to all of you! (*Puck, terrified, is afraid of understanding him.*) Let me be, all of you! I'm not for any of you! I only love the one, just her, you understand? As for the rest of you, I couldn't care less! ("*Puck, full of fear and desolation, draws back a bit, without as yet getting up from the bed; Eric looks straight in front of him, speaking more and more quickly, in a rage.*") No, but just think, a man's sick, he doesn't have a mouthful to eat, he's starving to death, you might say, in front of your eyes, and you, you don't have anything in your heads but your idiotic love stories. (*Puck slowly stands.*) But now it's done with. ("*At the height of fury.*") I've had it! had it! had it! ("*He beats at the air with his clenched fist, feels an atrocious pain, and falls back half fainting on the pillow.*")

Puck ("*ready to cry, still refuses to believe definitely that Eric has gotten angry at her*"): You say that to *me*? You want to beat *me*? ("*She wraps herself in her wet cloak, waits for a word that doesn't come, murmurs vainly, leaning over Eric.*") I'm going away now . . . I'm going far . . . very far . . . ("*She waits a moment, watches Eric's face—vacant, contracted—he doesn't hear her; she blows out the lamp and leaves like a shadow.*")

*Lake. Thin fog on the surface. A steering oar floats on the water. Tiger, soaked and lamentable, howls mournfully. The empty Dobbersberg boat drifts on the lake. White fog hiding the mountains.** "Four boats are searching the lake, with poles, lines and nets. The motor-powered rescue boat zigzags from one to the other."*

Voice: Have you found anything?
Voice: Nothing . . .

"*The Baron de Dobbersberg is kneeling at the stern of the rescue boat. He looks as though he has lost his mind. He is silent, indicating with his emaciated hand first one direction, then another. Two valets follow his directions, peering into the water and stirring it with poles.*"

Dobbersberg: If she's in the lake, we'll find her.

"*Another boat in which are Brindel, rowing; Matz, at the*

---

* See Variant III at end of text.

rudder; a fisherman, rowing; and Eric. Eric in the bow, in a bathing suit under his robe. His lips are pressed together. There are lines on his face. A moment later, Brindel points to a spot in the water and Eric dives. Two boats full of fishermen drag a net. They move forward little by little. One of the boats stops." Brindel's boat approaches; Eric, hanging onto the side, looks down into the water, then dives.

Voice of a fisherman: There's something holding it. We're caught.

Eric dives below the surface; his hair floats backward; distorted music of Puck's song. He thinks he sees Puck at the bottom of the lake, wrapped in her cloak. He swims closer; the corpse transforms itself into a tree trunk and floating algae. The edge of the net is caught on a broken branch; Eric unhooks it with difficulty, "then seems to collapse onto his side, his arms without strength, and exhales all his air, which rises in bubbles toward the surface." The music becomes the sound of bells, then the sound of bubbles bursting on the surface. Anxiety in the boats. The fishermen pull on the net. Uneasy faces. They hoist on board Brindel's boat the net containing the body of Eric. He is laid flat.

Brindel: No, no . . . the head lower than the feet . . .
Fisherman: He shouldn't have tried to dive, in the state he was in.
Second fisherman: Yes, look at his arm . . .
Brindel: It's always the same thing with accidents. For one that gets drowned, three more drown trying to recover the body.
First fisherman: We can't leave him like that . . .
Second fisherman: He'll have to be taken to the hospital.

Dobbersberg's boat arrives; he is anxious, having seen in the distance a body being brought up.

First fisherman: We still haven't found anything, Monsieur le Baron. But here's the swimming instructor, who's in pretty bad shape.
Brindel: He tried to dive . . .
Dobbersberg (shouts to Brindel): Take him back to shore while

there's still time. (*To the fishermen.*) You others, keep looking.

"*Convent. Bedroom. In the shadows we follow several hands
bringing things on a tray (vials, glasses, medicine bottles) and
we see Eric in a not-too-hospital-looking bed.*" Coif of a nun
seated at the head of the bed. Very agitated, Eric murmurs
words, first indistinct, little by little comprehensible.

Eric (*delirious*): You're made of gold . . . (*Shot of the empty
diving-board.*) In the sun, your arms, your legs, your downy
skin . . . a statue made of gold. (*Shot of Puck's cabana; her
voice.*) . . . and a fiancée? Do you have a fiancée? . . . Go
away, go away . . . No, stay . . . Oh, I don't know what I
want! (*Shot of the empty boat; Dolly's voice.*) Will you go
back again tonight to see her on the other shore? (*Voice of
Eric himself.*) Not tonight, not tomorrow, not ever . . . I
promise you, dear . . . (*A hand wipes the sweat from his
forehead; he comes to himself.*)

*Upper gallery of the convent. The Mother Superior in con-
versation with Dobbersberg. "He has a sad, unresigned air.
The Superior has the resignation of a Christian and the professional indifference of a nurse, but she isn't callous."*

Mother Superior: Oh, it was only a scratch at first; a little
attention and it would have healed easily. But with insuffi-
cient care, the wound has become infected. And so, this
fever, that tires him out so . . .
Dobbersberg: Yes.
Mother Superior: He was already very feeble; the poor boy
wasn't getting enough to eat and wouldn't admit it; he's so
proud!
Dobbersberg (*nervous, wants to persuade her that Eric's health
would not be further damaged by giving him, Dobbersberg,
a little reassurance*): The poor boy . . . But, you know, just
a few words would do . . . If he could only remember
something Puck had said. Perhaps it would put me on the
right track. I know they saw each other often, and Puck
confided in him more than in anyone else.
Mother Superior: I understand your great trouble, Monsieur de

Dobbersberg. But until after the operation, we must avoid anything that might raise his fever. (*The baron is no longer listening; he is thinking only of Puck.*)

Street corner in Salzburg. "We recognize the slim silhouette of Puck approaching a huge policeman. She raises her head to him; she is asking her way. The policeman responds with explanatory gestures." She reaches a huge building with a sign: LYSSENHOP & CO. Establishing shot of the offices. Puck hesitates a moment, then decides to enter. Dolly's office—she is her father's secretary. Table covered with papers, telephone, "and several elegant accessories (clock, mirror, lighter, paperknife, ashtray), which excuse the presence of so young a woman in such a gloomy place. Dolly, already astonished at what Puck has told her and full of projects she wants to put into execution immediately, listens to Puck without closely looking at her, merely throwing several glances at her; she is rather disturbed by this new affirmation of Eric's love."

Puck (*half seated on the desk, very naturally*): . . . If he hadn't been sick, he wouldn't have sent me away so brutally, but all the same he would have sent me away. He was a little delirious and that's why he was brutal. But when he said he loved you, he wasn't delirious then.

Dolly (*seated, "feels she needs to prove her modesty"*): He loved us both a little . . .

Puck (*gravely, to convince her*): No, no . . . He loved nobody but you, and a lot. He called me his little comrade. I wasn't even his friend.

Dolly (*"seems now to have a whole plan in her head; she asks with an exact sense of what must be done"*): Who's taking care of him now?

Puck: He's all alone.

Dolly: I'll telephone Brindel.

Entrance hall of the hotel. Behind his counter, the porter, Eggenhofer, "is sorting keys as solemnly as if he were taking part in a mass. In front of him, the Manager, much less ceremoniously, is filing his nails. We don't know if the two men are trying to conceal emotion with banalities or are trying to persuade themselves that they are moved by an event that would be worth no more than a paragraph in a newspaper."

Porter: They told me it could be all up with him.
Manager: That would be a shame. So young, so athletic . . .
Porter: If he comes through, it'll be minus an arm.
Manager: In that case, it's hard to know what to wish for him.

Vefi's bedroom. She prays in front of a crucifix, a large rosary in her joined hands.
Pool. Small combined office and ticket window belonging to Brindel, who is on the telephone. Nearby, M. Mayreder wants to speak to him; Brindel makes impatient signals for him to be quiet. Without Brindel's noticing, Matz has picked up the other receiver.

Brindel: . . . No, Mademoiselle Lyssenhop. He isn't there any-
   more . . . He's been taken to the hospital . . . No, Mademoi-
   selle Lyssenhop, they say it's serious . . . No, Mademoiselle
   Lyssenhop, not critical . . . But they're not sure of saving
   his arm . . . No, Mademoiselle Lyssenhop, they can't wait.
   The doctor says that the longer they wait . . .
Dolly (*in her office, near Puck, listens soberly then concludes,
   speaking low and briskly*): All right. I'm coming. I'll be at
   Lac-aux-Dames in a few hours.
Brindel (*nods his head*): Good, Mademoiselle Lyssenhop.
   (*Matz has hung up without being seen.*)

*Hospital. Eric in his bed, half awake. Matz seems to be wait-
ing near him.*

Matz (*softly*): Eric, old boy, you're awake, aren't you?
Eric: Why?
Matz: Because otherwise you might think that you'd been
   asleep. And that wouldn't be nice for Dolly.
Eric: Dolly?
Matz: She's coming . . .
Eric: When?
Matz: Right away.
Eric: How do you know?

Matz: She telephoned Brindel. I heard it all. Afterward, I ran
here.

Eric: Dolly? (*The doctor is now close to his bed. He takes
Eric's pulse.*)

Doctor (*softly*): My poor boy, I'm telling you because I
promised to keep nothing from you. You should have been
taking better care of yourself for a long time now. (*More
clearly and emphatically.*) We might have avoided the operation, but now it's necessary, urgent. This morning you were
full of courage.

Eric: I am still. But, Doctor . . . I'm waiting for someone.

Doctor ("*threatens him kindly*"): If we wait, I can't answer for
anything.

Eric ("*invincible stubbornness*"): Someone will come, I know.
Someone I have to see again first.

Doctor: My boy, you're risking your arm.

Eric: If I must.

Doctor: But you're also risking your life.

Eric: All the more reason! . . . Not before, Doctor. Not before.

Doctor (*to the Mother Superior, who enters and looks at the
sick man gravely*): Mother, did you hear? In that case, I
must disclaim all responsibility; I can't answer for anything . . . ("*The Mother Superior makes a slight sign of
assent, hoping that Eric will allow the operation all the
same*"; *the doctor leaves.*)

*Covered walkway of the hospital. Dolly and Puck advance
in silence. Puck stops. Dolly takes her by the hands, but Puck
resists, shaking her head.*

Puck: No, no; I don't want to see him again . . . That is, I don't
want him to see me. He's already nearly forgotten me, I'm
sure of it. As soon as you have news, I'll go away. ("*She is
already going; Dolly does not dare detain her; Puck smiles
faintly and says again, to be exact, to reassure her.*) I'll wait
outside.*

---

* See Variant IV at end of text.

Eric's bed. "He makes an effort to raise himself on his good arm and smiles when he sees Dolly enter; she appears in the door and slowly, a little timidly, approaches his bed."

Eric: Dolly . . .

Dolly: Eric . . .

Eric: I knew that . . .

Dolly (fervently): No, don't talk. Only look at me . . . I don't need your words to understand you. I wanted to tell you . . .

Eric: . . . tell me goodbye. You know I . . .

Dolly: I know everything. Eric. I even know you put off the operation to see me first.

Eric: Yes, I didn't want to go without telling you goodbye.

Dolly ("overcome with emotion, wants to give Eric hope"): Go, Eric? You're not going anywhere, now that I've found you again! *(He listens.)* Forever, Eric! Forever! *(She is on the point of crying.)* And what I wanted you to know is that I'm yours, whatever happens. Papa can't do anything about it. I'm yours even if you're penniless. I'm yours even without . . . *(She can't finish and sobs.)*

Doctor (enters, approaches Dolly, who is in tears on the bed): Mademoiselle Lyssenhop . . . I must warn you that every minute of delay makes the situation more grave and the result of the operation more uncertain.

Dolly (raises her head): Eric! Now you know what I wanted to tell you. *(She looks for encouragement from the doctor.)* Doctor! Doctor; I have so much faith.

Doctor: Yes, mademoiselle . . . But we must hurry.

Between the arches of the convent, Puck stands and waits, looking into the distance. Matz waits in a chair in a sort of anteroom; "he looks disturbed and stares at his right arm as if fascinated." Eric's empty bed. Dolly seated by the bedside. "She is grave and dignified, immobile, conscious of the danger; her emotions are greatly moved, but she does not show it; she is courageous and she hopes." The operating room; we see only the actors' faces leaning forward: "first a sister who stares fixedly, attentively at Eric's face (this is the anesthetist); then another, looking at the doctor work on the arm while she nervously bites her lips; the third is perfectly calm, passing a probe to the doctor, who is frowning behind his glasses." Then, with a sigh, he looks at the sister nearest him with a relieved air. Vague smile from the third sister, still occupied with Eric, whom she is looking at attentively, but with less anxiety. Expansive smile from the second sister, who is too keyed-up to stay at her spot and leaves, full of joy. Bedroom. "Dolly, near the window, looks out without seeing. She quickly turns her head toward the door as it suddenly opens. The second sister appears, as happy as a baby, overflowing with joy."

Second Sister ("low but intelligible voice"): He's safe! ("Dolly, who was hoping with all her strength, is not surprised, but still she is as if stunned; she looks at the sister with a calm, tired smile and closes her eyes.")

Convent parlor. "An unheard-of racket fills the room, where ordinarily conversations are whispered rather than spoken and where a man's voice is almost never heard."

Lyssenhop: Incredible! It's incredible!
Brouhaha from the sisters (who are surrounding him and trying to quiet him in sharp and overlapping voices): Be quiet, monsieur! . . . If someone heard you! I beg of you . . . There's not a thing we can do!
Mother Superior (attracted by the noise, arrives, indignant): A little quiet, if you please, monsieur!
Lyssenhop (bows respectfully but responds in a rather irreverent tone): I'm perfectly calm!
Mother Superior: Remember where you are! In such a place, an outrage like this . . .
Lyssenhop (isn't going to let himself be imposed on by a bunch of black habits): There's no outrage. But I want to see my daughter! I won't stand for her behaving like a . . . like a slut!
Sisters (horrified): Oh!
Mother Superior (indignant): Oh, monsieur! Such a word!
Lyssenhop ("his anger does not diminish, but he momentarily sweetens his tone in mockery of the Mother Superior"): A very innocent word, Mother, compared to what my daughter

deserves! (*Then he explodes again, gesticulating.*) Now, where is Monsieur Heller? I want to speak to him. (*Terror from the sisters, who draw away from him.*)

Mother Superior (*brave and firm*): For the moment, monsieur, he cannot see anyone.

"*A smiling, self-assured gentleman has just entered; he approaches Lyssenhop.*"

The Unknown: Even I, monsieur, haven't been able to talk with him. And I have something particularly urgent to tell him. (*The Mother Superior and the sisters have left.*)

Lyssenhop (*suspicious and brusque*): But who are you, sir?

The Unknown ("*seems rather pleased with himself; since he entered he has been sporting a little satisfied smile, a smile in the eyes*"): I am Monsieur Meyer, Benjamin Meyer, to whom Monsieur Heller entrusted his patent. (*Meyer pauses briefly to make an impression on Lyssenhop, who remains impassive—speechless—and adds with a careless air:*) The good news I'm bringing to him will contribute, I'm sure, to his quick recovery.

Lyssenhop ("*still unable to get over it; he is ready to get angry again, actually furious at himself for having been wrong*"): What? Is this thing really serious?

Meyer: Serious—? But, monsieur . . . monsieur?

Lyssenhop (*quick nod*): Monsieur Lyssenhop.

Meyer (*bows, with ease and satisfaction*): But Monsieur Lyssenhop, I'm bringing him a fortune. A gold mine, an invention of genius. I've already signed contracts for marketing . . .

Lyssenhop (*interrupts Meyer's discourse; "he is calmer, he feels that he is beaten, he is ready to come to terms; he begins walking up and down again, according to his habit, speaking with a dry humor*"): Ah, in that case! . . . In that case! This changes the situation a bit . . . I admit, Monsieur Meyer, that this whole story of an invention, a patent . . . and even your own existence . . . it all seemed a little problematical to me. There are so many Meyers in business.

Meyer (*with raillery*): One has to find the right Meyer. ("*The two men laugh with an effort at complaisance toward each other and go toward the door, which Lyssenhop opens.*")

Matz (appears and regards the two astonished men without the least timidity): What do you want, messieurs?

Meyer: Listen, my boy, we'd like to see Eric.

Matz: So sorry, but it's impossible for the moment.

Lyssenhop: But . . .

Matz: I am Monsieur Heller's secretary . . . How can I help you?

Lyssenhop (he and Meyer are simultaneously reassured "and irritated to have to deal with this little boy"): Tell Monsieur Heller that it's Monsieur Meyer.

Matz: Meyer?

Meyer: Yes. His friend Meyer.

Matz (absolutely stupefied): The letter Meyer?

Meyer: The Meyer from America.

Matz ("speechless an instant, mouth open, is going to shout, but turns back toward the two men, grabs the door, and shuts it in their faces"): No! No! Not all of you at once! Not all of you at once! Come back in an hour!

Terrace of the hospital. "Eric, lying outside in the sunlight, is resting with closed eyes. Dolly is beside him, looks at him, waits for him to open his eyes. He opens them, smiles. She smiles." From far away we begin to hear Puck's song.

Lake. Puck in her boat rows into the distance; she is singing. Her face is very sad. "A salmon leaps in the light to catch one of the last mosquitoes of the summer. Puck's boat draws away into the distance."

Puck (sings):

> On the other shore,
> The fires and feasts
> And the blond girl
> Have taken him.
> The lake, the mirror
> Of our faces
> With mouths joined,
> Reflects me alone,
> Mouth that sings,
> Eyes that stream
> With tears? No, no,
> With droplets of moon . . .

Variants

I. Lovers' quarrel, second version; no intervention from Brindel; the sequence begins directly on the diving board.

Pool. Diving board. Seated, their legs dangling, "Dolly and Eric argue animatedly but in low voices and without gestures; they are very angry with each other.

Dolly: You're a tyrant . . . a tyrant . . .

Eric: Me? That's the limit!

Dolly: And vain too . . . You forbade me to go to the dance just to exercise your authority over me . . . What did it matter to you if I went?

Eric: And what did it matter to you if you didn't go?

Dolly (reproaches him kindly): We would have danced together; why didn't you come?

Eric (sulking and brusque): I had good reasons . . .

Dolly (gets up with an exasperated laugh): Ha! ha! Were they blondes or brunettes, your good reasons? With you it's always women!

II. (Same scene, continuing; first version)

Dolly (exasperated laugh): Ha, ha . . . was it a blonde or a brunette, your good reason?

Eric (angry): Dolly, listen, don't be stupid!

Dolly (sulks): They're all after you . . .

Eric: Who?

Dolly: The women! The little Dobbersberg, another pretty idiot! The countess, the swimming pupils. Do I know? . . . (*Ready to cry.*)

Eric (scolds her): Dolly, there are times when you behave like a three-year-old. You don't want to understand anything, even the most obvious things.

Dolly: What?

Eric ("undertakes a full-dress speech to justify himself; his shyness disappears. As he speaks, Dolly stops whimpering and observes him"): You don't understand that I don't have eyes, thoughts, senses except for you. It's unbearable. I'm only a man, Dolly, and a man in love! You're there every day, so close to me and so far away . . .

Dolly (*moved*): Ah, you've finally decided!

Eric: What?

Dolly ("*leans her shoulder against his and throws him a look that embraces his whole bronzed body*"): To talk to me a little instead of looking at me like some wild animal, like an animal biting its chain! In all the time since I've met you, what have I learned about you? That you swim divinely . . . that you're waiting for a letter that never arrives . . . and that you're handsome . . .

Eric (*gets up and moves away, "enchanted but disturbed*"): Dolly . . .

Dolly: But the whole world can see that, that you're handsome. I don't know any more about you than the first woman passing by.

Eric (*tortured*): I can't tell you everything, Dolly.

Dolly (*offended*): Oh, well, then, don't say anything.

Eric (*explains*): I don't have anything bad to hide. But why should I disturb your existence when you haven't a care in the world? You have autos, silver slippers, dresses the color of moonlight . . . In short, you are the Lyssenhop girl.

Dolly (*humble*): It's not my fault.

Eric: I know, dear. But I can't speak to you, of all people, about a world you don't know.

III. Scene of Puck's supposed drowning; added MS leaf.

Steering oar.

Tiger howling in the drifting boat on the lake.

Puck's cabana. Lenitchka crying in a corner. Dobbersberg is there searching through some papers: "And you didn't find any letters in her bedroom either?"

Farmworkers bring out horses from the stable and get ready to mount them (hurry and bustle in the farmyard).

Farmworker sounds horn on mountain pasture (fog).

The remains of the party in the court of the Dobbersberg chateau. Burnt-out lanterns. Tables not yet cleared. Candelabras. Groups of guests, with drawn faces, whispering in corners.*

---

* At the bottom of the leaf is added this penciled inscription: "Simili Bojan, hysterical attack." This is the only allusion to an eventual direct appearance by Puck's mother. Through Puck herself, we have learned earlier that she is the daughter of Camilla Bojan, "the Bojan of the Vienna Opera."

IV. Scene of Puck's and Dolly's arrival at the hospital; first version.

Inner court of the convent. Fine weather. Through the arches, we see the lake and the mountains. Facing the lake, near a little table on which is a cup of tea, Eric is seated in an armchair. "Tiger is lying next to him. Nearby, in a covered walkway of the convent, Dolly and Puck advance in silence; they approach from the corner of the walkway. Puck stops; then she takes a step back to rejoin Dolly, who has stopped a bit further away, at the corner. Dolly takes Puck by the hands and wants to draw her forward, but Puck resists, shaking her head."

Dolly: Come.
Puck: No, not me.
Dolly: Yes, see how worried he is.
Puck: Not about me.
Dolly: Come, he'll be so happy.
Puck: Not because of me.

Tiger pricks up his ears, Eric caresses him, but the dog goes away as Eric calls him in vain. Tiger crosses Dolly's path and bumps up against her as she arrives alone, then he turns the corner, running. Eric has turned to follow the dog with his eyes; he sees Dolly.

DIVINE

The investigations to discover the whereabouts of Colette's manuscript for *Divine* had even less success than those for *Lac-aux-Dames*. We were forced to the ultimate solution, the same that Maurice Goudeket had suggested for Marc Allégret's film—to run the film and make a stenographic copy of the words. The text that follows is thus a transcription, as faithful as possible, of the sound track of the film *Divine*, a transcription made through the courtesy of the Cinémathèque Française. It goes without saying that even after all precautions have been taken, the result of such a method cannot be absolutely without imperfections; for example, we have no assurance that the print projected is definitive and free of cuts. But at least the result offers us a reasonably precise general idea of the film, and thus of the text written by Colette.

There is little on the project in her correspondence, merely a fleeting allusion in a letter to Mme Léopold Marchant in August 1934: "After [the novel *Duo*] the film for Mme Berriau will darken my days." An allusion full of interest: for us, of course, *Divine* is today above all a film by Max Ophuls—that is to say, by one of the greatest directors of the modern cinema, who before his death in 1957 gave us *The Earrings of Madame de . . .* , *La Ronde*, and what many consider to be his masterpiece, *Lola Montès*. But in 1934, Ophuls was merely another exile from the Hitler regime, his reputation in France resting on a single film, *Liebelei* (1932), which had superficially catalogued him as a specialist in Viennese operetta. His true merit had not yet been discovered, and it was thus logical to think of *Divine* as a film "for" the far more influential Simone Berriau, already a producer in her own right and later to be the director of the Théâtre Antoine. The first film of her Eden-Productions, *Itto*, directed in Morocco by Jean Benoit-Lévy, had won the Grand Prix du Cinéma Français; the second production was *Divine*.

Berriau had become a friend of Colette's, who marveled at her all-conquering energy, and she had invited Colette several times to her farm of Mauvanne, near Salins d'Hyères. At Mauvanne were filmed the exterior shots of *Divine*. One of the *Lettres de la Vagabonde*, to Mme Marchand, describes "Simone Berriau's great vineyard, near Hyères, and its more than a hundred hectares of vines, of peach trees, of almond trees, and the enormous farmyard." And since the letter dates from summer 1935, we may be allowed to suppose that Colette went there to watch the filming. We know also, through the second part of "Backstage at the Studio," that she was also present during filming at the Billancourt studios, this time in midwinter. She recounts the ups and downs of the filming, the difficulty of the working conditions, and the fevered atmosphere in the uncomfortable studio with the same horrified empathy that she showed at Rome in 1917 during the filming of her *Vagabond*.

It must be admitted that she "followed" the filming of *Divine* much more closely than that of *Lac-aux-Dames*. This is doubtless due to the fact that this time the scenario had really come from her pen. Granted, the phrase preceding the credits "the first scenario written directly for the screen by COLETTE," didn't quite reflect the real situation. Colette had already written a scenario for Musidora in 1917–1918 (*La Flamme Cachée*; *The Hidden Flame*); moreover, *Divine* was not an original work but was inspired by her *Backstage at the Music Hall*. However, *L'Envers du Music-Hall* was not a novel or a series of stories, but a collection of impressions and sketches, and it had in fact been necessary to invent a story line for the film. This plot had been created with the help of Ophuls, Jean-Georges Auriol, and Colette de Jouvenel, if we are to believe the credits. Colette was credited only with the dialogue. We can nevertheless allow ourselves to view her as the real intellect behind the overall plot and dramatic progression of the film, even if only a few scenes—the showgirl nursing her baby in the dressing room, the strategy for dining free in the restaurant—were inspired directly by *L'Envers du Music-Hall*.

The advertising was built around the theme, "a great film about the music hall and nature": a naive formula that has the advantage of summarizing the two aspects of the film, the rustic and the citified. But the unassured articulation of these two antagonistic themes explains in part the relative failure of the film. The work seems to be based on a schematic opposition between an unhealthy environment (the music hall, debauchery, artifice, drugs) and a healthy one (the country, the outdoors, animals, simplicity). The film's heavily underlined opposition is summarized by two masculine cardboard figures, one no more credible than the other: Philippe Hériat as a pitiably maleficent fakir and Georges Rigaud as an awkward milkman—who can in no way be compared with the poetic milkman of Prévert's *Drôle de Drame* (1937). This contrast, expressed awkwardly in the story, is nevertheless at the heart of much of Colette's writing. Claudine Jardin has remarked that her heroines "always return to the nourishing countryside after that great evil, city life." How, though, could this fundamental attitude have found such unconvincing expression on the screen?

The reason for its failure is probably simple enough. One need only see, or re-see, the film, to comprehend that the director is infinitely more at ease painting the urban milieu, evoking the artificial and baroque universe of the music hall, than in the country scenes. Max Ophuls' fine touch suited only half of the diptych—the half that prefigured, in miniature, his *Lola Montès*, the half that the scenario of *Divine* clearly invites us to condemn. From this comes the profound disequilibrium of the film: Ophuls was not the man to plead the case that Colette had prepared. His film has nevertheless found defenders;

François Truffaut sees in it, not without some hyperbole, "a little masterpiece of verse and healthiness" and even "a true little Renoir."

Countryside. Plowing scene. Furrows. A horse, a plow, two women. Accompanied by her mother, Ludivine is behind the plow. She is singing.

Mother: Your're not shy about singing, you!
Ludivine (interrupting herself): When I sing, I feel on top of the world.
Mother: Yes, and then you get ideas.
Ludivine (gaily): No need to get them. I've got them and I'm holding on to them!
Mother (realist): And not a lot else . . . And you a pretty girl!
Ludivine (confident): Just wait, Mama, things can change!
Mother: Wait?
Ludivine: Of course . . . wait for a letter!

The neighboring road. Noise of an auto. An elegant convertible brakes and stops. From it descends a young woman, in city clothing, who hails the two working women.

Young woman (calling): Hey, there! Hey!
Mother (vaguely hostile): What does that one want?
Ludivine: Oh, I dunno! (*The young woman comes toward them, making little affected jumps across the furrows.*)
Mother (protests): Be careful of where you put your feet, madame, we have enough trouble making things grow!
Young woman (joins them): Madame yourself, don't you recognize me? *Bonjour,* Madame Jarisse!
Mother (exclaims): Oh, it's little Roberta! But what are you doing in the country? (*Embraces.*)
Roberta (pretends to lament): Oh, my poor little shoes and my stockings!
Ludivine (teases): Aren't you the great lady!
Roberta (affected): Oh la la!
Ludivine: It's not like springtime in Paris, is it!
Roberta: Come, let's go back to the house! (*They leave horse and plow where they stand and go toward the road.*)
Ludivine: You must have stories to tell us!

Roberta: I'll tell you all about it. Am I happy!

Ludivine: It's nice of you to come back to see your hometown. It's pretty here, isn't it?

Roberta (*still chirping affectedly*): Oh, you know, the country-side, the fresh air!

Ludivine (*they have reached the auto*): Oh, you've bought a car? It's great!

Roberta: And what a car! Come on, get in! Look, seven horse-power, convertible hood, high and low lights, radio . . . Isn't it pretty? Of course, it's not a new car, but it's super-luxurious.

Farm Kitchen. The three women are eating. The newcomer is devouring everything.

Ludivine: You sure were hungry.

Mother (*serving Roberta and her daughter*): Everything's very simple here; there's just soup . . .

Roberta (*enthusiastic*): Oh, soup, gorgeous soup! Marvelous, I haven't had any for three years!

Ludivine: Would you like a bacon omelet?

Roberta (*serious*): All right, but not too much fat; I've got to take care of my figure.

Ludivine (*teases*): Oh, your figure!

Mother (*to Roberta*): At least you've got a good appetite!

Ludivine (*sincere*): You're superb!

Roberta (*false modesty*): I don't complain.

Ludivine (*curious*): Is it true what they say—that you're acting in the theater?

Roberta (*eating*): It sure is! And I dance, too.

Ludivine: Where?

Roberta: At the theater where I act, the Empyrean. I'm pretty happy, except that I broke a bone. Look, there. (*She shows her leg.*) I have to take two weeks off, so I said to myself: why not take advantage of the opportunity to see Grandma and the old hometown. I was dying to . . .

Ludivine (*teasing her amicably*): You couldn't have been dying all that much, since it took you so long to get around to it.

Mother (*amused, intervenes*): Heaven, hear them!

Ludivine (*sudden idea*): Mama, what would you think if we put Roberta up for the night? It's getting dark already . . .

Mother (doesn't say no): If you don't mind sharing your bed with her . . .

Ludivine: It's lucky that we're skinny!

Ludivine's bedroom. The two girls are getting undressed, chattering gaily. A big country bed with an eiderdown.

Roberta (looking at Ludivine): You know, talk about figures, yours isn't bad. What are you going to do now?

Ludivine (misunderstanding): Me? Nothing until tomorrow morning. The hens are shut in for the night, I've pumped up the water, I'm going to bed.

Roberta: I don't mean that! I mean with your life! Are you going to get married?

Ludivine: Married? To what? I'd rather go back to the candy factory.

Roberta (practical): How much would you make?

Ludivine (knowledgeable): Eighteen francs a day.

Roberta: What about if I found you a job for forty francs a day?

Ludivine (impressed): No kidding! Where'd you find a job like that?

Roberta (explains): I'm going on a tour with the old revue that we're doing now. You could take my place in the new show, the one we're rehearsing. Because I really want to go to Cairo, for *business** . . .

Ludivine: For what?

Roberta: That's English. Don't worry, you'll get the hang of it! Listen, get up, I have an idea. Go over to the window, walk naturally . . .

Ludivine: Why?

Roberta (insists): Do what I say. Go on!

Ludivine: All right! (*She walks calmly toward the window.*)

Roberta (protests): Not like that! I said, walk naturally. Pretend you're on stage, you're the Queen of the Fountains. Look, like this, don't you think it's great? (*Walks, swaying exaggeratedly from side to side.*)

Ludivine (bursts out laughing): Oh, that's ridiculous!

Roberta (annoyed): And why are you laughing?

---

* In English in the original.

Ludivine (*laughs*): Is that how the Queen of the Fountains walks?

Roberta (*patient*): Kid, you've got a lot to learn. And to start with, don't laugh at me when I'm knocking myself out to do something for you. Come on, now, follow me! (*She begins the motion again.*) Watch and do like I do. One, two, one, two . . . (*They do a comic snake dance up and down the room, Ludivine making herself imitate Roberta; a sudden noise stops them.*)

Ludivine (*alert*): Mama! (*They stop the movement, gallop to the bed and dive in like urchins. Ludivine whispers.*) Pretend you're asleep. (*The mother opens the door, sees them "sleeping," and retreats. A clock chimes. In the dark, the conversation begins again, whispered underneath the covers.*)

Roberta: If you have to get up on a stage and show your figure . . .

Ludivine (*interrupting her*): Oh, don't worry about it!

Roberta (*continuing*): What will your mother say?

Ludivine: Nothing, if it's a real job and I'm not doing anything wrong.

Roberta: Are you afraid of going to Paris?

Ludivine (*tranquil*): Me? Did you see me being afraid of anything when we were kids? There's not much I'm afraid of.

Roberta: Obviously, it's not the Folies-Bergère, it's sort of a hick production, but you know, if you really distinguish yourself . . .

The "Empyrean," a little neighborhood music hall. Roberta leads her friend backstage. Bustle. Continuous movement. Music. Troupe of girls.

Employee (*in the corridor*): Hey, Roberta, how's the gam?

Roberta (*still moving*): So-so. Listen, have you seen Victor?

Employee (*gestures*): He ought to be over there, in the prop shop. (*They move toward the prop and costume shop, continually bumping into other people.*)

Roberta (*to a middle-aged woman*): Good morning, Madame Gaby! (*To Ludivine.*) That's the ballet mistress. Morning, everybody! (*Responses, exchanges of greetings.*) Hi, Dora!

(*Through a perpetual bustle, we approach a group where a middle-aged man is speaking angrily; we hear several phrases.*)

Middle-Aged Man (*furious*): Chicks with good legs I can get thirty-six of 'em in an hour! I'm not going to take this prima-donnaing. Understand?

Roberta (*aside to Ludivine*): That's the director, but you're not going to have anything to do with him yet. Under two hundred francs, Victor does the hiring. (*She suddenly stops and turns to face Ludivine, looking upset.*) I forgot: "Merde, double *merde*, and *merde* again"; that's supposed to bring you good luck! (*Calls to the stage manager.*) Victor!

Victor (*occupied*): I'm here, I'm here, but I'm busy!

Roberta (*not impressed*): Here she is!

Victor (*turns around*): Here who is?

Roberta (*shows Ludivine off*): My replacement!

Victor (*briefly considers the young woman*): H'm. What's her name?

Ludivine: Ludivine Jarisse.

Victor (*Parisian snob*): Do you have to hinge your name in the middle to get it around corners? Why not Artemisia? (*Calls from near by: "Victor!"*)

Roberta (*insistent*): Take a look at her!

Victor (*with a connoisseur's eye*): Not a bad head. She looks as stiff as a board.

Roberta (*praising the product*): You haven't seen everything; look at her legs! (*She lifts Ludivine's skirt; Ludivine is very embarrassed.*)

Victor (*a bit shaken*): H'm, yes . . . What did you say her name is?

Roberta: Ludivine Jarisse.

Victor (*decided*): That's not a name, it's a catastrophe! We'll call her Divine. (*Yells: "Victor!"*) All right, she'll be good fresh meat for the slave market! (*Leaves hurriedly.*)

Roberta (*enthusiastic; taking Ludivine's arm*): See, as easy as pie! Now you're Divine! (*Continuing.*) And now, let's go home!

Roberta's apartment. She's showing her friend around enthusiastically.

Roberta: I'll let you have my apartment while I'm gone. It'll be to the advantage of both of us. Look, here's the entry-way, the living room—and I only pay two thousand francs a year. Nice, isn't it?

Divine: Yes, it's really pretty! (*The visit continues, lively as ever; great mess in all the rooms.*)

Roberta: And I even have a piano. (*Shows it in passing.*) And here's the bedroom. I've got a huge bed!

Divine: But your car—how do you ever afford your car?

Roberta (*slightly false assurance*): Oh, the car, that's another thing. Obviously, it's not from what I earn, but I worked it out . . . (*Continues.*) Right now, of course, it's a little messy, but, after all, when a person's just leaving . . .

Divine (*placid*): Oh, of course.

Roberta (*finishing the tour*): There, that's the bathroom and the kitchen, and the landlord is going to put in hot water.

Divine (*practical*): When?

Roberta: He hasn't told me when.

Divine (*considering the state of the kitchen, the scattered cooking utensils, etc.*): It's really quite a mess.

Robert (*suggestively*): Oh, but it doesn't matter, Divine! When I'm gone, you can arrange things to suit yourself!

Shot of the apartment, in perfect order. Staircase of the building. A little boy throws his schoolbag down onto the next landing, then slides down the banister; arriving on the landing, he discovers that his bag has knocked over a bottle of milk in front of a door. Not overly troubled, he descends the staircase normally, whistling, and crosses the path of Divine, who is ascending; he greets her hypocritically. On her landing, Divine discovers the small disaster and begins to clean it up. The concierge arrives.

Concierge: I suppose you think I'm your maid?

Divine (*preparing to sponge it*): Bonjour, Madam Nicou. It wasn't my fault, but I'm cleaning it up.

Concierge (*dignified*): You should tell the milkman to ring the doorbell; that's obvious! (*Leaves. The ballet mistress comes down the stairs.*)

Divine: Bonjour, madame.

Ballet mistress: Up already? I thought you began work at eleven.

Divine: Yes, but I can't get used to not getting up early. So I do my shopping in the morning, and it gives me a walk.

Ballet mistress: What are you doing there?

Divine (sponging): I don't know who's spilled the milk . . .

Ballet mistress (maternal): That develops the arms and the chest. You need that, you know; I've noticed! Lift your chin, throw back your shoulders. Are you doing the exercises I showed you?

Divine (docile): Yes, madame.

Ballet mistress (sees Divine's bag of groceries): You eat all that bread? Stick to the crust, the rest of it makes you swell up. But don't starve yourself either; you have to be in condition to wear the costume for the fountain spectacle. I have it here. Want to see it?

Divine (sincerely): Oh, yes, madame!

Ballet mistress (showing her): You see, there, those are pearls. There, that's spun glass. All the rest, that's your skin. Remember that, will you?

Empyrean Theater. Rehearsal, very lively. Songs. A dance being rehearsed.

Victor (directing the movement): Gently, kids! This isn't the first time you've gone through this. Smile, for Pete's sake! . . . Good! Graceful!

Music and songs. Shout: "Curtain!" An observer is very attracted.

The Man: René, she's charming. What bearing! (*Animation, babble.*)

Victor (directing): There, *con amore*, passionately!

The Man (doubtless one of the angels of the production): Divine, you're stunning! Listen, I've absolutely got to do something for you! (*Noises; a quarrel begins around an actress; the man continues.*) I'll give you a solo to sing!

Divine (suspicious): Why?

Man (insisting): A solo, you understand, that's a solo in front

of the curtain, with the spotlight on you, you'll be a hit right
away. It's the beginning of your career!

Divine (*not beating around the bush*): I wasn't hired to sing
and I'm not here to make a career out of it! (*She escapes.
Babble of voices.*)

Nero (*the animal tamer, against whom Divine bumps at the foot
of the stairs backstage; he catches hold of her*): Oh, not so
fast, little girl! Let me look at you a minute. Geez, the dew's
still on you. (*He is old and greasily fat.*)

Girl (*to Nero*): Leave her alone, huh?

Nero: What?

Girl: Come on, get out of here. (*Divine has run away.*)

Nero (*elbowing match on the staircase*): Artistes first,
madame, please!

Dora (*hails Divine*): Cigarette?

Divine: No, they make me thirsty!

Dora (*insists*): A piece of candy? (*Divine accepts, then makes
a face.*)

Divine: Funny taste!

Dora (*persistent*): Oh, really? I've got others. Some snuff?

Victor (*interrupts this little game*): Come on, kids, come on!

Dora: Oh, him again!

*Entrance of Divine's building. A young man arrives. The
concierge stops him.*

Concierge: The milk, that's you?

Man: Yes, Madame Nicou.

Concierge: Listen to me a minute. Where's your delivery boy?

Man: He's sick.

Concierge: Listen: I don't know which of you two brought the
milk yesterday. But, please, ring when you get to that young
lady who just moved in on the third, don't just leave the milk
in front of the door. Somebody knocked it over, and my nice
clean steps were completely flooded.

Man (*interested*): There's a new young lady on the third floor?
Another artiste?

Concierge (*disdainful*): That an artiste? She never goes out,
and she never has callers, not so much as a cat. As far as
I'm concerned, that's no artiste.

Man (*gaily*): OK, Madame Nicou, I'll ring. Au revoir, madame!

Landing. The milkman rings. Divine sleepily calls from her bed.

Divine (*in a fog*): Who is it?

Milkman: It's the milk!

Divine (*only half awake*): What?

Milkman (*louder*): The milk!

Divine: Leave it on the mat outside the door! (*She sinks back into bed; another ring; grumpily she puts on a bathrobe and goes to the door, which she opens a crack, irritated.*) What *is* it?

Milkman (*bottle in hand*): I can't leave it!

Divine (*doesn't understand*): Why not?

Milkman: The concierge said I couldn't.

Divine (*annoyed*): The concierge, the concierge . . . Oh, for goodness' sake! Just when I wanted to sleep today. I came back very late last night. Fine, give it to me. Thank you.

Milkman (*lively*): *Au revoir!* (*She has closed the door; he rings.*)

Divine (*opens the door again, bewildered*): What is it now?

Milkman (*nicely*): If you don't mind, mademoiselle, let's arrange something. Every morning I'll ring three times, like this, and I'll give you a full bottle of milk. You'll give me the empty bottle. That way we shouldn't have any trouble.

Divine: Fine!

Milkman: Good mademoiselle. Au revoir, mademoiselle. (*He leaves.*)

The next day. The bell rings three times. Divine opens the door a crack.

Milkman (*gaily*): Bonjour!

Divine (*reserved*): Bonjour. (*Exchange of bottles.*)

Milkman: You wouldn't want to open the door a little more?

Divine: No need, thanks. (*She closes the door again.*)

The next day. Again three rings. Divine opens the door slightly more widely.

Divine and Milkman (*together*): Bonjour! (*Exchange of bottles.*)

Milkman (*obliging*): Thank you. You wouldn't need any eggs? We have fresh-laid eggs.

Divine (*skeptical*): "Fresh-laid" eggs—I know what that means in Paris.

Milkman (*sincere*): Oh, no, they really are fresh-laid, gathered at five this morning . . .

Divine: That wasn't what I meant to say; at twenty-four sous, they're much too expensive for me.

Milkman (*engaging*): Twenty-four sous, that depends.

Divine: On what?

Milkman: On the wholesale price at Les Halles.

Divine (*wavering*): Well, if they really are fresh-laid eggs . . .

Milkman (*shows her*): You can check it. Look, here: every day fresh eggs; the date is marked every day . . .

Divine (*hardly looks*): Really?

Milkman (*gives her the eggs*): Really, look!

Another day. Door open. Conversation already begun.

Divine: Let me have my bill today.

Milkman (*protests*): There's no hurry, mademoiselle.

Divine (*insists*): But there is.

Milkman (*does as she says, brings out a notebook, adds*): All right, if you insist. That's nine days, a half-liter of milk a day . . .

Divine (*corrects*): No, a liter, a liter!

Milkman (*ignoring the correction*): . . . a half-liter of milk, and two fresh eggs every day . . .

Divine (*again corrects*): No: once there were five.

Milkman (*imperturbable*): Yes, seven times two . . . eleven eggs.

Divine (*refusing to understand*): Why eleven?

Milkman (*detached*): There: that's eight francs eighty-five centimes; there's no hurry, we'll see each other again. Au revoir, mademoiselle! (*He leaves rapidly after having given her his bill.*)

Divine (*touched*): Thank you . . .

Entrance hall of the building. The milkman, leaving, meets the concierge.

Concierge: Say, isn't your delivery boy well yet?

Milkman (gaily): No, Madame Nicou, we're having a real epidemic!

Entrance of the theater. The doorman warns someone entering.

Doorman: Watch out! The police are with the boss.

Office of the director of the theater. He is talking with two plainclothes policemen.

Director (very animated): If I've decided to tell the police commissioner, it's because I couldn't figure it out by myself, right? After fourteen years of running this show, you can imagine what I've seen. Thefts, babies, sudden death!

Policeman (blasé): That's how it is.

Director (agitated): Yes, but when it's a matter of replacing three artistes in four days, no! That's the limit, it's unheard of, you can take it from me! (*Knock; someone enters; the director turns his anger on the intruder.*) Come in . . . What? I don't want any fucking interruptions!

Intruder (a woman, who tries to get a word in): It's Victor, he sent me to tell you . . .

Director (furious): Beat it! (*Continues.*) And now I learn that my theater's a drop for snow. Personally, I don't give a shit! The private life of my artistes isn't my business.

Policeman: Couldn't a packet of drugs have got in here accidentally?

Director (sarcastically): Oh, accidentally! Do you know people who sniff coke accidentally? Not me. And I'm the boss! (*Another knock; another intruder; the director blows up.*) Come in! Get out! I've had enough! (*He throws files at the intruder's head, who retreats. Another knock.*) Come in! (*It's Victor, who gestures to stop the director, who is ready to throw anything, it doesn't matter what, at his head.*)

Victor (advances): It's very important. You have to come downstairs, boss: she doesn't want to act the dancing girl anymore, she's afraid of the snake, she went out like a light!

Director (calling the policemen to witness): You see? There's something behind all this. That snake isn't mean, just as long as he isn't bothered . . . For this number I need someone with steady nerves. My theater, my cast, can't all be on drugs! I should be able to find one woman who's healthy and sane!

Stage of the theater. Rehearsal. Air of great activity.

Actress (*throwing herself forward*): *Voilà!*
Victor: I asked for the dancing girl with the serpent!
Actress: Just that?
Victor: Right, just that!
Actress: But about that serpent—is it a real serpent, the kind that squirms around?
Victor: Do I know! Ask the director, there he is.

Doorkeeper's lodge at the entrance. He is stopping everyone who enters.

Doorkeeper (*to a girl who's arriving*): Let me see your purse and your newspaper.
Girl (*astonished*): What's happening?
Doorkeeper: I have my orders; everybody has to do it.
Girl (*irritated*): Well, it doesn't make any difference to me! It doesn't make any difference, but I don't like it.
Doorkeeper: Can't do anything about it. They just gave me the order. All of a sudden, everything has to be checked.

Near the doorkeeper's lodge. New arrivals. They catch up with the gossip. Whispering groups.

Girls (*calling*): Divine, Divine!
Doorkeeper (*to the group*): Morning, kids. Show me the purses.
Girl (*provocative*): You can look at anything you want!
Another (to Divine): Come with us, we'll all leave together!
Doorkeeper (*to one who's sneaking away*): Hey, you there! Let me take a look at that!
First girl (*whispers to her neighbor*): Go on, take care of Boutin!
Doorkeeper (*ready to take off after her*): Hey, you there, are you going to let me see that!

Colette did both the adaptation and the dialogue for Divine *(1935), which was based on her* L'Envers du Music-Hall. *Directed by Max Ophuls, a recent exile from Nazi Germany, it starred Simone Berriau as a music-hall performer, and Georges Rigaud as her milkman lover.*

Photo courtesy Cinémathèque Française

One of the more famous scenes in Divine *showed an infant, who had been smuggled backstage by his chorus-girl mother, being breastfed. Portions of the film prefigure the style that Ophuls was to bring to maturity in his breathtaking* Lola Montès *(1955).*

Photo courtesy Cinémathèque Française

Girl (*coming into the lodge*): Boutin, I want an apple.

Doorkeeper (*busy but not suspicious*): Take it, then.

Girl (*takes one, slinks into the lodge, charms the man to distract his attention*): You're a love! (*Caresses his head.*) You've got good-looking hair. You shouldn't comb it like that!

Doorkeeper (*half-conquered, half-uneasy*): I know I'm handsome, but enough is enough! If my wife saw this . . . (*Laughs, movement, babble.*)

Another girl (*already for away from the lodge*): Here, take this! (*Passes a large handbag to her neighbor.*)

Neighbor: What is it? (*The purse passes from hand to hand.*)

Rehearsal. Continual bustle everywhere, like a beehive.

Victor (*brusquely*): Here, you, you're going to do the dancing girl with the serpent.

Divine (*surprised*): Why me?

Victor (*busy*): I don't have the time to explain, I'll tell you afterward! (*Yelling to a lighting man.*) René! Look at me; focus the spot on my face!

Divine (*searching for information elsewhere*): Monsieur, can you tell me anything about that serpent?

Set designer (*following his idée fixe*): The serpent will be striped black and white, with a cross on the stomach and a cross on the back. If the serpent doesn't have a cross on his back, it will ruin my whole decor! (*He goes off; she accosts Nero.*)

Nero (*the pot-bellied trainer*): Ah, there you are, little one!

Divine: Monsieur, could you tell me anything about that serpent?

Nero: The serpent? Oh, yes, I understand; it's the first costume rehearsal. Does it make you nervous?

Divine: Yes . . .

Nero: Oh, get along with you, kid!

Divine (*insists*): You can't tell me anything?

Nero (*grotesque*): Tell you anything? But I can tell you everything and even do everything with you, my Andalusian! (*He tries to press her against him; she escapes.*)

The stage. The rehearsal continues. A group of girls go through their number spiritlessly.

Victor (furious): You're driving me crazy, you herd of mechanical sheep! Stop and get your asses out of here! (*Screams burst out in another corner.*)

Actress ("Poison"): The director! Where's the director! (*Loud and angry.*) My ring! I can't find it! It's been stolen. You can keep looking for it, but until it shows up again, I'm going! (*As a parting shot.*) The police would do well to look a little more closely at this theater!

Victor (beside himself): Goodbye and good luck, lady! (*Aside.*) You bitch! One well-aimed shot, that's the only way! (*Loud voice.*) Shall we begin?

Divine (catches hold of him): Monsieur Victor, please, what is it I have to do with the serpent?

Victor (takes her aside, explains): You stand calmly in front of the altar, without moving . . . (*Cries, tumult; Victor, interrupted, addresses himself to an actress.*) All right, keep it, so much the worse for you, madame! A lot of good it will do you, you'll see! (*Calls: "Victor!" Brouhaha; he comes back to Divine.*) I was saying, you stand calmly in front of the altar. You look into the eyes of Lutuf-Allah . . . (*Calls suddenly.*) Lutuf-Allah! (*The fakir appears.*) Ah, here he is. (*He brings Divine over to him.*)

Divine (by the fakir): Monsieur, I came for the serpent . . .

Fakir (superior): What's the matter? Look me in the eyes . . . You aren't afraid, are you?

Divine: Yes . . .

Fakir (cajoling): Give me your hand, let me feel your pulse. There, it's calmer. I'm your friend, darling!

Director (exploding): Three-quarters of an hour! Monsieur Pierre-Paul, I beg you, make up your mind! Come on, curtain!

Fakir (coming forward): I think we're going to rehearse without the serpent.

Set designer (protesting): What, without the serpent? My decor is designed to match . . .

Fakir (firm): Sorry, without the serpent!

Set designer: Very well, very well, but I refuse to take any responsibility!

Fakir: I don't want to risk it today, with everybody so nervous. I guarantee you, on opening night, the number will be perfect.

Director (resigned): I've survived forty-four revues, I'll make it through this one. The important thing is, let's get going. Curtain, rehearsal! We open day after tomorrow!

Theater. Audience. The curtain is up. Director's box. He is with a guest.

Guest: Very pretty, the set! Astonishing local color . . .

Director (satisfied): And not at all expensive!

Onstage. The revue is taking place. Music. It is the scene with the serpent.

Fakir (solemn): "Are you my faithful servant?"

Divine (conscientious): "Yes!"

Fakir (as above): "Then you will have to face danger!"

Divine (as above): "Yes!" (*He hands her the serpent.*)

Director's box. He is nervous.

Director (to his guest): All we can do now is pray.

Onstage. The serpent, which is enormous, slowly winds itself around the body of Divine, who stands, stoic and immobile. The music has stopped.

Fakir (whispers): Look at me! Stay calm, little girl. (*The head of the serpent reappears very close to Divine's face, which the beast inspects; Divine tries not to stir; drums.*) Hold it, hold it. Stay calm! Look at me. Now turn toward the audience! (*Divine, the serpent wound around her, turns and bows to the audience; the fakir continues.*) Magnificent! you have to smile when you do that, otherwise they'll think you're afraid . . .

Applause. Revue continues with a song: "In the land of the dancing girls . . ." Backstage, with the serpent unwound, Divine faints; the fakir busies himself around her. Onstage the song continues. Bustle around Divine.

Dora (to fakir, half-teasing, half-serious): Do you like her?

Fakir (detached): Yes, but not for what you think . . . Perhaps, yes, for what you think! (*He takes Divine in his arms; little by little she comes to herself.*) Do you feel all right, here against me?

Divine (*only half-conscious*): Yes . . .

Fakir (*pushing his advantage*): Would you like to come to my place one evening?

Victor (*says to another witness of the scene*): It's a shame the poor kid should fall into the hands of that painted nothing! I mean that Lutuf-Allah!

Fakir (*gets ready to put Divine down on some trunks; to those who are there*): Gently! You see she's not feeling well. Something to cover her . . . (*He wraps her up.*) Better?

Divine (*suddenly all right again*): Yes . . .

Fakir (*reassuring*): It'll be all right. Tell me, do you live alone in Paris?

Divine: Of course!

Fakir: Then if you need someone you can have confidence in, just let me know!

Divine: Thank you . . .

Doorkeeper's lodge. A policeman in plainclothes passes by.

Policeman: Anything special this evening?

Doorkeeper: Yes, it's the first night!

Policeman: No, I mean have you checked everything coming in?

Doorkeeper: The same as I've done ever since I got the order. Nothing comes in here unless I've seen it with my own eyes.

Policeman: Good. Then I'm going up to see the rest. The serpent wasn't bad. Us policemen, you know, we've seen it all before, but the serpent and the girl, that was real art!

Backstage. Dressing room of the actresses. Everyone busy.

Actress: Did you hide it all right?

Another: Of course, don't worry, they won't get you.

First actress: Don't anybody touch it until I get back! After the next number, I have a minute . . .

A lively quarrel breaks out between two girls in another corner of the room. We catch several snatches of it.

First Girl: Oh, that's not bad!

Second Girl (*furious*): Shut up about your morphine injections and mind your own business, huh? Do I ask what you stuff up your nose?

Third (*intervenes*): Hey you, hurry up!

Fourth (*goes toward the door*): I'm going to keep watch.

Third (*calls to her*): If you see Victor, tell him we're stripped, he can't come in! (*The mysterious handbag of a moment ago is opened; a baby appears.*)

Everyone (*in chorus*): Oh, isn't he lovely! Isn't he sweet! Adorable! (*Etc.*)

A girl calls, "Watch out!" We hear whispers: "Here, take him." The mother takes the baby and, very naturally, begins to suckle it under the tender gaze of everyone present.

Backstage, preparations for the climax of the revue. On-stage, the revue is in progress.

Man (*orders*): Ready for the Slave Market!

Showgirl (*confides*): Twenty-four steps on the Grand Staircase, twenty-four steps to walk down all alone—it's sublime! (*On-stage, a happy singer is giving his all.*)

Victor: All right kids! (*The human pyramid is laboriously set up.*)

Nero (*near Divine, half-audibly*): I haven't seen anything yet, but . . . ain't I smart! In a minute, I'll be able to admire you!

Divine (*cry of revolt*): No!

Victor (*alerted*): Who's talking up there?

Nero (*half-audible*): Shut up! (*The singer has finished; applause.*)

The show; it's the Slave Market number. To the sound of a drum and under the cracks of Nero's whip, the showgirls undress one by one. Divine, on top of the pyramid, shows strong apprehension at the voyeuristic looks of the audience. When her turn comes, she refuses to undress, in spite of Nero's threats; when he insists, she grabs his whip.

Nero (*under his breath, pulling at his end*): Let go!

Divine (*pulling hers*): No!

Nero (*furious*): I tell you, let go!

Divine (*enraged*): No! No! (*She finishes by ripping the whip*

*away from him and immediately and energetically hits him.
He falls down the stairs. Feminine shrieks. Cries of outrage.*)

*Director's box; he is horror-stricken by the scene, then over-
come by fury.*

Director: That's the limit! (*He begins to put his leg over
the side of the box, then thinks again, calls "Curtain!" and
runs toward backstage, exasperated.*) She'll pay for it, I
swear she'll pay!

Victor (*halts him*): What's the matter?

Director (*showing the strain*): Why doesn't the orchestra start
the Paradise Ballet? I want the Paradise Ballet! (*We hear
applause.*)

Victor (*to the director*): They're clapping!

Director (*taken aback*): Where?

Victor: In the theater, naturally!

Director (*taken aback*): For her?

Victor: Naturally! (*Rushes off.*) I'll be back in a minute!

*Another part of the backstage area. A man—doubtless the
"angel" we have already seen courting Divine—accosts her as
she strides toward the dressing rooms.*

Man: Where are you going like that?

Divine (*impassive, stubborn*): Let me go. They told me I'm
through here.

Man: That's not right. You were very good, very amusing. I
assure you!

Divine (*stiff*): I assure *you*, no!

Man (*insists*): Yes—for the house! If you stay, you do that
for us every evening, you understand? Every evening . . .

Divine (*incredulous*): Really? And hit him?

Man: You like that?

Divine: Yes, I do.

Man: Am I being kind to you?

Divine: Yes, monsieur, very kind!

Man: Then are we going to be good friends?

Divine (*reserved*): Yes, monsieur.

Man (*wishing to clarify the situation early*): Would you allow
me to accompany you home this evening after the show?

Divine (decidedly): No, monsieur.
Man: Why not?
Divine (firm): Because I'm going out!

A little restaurant; the dinner hour. At one table, a group of showgirls, including Divine. Several moments' whispering among the four girls, then:

First showgirl (loud voice): I can smell *choucroute!*
Second showgirl (same): No, I smell smoked eel!
Third showgirl: Oh, if I had even one cent, I'd get myself one of those *choucroutes* with boiled potatoes and mustard!
Second showgirl: And I'd get butter with my smoked eel!
First showgirl (to Divine): How about you, aren't you hungry? Or don't you have any imagination?
Divine: Both!
First show girl (still in a loud voice): No money, then?
Divine: No. *(She thinks.)* I smell a mushroom omelet!

All this at the top of their voices. Music. The group's speeches finally attract the attention of an elderly man, seated alone at a table. He calls the waiter and orders everything the girls have been talking about—that is, "Two choucroutes, a smoked eel with butter, a mushroom omelet," everything to be put on his bill. The four girls are served. This was the goal of the operation.

First showgirl (to Divine): You see, it's that easy. Only it doesn't always work. *(Music.)*
Second showgirl (with vivacity): Bon appetit!

When they have finished, the four girls get up and pass in review in front of the table of their generous benefactor.

First showgirl (detached tone): Thanks very much! Au revoir, monsieur!
Divine (same): Au revoir, monsieur! I want to get back to my husband now.
Second showgirl (same): Thank you, monsieur, I have four kids waiting for me!
Third showgirl (same): As for me, monsieur, I have to catch my bus. Yes, my bus! *(They vanish, laughing.)*

*Divine's building. As she comes home, she finds on the
landing the milkman, waiting for her, a basket in his hand.*

Milkman: Yes, it's me, the milk, mademoiselle. I was just
passing by . . .

Divine (amused): Do you bring the milk in the middle of the
night now?

Milkman (gaily): No, not exactly, but it could happen . . .

Divine: Did the concierge let you come up?

Milkman: The concierge? I've got a flirtation going with her!
And besides, when she knew it was flowers for your first
night . . .

Divine: Oh?

Milkman (gives her the basket): So!

Divine (touched): Thank you! (*She looks at the contents.*)
But why are you giving me all this?

Milkman: For friendship . . .

Divine (happy): Apples . . .

Milkman (proud): Yes, from our orchard. They look good, don't
you think?

Divine: And cowslips!

Milkman: Cowslips?

Divine (shows him): What do you call them?

Milkman: In Paris, they call them primulas.

Divine: They're cowslips! Already?

Milkman: They aren't garden flowers. They grow on the edge of
the fields. Just now the grass is full of them! (*A little
intimidated.*) I came . . . I came to . . . I brought you these,
because I thought . . . at least . . . (*Suddenly the light goes
out.*)

Divine (moving quickly): It's the timer on the hall light. Don't
move, I know where it is! I've found it, I've found it! (*Light
again in the staircase.*) There! Au revoir, monsieur . . .

Milkman (just leaving, thinks again): I wanted to ask you
something . . .

Divine: What?

Milkman: When you give me back the basket, could you put in
it—not a good seat, mind—but a pass for the theater?

Divine (immediate reflex): You'll have trouble spotting me in
that crowd, and with the kind of role I play . . .

Milkman (playful): I'll rent binoculars!

Divine: Only, I should warn you that the management doesn't give passes until the revue's been going a week, and you still have to pay eight francs taxes.

Milkman (practical): Is it worth it?

Divine: Yes, but it'll cost you sixteen francs . . .

Milkman (composedly): Only eight.

Divine (false ingenuousness): I didn't think you would go alone . . .

Milkman (calmly): Of course I'll go alone. Au revoir, then!

Divine: Au revoir!

Milkman (descends several steps then calls): One more thing!

Divine (turns around): Yes?

Milkman: Say goodbye like you do every day?

Divine (gaily): Au revoir, milk!

Milkman (joyous): See you soon! *(He leaves.)*

Concierge's lodge. Dark. We hear the milkman's voice.

Milkman: Door, please. *(He knocks.)* Door, please!

Concierge (lights up, opens the door for him, checks): Two o'clock . . . He's just leaving. She's an artiste after all!

Divine's bedroom. Day. She is writing a letter, then reads it aloud.

Divine (reading): "Dear Mother, Please forgive me for sending you a very small check. Life in Paris is more expensive than we thought. I don't believe our revue is having a big success . . ."

At the fakir's apartment. He is no longer in his gleaming stage costume but in an elegant lounging suit. He is conversing with Dora.

Fakir: The fiftieth night is a pretext that should work. It must work . . .

Dora: I've done everything; I've sent flowers to her, I've brought her candy, I've gone with her to visit her apartment, I've even given her silk stockings!

Fakir: That's nothing, that's . . .

Dora (continuing her report): . . . I gave her cigarettes! I *courted* her! There is nothing to be done with that woman, nothing; she's a hick!

Fakir (*meditating on his plan*): It's got to work! I'll tell her very simply: It's not a big party, you know; two or three friends . . .

Backstage. Music. The fakir invites Divine according to his plan.

Fakir: . . . good music, good champagne, a good sofa, everything's good at my place. You'll come, won't you?

Divine (*natural*): Of course!

At the fakir's. Dora is already there. There is a "boy" to serve. Arrival of Divine in street clothes.

Dora (*welcomes her*): Slip out of your dress! (*Pause.*)

Fakir (*to the boy*): Tea!

Dora: Well, sit down!

Fakir (*to the boy*): The tea, do you hear me? (*To Divine.*) Well, come on; be the young lady of the house and serve yourself first!

Divine: No, thank you.

Fakir: Why? Don't you like it? What would you rather have?

Divine: I'd rather have a sandwich . . .

Fakir (*calls*): Boy!

Dora: While you're waiting, have a little champagne!

Divine: Oh, that would be nice. (*Dora serves her.*) Not all the way to the top! Champagne makes me fall asleep.

Dora: Make yourself comfortable. Would you like a kimono?

Divine: A what?

Dora: A kimono.

Divine (*suspicious*): My dress is comfortable.

Dora (*brutal*): "My dress is comfortable!" Well, screw you, darling! You take your dress off easily enough on stage! The whole world has seen what you've got under your dress!

Fakir (*near the door*): Boy, is everything ready?

Boy: Yes, monsieur.

Fakir: Then, boy, you can leave.

Boy: Yes, monsieur.

Fakir: And, tomorrow, not before eleven! (*He closes the door behind the boy and rejoins the two women.*)

Dora (roughly, to Divine): Get undressed, do something! Did you come here to twiddle your thumbs? Why did you come?

Divine (crisp): Because you invited me. I can leave, you know!

Fakir (intervening): Enough, all right? *(Pause.)* Take my hand, come here a moment. Come here, be calm. There, come and sit down. Friends! Like that. Just friends. Don't be afraid! Dora . . . *(He makes a sign to her to push the tray closer; persuasively, to Divine:)* You have confidence in me? You know I'll never give you anything but good advice! You've already smoked? Smoked . . . I don't mean cigarettes . . . No, you've never smoked! *(Dora has brought the tray with smoking accessories closer; Divine kicks it over.)*

Dora (furious): Look what she's done! Idiot!

Divine (in a passion): What did you say?

Dora (same): Idiot!

Fakir: Now, then!

Divine (same): That's it! *(Suddenly a forceful knocking is heard.)*

Voice: Open up! Police!

Fakir (low voice, to Dora): Put it above the window, you understand, above the window!

Divine (uneasy): What's wrong? *(More heavy knocking at the door.)*

Voice: Are you going to open up?

Fakir (draws Divine toward the service entrance, while Dora rushes around clearing up): Go quickly! I don't want you to be found here; it'd get you in trouble! Go on, everything will be all right . . . Don't lose your head, that's all! Go on, take this. *(He hands her a package.)* Go that way, take your purse. That way, go, put this in your purse. If they ask you anything—I'll explain everything—you're the maid from the fourth floor. Understood?

Divine (stubborn): But why?

Fakir (pushes her out): Go that way. You're the maid from the fourth floor. Go on, get moving!

Voice (after more knocking): OK, we're coming in!

Fakir (goes to open it composedly, as if he were used to this sort of thing): Can't a man get any sleep around here?

First policeman (appearing): It's me again!

Second policeman: Yes, it's us again. *(They enter)*.

Dora (false amiability): So kind of you to call. You've come at just the right time! Please come in.

In the fakir's dressing room. Later. He is with Divine. Dora isn't there.

Fakir (pleasantly): It's been three months now since the cops were here, and no one knows that you were with us. I've always played straight with you!

Divine (keeping her distance): You?

Fakir: Yes, I have. Dora and I held them off, and it's thanks to me you got away.

Divine (dry): With your packages?

Fakir (changes his tone a little): With my packages, precisely. And it would interest the gentlemen of the police very much, even now, to know you were with us that night.

Divine (her hackles raised): And would it interest them to know what I took away with me that evening? Packages of . . . cigarettes?

Fakir: It certainly would!

Divine: Suppose I told them.

Fakir: You won't!

Divine: Because?

Fakir: Because you're not the kind that tells . . . (*Pause.*) That's why you're going to find the man that'll be sitting this evening at the bistro across the street, reading a Spanish newspaper, *La Publicitad.* You'll turn over to him what I'm going to give you. It's the last time.

Divine (unbelieving): You've been telling me that for three months.

Fakir: You'll go?

Divine: No!

Fakir (looks for a package which he gives to her): Do you have the money?

Divine (hostile): Is that all? Can I go?

Fakir: Here's two hundred francs.

Divine: I don't want it! (*Knock at the door.*)

Victor (outside): Come on, open up; it's Victor! (*He enters; to Divine.*) What the fuck are you doing here? Go change your costume . . . (*To the fakir.*) I don't want any of that. I've already told you! (*To Divine.*) If he bothers you, just tell me; let's go! (*Divine and Victor leave.*)

Dora (*enters*): Will she do it?

Fakir (*superior*): Of course! I have her in the palm of my hand . . .

Dora (*skeptical*): To listen to you, you have all the women in the palm of your hand. It's not as easy as that. If she isn't willing this evening . . . You make me sick!

Showgirls' dressing room. Two girls.

First: Oh, shit! It's like a morgue in here . . .

Second: What's eating you? Troubles?

First: And all this to earn forty francs a day.

Second: What do you want? It's our life.

Backstage. Victor approaches the fakir.

Victor: Say, do you have a mother?

Fakir (*haughtily*): Naturally I have a mother, my boy. I've got nothing but mothers.

Victor: All right, there's a call from your mother in the office . . .

Staircase backstage. Divine and the ballet mistress cross paths.

Ballet mistress: Now, child, hurry up! You're late . . . Are you cold?

Divine: No, madame.

Ballet mistress: Have you eaten?

Divine: Yes, a little . . .

Ballet mistress: A little! You've been looking very thin recently . . . I hope you're not in love, are you?

Divine: Oh, not that, madame, not that!

Ballet mistress: I've seen so many of them come and go, kids like you! I'm telling you . . . because once you lose your health . . .

The office. The fakir is at the telephone, while the show goes on; bursts of music.

Fakir: Yes, it's me! Talk . . .

Person on phone: . . . otherwise, we're all screwed! Shorty nearly bought it, and he spilled it all at the hospital, everything they wanted to know. So watch out this evening; when you leave, you'll be followed. You'll be followed.

Fakir (everyday voice): Thank you for telephoning, Doctor. I hope this evening won't be so bad . . . Au revoir, Doctor, au revoir. (*Hangs up.*)

Victor (in the passageway): Bad news?

Fakir (evasive): It could be better. (Music. The show continues).

Police Commissariat; a policeman in plainclothes is telephoning.

Policeman: This is the Commissariat, Eighth Arrondissement . . . arrest whoever delivers a package to the man with the Spanish newspaper!

Cafe. A man is seated reading a Spanish newspaper, La Publicitad. *His eyes follow Divine, who enters, seems to be heading toward him, passes him, and goes toward another table, at which the milkman is waiting for her.*

Divine: Oh, you're here! Did you have a good time?

Milkman: Thank you very much for the tickets; they gave me a very good seat, the fifth row of the orchestra . . .

Divine: Did you enjoy yourself?

Milkman (sincere, but not delirious with enthusiasm): Yes, yes, it was very good. Waiter! I must compliment you; you're here exactly on time, exactly! Not at all like an artiste . . .

Divine: But, you know, I don't take myself for an artiste! I don't have the vocation . . . (*She laughs.*)

Milkman: Would you like to change jobs with me?

Divine (gaily): Right away!

Milkman (teases): You couldn't ever get up at four in the morning— worse, go to work at four . . . Open up the henhouse . . .

Divine (continues joyously): . . . give them their food . . .

Milkman: . . . and water . . .

Divine (laughs): . . . grind the coffee . . . wash the dishes . . . (*Sound of voices from the cafe.*)

Milkman: . . . saw the wood, and gath—
Divine (interrupts him and continues, laughing): gather the eggs!
Milkman (continues the game): And, in the afternoon, lead the animals to water . . .
Divine: . . . and bring in the hay . . .
Milkman: . . . clean the rabbit cages! (*They laugh.*)

Front of the theater. Two plainclothes policemen seem to be waiting for someone to leave.

Policeman (raising his eyes): Look, there's hardly any light left!
Second policeman: But what the heck is he doing to take this long?
Doorman (in the theater doorway): He always takes a long time, that one!
Policeman: It's strange! He certainly hasn't come out . . .
Doorkeeper: No, I would have seen him.
Policeman: It's not normal.

Interior of the theater. In his dressing room, the fakir hurriedly destroys papers by burning them. He leaves before the fire is out.

Doorkeeper (calls): Is anybody still up there? Anybody still there?
Fakir (distant voice): I'm coming! Don't put out the light. (*A pause.*)
Doorkeeper: Hey, up there, shake a leg!
Fakir: All right, all right, I'm coming! (*Another pause.*)
Doorkeeper (getting impatient): Hey, there, are you finished?
Fakir: I'm coming, I'm coming! (*He arrives and leaves the theater.*)

A walk in the rain. Divine and the milkman. His name is Antonin.

Antonin: Just the same, I think we would have done better to take a taxi.
Divine (relaxed): It doesn't matter to me if it rains; I love to walk home, it doesn't matter what the weather is! I don't often get a chance to get outside. Think of it: since

I've been in Paris, I've gone only maybe three times to the Bois de Boulogne . . .

Antonin: I can offer you better than that.

Divine: What?

Antonin: A walk in the country. An hour's ride; it would do you good. Wouldn't you like that? Would you like me to come get you some Saturday afternoon?

Divine: Oh, but I can't! Remember, I do matinees on Thursday, Saturday, and Sunday!

Antonin: That's annoying because I can't . . . because the boss only gives me Saturday afternoon . . .

Divine (*dreams*): Still, a walk in the country . . .

Antonin: With everything open and aboveboard.

Divine: That's a nice way of putting it. It's the first time I've heard that said since I've been in Paris.

Antonin (*comes back to his idea*): It's a shame, because after all, a walk in the country . . . Of course, not in weather like this! Are you sure it's not possible? I'll come by to get you tomorrow morning!

Switchboard rings. We hear announced: "Fire at the Empyrean-Montmartre!"

On Antonin's truck, an old Citroen, Divine reads the newspaper attentively.

Divine (*stupefied, reads aloud*): "A fire early this morning destroyed a portion of the Empyrean-Montmartre Theater. The management has announced that because of repair work, which they will complete shortly, the show will not resume performances until next Tuesday evening . . ." (*Commenting on what she has just read:*) It's terrible!

Antonin (*joyful*): No, it isn't terrible. That will let you stay a few hours more in the country air; you need it! Look at the weather, the flowers are out everywhere. It's real spring . . .

Divine (*worried*): Yes, but I'll have to get back . . .

Antonin: Why?

Divine: I have to pick up my paycheck. I'll have to go there this evening . . .

Antonin: Then I'll bring you back this evening! But don't think of it now. (*The truck rolls away into the countryside.*)

They arrive at a farmyard. Joyful music.

Antonin (*happy*): Voilà, we're here! Come tour the place. See where the eggs I bring you every morning come from. (*They find themselves in a poultry yard. Innumerable fowl. A dog barks.*)

Divine (*conquered*): Here, chicky, chicky, chicky! (*She kneels in front of a brood of chicks and cradles one in her hands.*)

Antonin: Here are some new members of the firm! You like this, don't you?

Divine: I do like it. You can't know what all this means to me.

Antonin (*leaves her*): Yes I do, yes. I'll leave you with your little friends and run over to the kitchen to make a good lunch.

Divine (*uneasy*): But, tell me, what will the owner say when he sees us poking around?

Antonin (*joyful*): He won't mind at all, because the owner— is me.

Backstage at the theater. Police investigation. Everyone is there.

Policeman (*plainclothes*): No one has anything more to say? Now then, does anyone have anything more to say?

Actress ("*Poison*"): Yes, I do, Inspector! I'd like to draw your attention to this so-called Divine. I have to tell you something about her. Obviously, you don't know that in the Slave Market number, I had a magnificent scene, with twenty-four steps to go down all alone, and that little nothing used underhanded methods to try to steal my scene!

Policeman: We don't care about that.

Director (*furious*): Right, we don't care!

"*Poison*" (*ulcerated with resentment*): Oh, in that case, I don't have any further business here.

Director: No! (*She sweeps out with a great motion of infuriated dignity.*)

Policeman (*calls after her*): But stay around where I can reach you! (*To the others.*) Who's not here? Monsieur Lutuf-Allah! Mademoiselle Dora and Mademoiselle Divine! (*Giving an order.*) When they show up, have them wait in the corridor backstage; don't let them go away! (*Protests from the group.*)

Girl: This is a dictatorship!

A man: Do you know what a dictatorship is?

Girl: Yes; it's when the police are in the dressing rooms and the artistes are in the corridor!

Showgirl (to her neighbors): They're looking for Divine!

Another: The pigs! But she hasn't done anything!

Dressing room of Divine (and other showgirls). The police are searching her dressing table.

Policeman (indicating what he's found): Powder, Love Apple Red rouge . . . Ahah!

Second policeman: What is it?

First policeman: Postcard from Cairo! (*Reading.*) "Wish you were here at the Pyramids. I hope that you have your car now, too, and that everything is the way you want it." (*Calls the stage manager.*) Victor, Victor!

Victor (enters): Here!

First policeman (asks him): Do you have her address, this so-called Divine?

Victor: The dancer?

First policeman: Yes!

Victor: From here, from the theater? You think we have their addresses?

First policeman: Go look at your register and bring those women in here . . .

Victor: All right. Right away?

First policeman: Yes, right away!

Victor (leaves; yells to the backstage generally): Everybody into the dressing rooms! (*The troupe obeys.*)

Policeman (interrogates Divine's companions, now reassembled in the dressing room): You didn't notice anything peculiar in the behavior of this Divine?

First showgirl: No, monsieur!

Policeman: And you?

Second showgirl: Yes, monsieur!

Policeman (attracted by the scent of a clue): Ah! What?

Second showgirl: She was very nice, very decent . . .

Policeman: And?
Second showgirl: That's all.
Policeman: That's all?
Second showgirl: Of course! You don't think that's peculiar? It's obvious you've never worked in a music hall.
Policeman (sarcastically): Ah, Madame is a comedian?
Second showgirl (imperturbable): No, monsieur, an acrobatic dancer . . .
Policeman (changing the subject; to the whole group): Does anyone know her address?
Several voices: Yes . . .
Policeman: Where does she live?
A showgirl: 13, rue Ordener.
Another: That's not true: 146, avenue des Champs-Elysées.
A third: No, that's not true: she lives in Arcueil.
The second girl: Oh, yes, that's right, she was always worried about missing her train.
Policeman (bewildered): This is getting complicated. *(Knock.)* What is it? Come in. *(Enter Victor.)* Now, do you have this person's address?
Victor: Yes: 4—that's two times two—place du Trocadéro.
Policeman: 4, place du Trocadéro? *(Suddenly furious, to the showgirls.)* Say, are you trying to make us look like idiots?
Several voices (hypocritical protests): Oh, no, Inspector!
Second policeman (subtle): Listen, I think we should send someone to these four addresses; she seems to live everywhere! *(Chatter of voices.)*

Street in front of the theater. Crowd. The milkman's truck draws up.

Divine (uneasy): What are all these people doing here?
Antonin (reassuringly): It must be because of the fire. Perhaps they're volunteer firemen. I'll go for you and get your paycheck . . .
Divine: They don't know you, they won't want . . .
Antonin: I'll go see what's happening! *(He leaves her in the truck and approaches the theater.)*
Gendarme: No one's allowed to enter, monsieur!
Antonin: I'm a fireman!

Gendarme: What do you want?

Antonin (decides to parley): I've come on business . . .

Gendarme: Do you belong to the theater?

Antonin (evasive): More or less!

Gendarme (firm): No, monsieur, no one comes through!

Antonin (insists still): Just to say two words . . .

"Poison" (bursting out of the theater): Monsieur, tell those gentlemen from the police that I'm going home! I'm ill. I'm at their disposal in my apartment. I've never been involved with the police in my life! (*She noisily moves from the theater into the crowd.*)

Antonin (to the gendarme): Is is true that they're searching everyone?

Gendarme: Yes, everyone, everyone!

In the street, further away, two plainclothes policemen see Divine in the milkman's truck; they consult a newspaper photograph and recognize her.

First policeman: Recognize her? She's the one!

Second policeman: We should take her in . . .

First policeman: Let's see! (*They approach the truck.*)

Antonin comes back toward Divine, sees the pair of policemen, comprehends their intentions, rapidly gets into the car and addresses the young woman in an unconcerned voice.

Antonin (loud voice): Say, did you remember the scooter for the kids?

Divine (surprised a moment, quickly gets into the spirit of the game): Yes, and also the wool for your sweater.

Antonin (same): Great! We'll have Mom knit it. (*The disconcerted policemen stop in their tracks. The truck moves off.*)

Divine (further away, as the truck rolls on): You were very nice. You got me out of that with the story about the scooter, and this and that . . . But tomorrow I have to go explain to the police!

Antonin (resolute): I'll go with you. But first we're going to city hall!

City hall. Antonin familiarly greets the clerk. Divine is with him.

Antonin: Good morning. I have something serious to tell you: I want to marry Mademoiselle . . .

Clerk: Fine. I'll take it all down. It won't be too hard as far as you're concerned, old friend! Yes, mademoiselle, this Antonin is an old buddy of mine! We played marbles together. (*He opens his register.*) But you, mademoiselle, I don't know you. Would you mind giving me your name, your age—in short, all the necessary information?

Divine: Ludivine Jarisse . . .

Clerk (*hesitates a second, then stands*): Just a moment, please! (*He leaves his office and joins his wife in the apartment across from it. Excitedly, to his wife.*) You'll never guess what's happened! It's amazing, I've found her! Where's yesterday's newspaper? Where is it?

Wife (*astonished*): You're so nervous! (*He whistles to call his son.*)

Clerk (*more and more agitated, to his son who arrives*): Arsène! If only she doesn't escape! Come here, listen to me carefully: you're going to go to the front door, you're going to double-lock it, do you understand? So that they don't notice anything . . . Where's the newspaper?

Wife (*brings it to him*): Here it is, here it is! You're so nervous! What's the matter?

Clerk (*paper in hand, exultant*): It's her, without any possible doubt, it's her! Drug traffic . . . and I'm the one who found her! I have to call the police . . .

Office next door. The two young people, alone, wait for the clerk to return.

Antonin (*reassuringly*): Now, whatever happens, you're not alone: I'm here.

Divine (*still uneasy*): If only it works out!

Antonin (*confident*): But of course everything will work out! Here, let's see: even, everything will be fine; odd . . . (*One by one, he picks the petals from a daisy.*) One, two, three, four, five, six . . .

Clerk's apartment. He is telephoning to the police.

Voice (*on the telephone*): Hello, hello? Who? Ludivine Jarisse?

Clerk (*proud*): Yes, commissioner, she's here, in the room next door. It was I who found her!

Commissioner's voice: Well, don't make a fool of yourself! The affair was cleared up last night. We know everything! The young lady isn't involved.

Clerk (*disappointed*): Ah, good! Fine! I know what I have to do . . .

He returns to the office, where Antonin is continuing to pick petals from his flower.

Antonin (*Divine counts with him*): Sixteen, seventeen, eighteen, nineteen, twenty . . .

Clerk (*friendly*): And now, my dear friends, my very best wishes! And I hope that soon . . . (*Relieved smiles from the two young people; joyous music.*)

SIMONE BERRIAU REMEMBERS
FILMING DIVINE

An extract from *Simone Est Comme Ça* (*Simone's Like That*), published by Robert Laffont, 1973):

We had engaged a thirty-year-old director who had put on numerous plays in Germany before becoming Anatol Litvak's assistant. Max Ophuls, who had made his debut in the cinema at the beginning of the sound era, had arrived in France preceded by a flattering reputation, at least in film circles; he had directed *Liebelei*, a bittersweet romantic film prefiguring *La Ronde*. With him, we produced *La Tendre Ennemie* (*The Tender Enemy*) . . . and *Divine*, a charming film nicely scripted by Colette, which unfortunately was a failure.

In spite of my reservations, I had to go back to acting in front of the camera during the filming of *Divine*, replacing at the last moment Yvette Lebon, who fell ill just as the cameras were about to roll.* I remembered for a long time the music-

---

* Yvette Lebon in fact appeared in the first scenes of the film as Roberta, the childhood friend of Divine, who introduces her to music-hall life.

hall sequence in which I had as a partner the writer and future Academician Philippe Hériat . . . and an interminable boa constrictor as thick as a tree trunk. I had to do whatever Hériat wanted. He was amusing himself by playing the role of a magician while I played his assistant and slave. He handed me the reptile, saying to me in a solemn voice:

"Are you my faithful slave? Then take this serpent!"

Max Ophuls had asked the assistant director to find him a fake serpent, which would be suspended like a marionette from fine threads invisible in the shadows. We began to film with the false boa, but it looked no more alive or terrifying than a doll stuffed with straw. It hung across my shoulders, moved in jumps, was ridiculous . . . I decided, as the producer, that the scene would be filmed with a real serpent, in spite of my aversion for reptiles. I had gone to see a snakecharmer at Clichy who introduced me to the most impolite boa living; it didn't have any empathy with me at all and curled up at the other end of the room the moment I arrived.

In spite of this obvious lack of elective affinities, I had it brought to the studio by its proprietor, who came to the filming with a knife in his hand, ready to intervene. The heavy boa did not seem at all cooperative when Philippe Hériat held it out to me, but it awakened from its apathy under the tropical heat of the sun arcs. It wound itself around my shoulders (I could hardly stand up under it!), slithered over my head, and came down again over my face. I had its tongue on my lips—the most disagreeable kiss I have ever known—when Ophuls cried "Cut!," mad with joy at the take, which we fortunately did not have to do again. Albert Wolff, who wrote the music for the film, watched the scene. He was white when it was finished. As for me, I fainted when the snake charmer took back his boa, which didn't want to let go of me!*

---

* Note the contrast with Colette's version of the same events in "Backstage at the Studio."

A COLETTE FILMOGRAPHY

1916 *Minne* (based on *L'Ingénue Libertine* [*The Innocent Libertine*]).
Adapted by Jacques de Baroncelli; directed by Musidora; starring
Musidora. Prod. Films Lumina. Made in Paris, December 1916.
(According to Francis Lacassin, this film was unfinished or never
distributed.)

1917 *La Vagabonde* (*The Vagabond*). Scenario Colette; adapted by
Musidora and Eugenio Perego; dir. Eugenio Perego; starring Musidora (Renée Néré), Luigi Maggi (Maxime Dufferein-Chantel),
Ernesto Treves (Adolphe Taillandy), Rina Maggi. Prod. Film d'Arte
italiana (Rome); distrib. Pathé. Filmed in Rome, April-May 1917;
released Paris, March 1918.

1918 *La Flamme Cachée* (*The Hidden Flame*), "a drama in four parts."
Scenario Colette; adaptation and editing Musidora; direction Musi-
dora and Roger Lion; starring Musidora (the student, Anne Morin),
Maurice Lagrenée (Armand, her lover), Jean Yonnel (Hubert, her
husband), and Le Gosset. Prod. Societé des Films Musidora; distrib.
Éclair. Filmed in Paris, October-November 1918; released Paris,
March 1920.

1931 *La Vagabonde*. Adapt. and dialogue Solange Bussi (additional
scenes by Colette). Dir. Solange Bussi (Solange Térac). Photog-
raphy Rudolf Maté and Louis Née; set design Franc-Nohain; music
Silviano; assistant dir. Colette de Jouvenel; starring Marcelle Chantal
(Renée Néré), Fernand Fabre (Maxime Dufferein-Chantel), Robert
Quinault (Brague), Jean Wall (Taillandy), Jeanne Fusier-Gir
(Margot). Prod. Pax Films. Released 1932.

1932 *Jeunes Filles en Uniforme (Maedchen in Uniform)*. Directed by Leontine Sagan from the play by Christa Winsloe; French text adapted by Colette. Artistic director Carl Froelich; scenario by F. Dardam and Christa Winsloe; photography Reimar Kuntze, Franz Weimayr; music Hanson Milde, Meissmer; starring Herta Thiele (Manuela), Dorothea Wieck (Frau von Bernburg), Ellen Schwanneke, Emilie Unda, Edwige Schlichter, Marte Hein "and one hundred young boarding-school girls." Distributed in France by Gaumont-Franco-Film-Aubert.

1933 *Lac-aux-Dames*. Dir. Marc Allégret from the novel by Vicki Baum; adaptation Jean-Georges Auriol; dialogue Colette; photography Jules Kruger and Ribault; set design Lazare Meerson; music Georges Auric; sound Hermann Storr; editing Denise Batcheff; script-girl Françoise Giroud; assistant directors Yves Allégret and Colette de Jouvenel; prod. Sopra Films–Philippe de Rothschild. Released Paris 1934. Starring Jean-Pierre Aumont (Eric Heller), Wladimir Sokoloff (Baron de Dobbersberg), Michel Simon (Oscar Lyssenhop), Eugène Dumas (Matz), Maurice Rémy (Count Stereny), Paul Asselin (Brindel), Romain Bouquet (owner of the inn), Guy Derlan; Rosine Deréan (Dolly), Simone Simon (Puck), Ila Meery (Anika), Odette Joyeux (Carla), Marulka (Vefi), Marie Deschamps, Germaine Reuver, Milly Mathis.

1935 *Divine*. Scenario by Colette (from her *L'Envers du Music-Hall* [translated as *Music-Hall Side-Lights*]). Adaptation Max Ophuls and Jean-Georges Auriol, with Colette de Jouvenel. Dialogue Colette. Dir. Max Ophuls; asst. directors Ralph Baum and Pierre de Hérain; photography Roger Hubert; set design Jacques Gotko and Robert Gys; sound Fred Behrens; music Albert Wolff; songs Roger Féral and J.-G. Auriol; editing Léonide Moguy; starring Simone Berriau (Ludivine Jarisse, known as "Divine"), Catherine Fonteney (her mother), Yvette Lebon (Roberta), Georges Rigaud (Antonin), Philippe Hériat (the fakir, Lutuf-Allah), Marcel Vallée (manager of the "Empyrean"), Paul Azais (Victor), Gina Manès (Dora), Sylvette Fillacier (Gitanette), Thérèse Dorny ("Poison"), Nane Germon (Zaza), Gabriello (Nero, the animal tamer), Jeanne Véniat (the ballet mistress), Jeanne Fusier-Gir (Madame Nicou, the concierge), Pierre Juvenet (the doorman), Lucien Callamand and Tony Murcy (two inspectors), Roger Gaillard, Floyd Dupont, Paul Lluis, Claude Roussell. Prod. Éden-Productions.

1937 *Claudine à l'École* (*Claudine at School*), based on the book by Colette and Willy. Adapt. and dialogue Jacques Constant-Robillard; dir. Serge de Poligny; photography Willy, Goreau; sound Maurice Vareille, Causset; music Paul Misraki; set design Jacques Krauss; ed. Maurice Serein; starring Max Dearly (Claudine's father), Pierre Brasseur (Dr. Dubois), Marcel Mouloudji (Moulou), Marcel Charvey (Duplessis), Leon Larive (Rabastens), Auguste Boverio (Lebarbu), Gouge (swimming coach), Louis Rognoni (examiner), Fred Marche, Maurice Marceau, Frank Maurice, and Blanchette Brunoy (Claudine), Suzet Maïs (Mlle Aimée), Margo Lion (Mlle Sergent), Jeanne Fusier-Gir (Mlle Griset), Katia Low (Anaïs), Jacqueline Valerio (little Soulié), Ketty Pierson (Juno), Jacqueline Dumonceau and Marthe Sylvain (the Jaubert twins), Zélie Yzelle (the maid), Solange de Turenne (Luce), Yolande Lavergne, Marlène Martin, Fanchette Mazin (students), Christine Renal, Janine Guyon, Irène Jeanning, Yodi Low. Prod. Films Régent.

1948 *Gigi.* Adapt. Pierre Laroche. Dialogue Colette. Dir. Jacqueline Audry. Photography Gérard Perrin. Set design R. Druart. Music Marcel Landowski. Starring Danièle Delorme (Gilberte Alvarez, known as Gigi), Gaby Morlay (Aunt Alicia), Yvonne de Bray (Mme Alvarez, "Mamita"), Hélène Pépée (Andrée), Yolande Laffon (Mme Lachaille), Madeleine Rousset (Liane), Colette George (Minouche), Frank Villard (Gaston Lachaille), Jean Tissier (Honoré), Paul Demange (Emmanuel), Jacques Henley (M. Lachaille), Marcel Rouzet, Louis Siccardi, René Marjac, Marcel Arnal (maîtres d'hôtel), Pierre Juvenet. Prod. Codo-Cinéma (Claude Dolbert). Filmed 1948. Released Paris February 3, 1949. Text of the film published in the theatrical supplement of *Opéra* (No. 11, Oct. 1949).

1949 *Julie de Carneilhan.* Adapt. Jacques Manuel and J.-P. Gredy; additional dialogue J.-P. Gredy; dir. Jacques Manuel; photography Philippe Agostini; set design René Moulaërt; music Henri Sauguet; director of production Mnouchkine; starring Pierre Brasseur (Herbert d'Espivant), Edwige Feuillère (Julie), Jacques Dumesnil (Léon de Carneilhan), Jacques Dacqmine (Coco Vatard), Marcelle Chantal (Marianne), Michel Lemoine, Marion Delbo, Sylvia Bataille. Prod. Ariane-Sirius. Filmed September-November 1949. Released Paris April 1950.

1950 *Chéri.* Adapt. Pierre Laroche; dialogue Colette; dir. Pierre Billon; photography N. Toporkoff; set design R. Druart; music Marcel

Landowski; starring Jean Desailly (Fred Peloux, known as Chéri), Marcelle Chantal (Léa), Jane Marken (Charlotte Peloux), Yvonne de Bray (the Girl-Friend), Suzanne Dantès (Marie-Laure), Marcelle Derrien (Edmée), Mad Siamé (Rose). Prod. Codo-Cinéma (Claude Dolbert). Filmed January-March 1950. Released Paris April 1950.

1950 *Minne, l'Ingénue Libertine (Minne, The Innocent Libertine)*. Adapt. and dial. Pierre Laroche; dir. Jacqueline Audry; photo. Marcel Grignon; set design Raymond Druart; music Marcel Landowski; starring Danièle Delorme (Minne), Frank Villard (Antoine), Jean Tissier (Maugis), Claude Nicot (Jacques Couderc), Simone Paris (Irène Chaulieu), Yolande Laffon (Blanche), Armontel (Uncle Paul), Charles Lemontier (Chaulieu), Jean Guélis (Le Frisé-Ramon), Pauline Carton, Dinan. Prod. Codo-Cinéma (Claude Dolbert). Filmed January-March 1950. Released Paris May 1950.

1950 *Colette*. Short subject by Yannick Bellon.

1952 *Lès Sept Péchés Capitaux (The Seven Deadly Sins)*. "L'Envie" ("Envy"), based on *La Chatte (The Cat)* by Colette. Dir. Roberto Rossellini, starring Andrée Debar (Camille), Orfeo Tamburi (Olivier); other directors: Jean Dréville, Eduardo de Filippo, Yves Allégret, Carlo Rim, Claude Autant-Lara, Georges Lacombe. Prod. Franco-London-Film. Released Paris 1953.

1953 *Le Blé en Herbe (Ripening Seed)*. Adapt. and dialogue Jean Aurenche, Pierre Bost, Claude Autant-Lara; dir. Claude Autant-Lara; photography Robert Lefebvre and Jacques Natteau; set design Max Douy; ed. Madeleine Gug; music René Cloérec; starring Edwige Feuillère, Pierre-Michel Beck, Nicole Berger, Renée Devillers, Charles Deschamps, Louis de Funès. Prod. Franco-London-Film. Released Paris January 1954.

1956 *Mitsou*. Adapt. and dialogue Pierre Laroche; dir. Jacqueline Audry; photography Marcel Grignon; set design Claude Bouxin; costumes Mireille Leydet; sound Coutelier; music Georges Van Parys; ed. Yvonne Martin; starring Danièle Delorme, Fernand Gravey, Claude Rich, Palau, Odette Laure, Denise Grey, Thérèse Dorny, Gaby Morlay, Jacques Duby, François Guérin, Max Elloy, Maurice Sarfati, Charles Lemontier, Maryse Martin, Jacques Fabbri, Gabrielle Dorziat. Dir. of production Jean Kerchner; prod. Ardennes Film (René Lafuite); Général Production; Eastmancolor. Released Paris November 1956.

1958   *Gigi.* Based on Colette's novel and the musical comedy by Alan Jay
       Lerner and Frederic Loewe. Adapt. Alan Jay Lerner; dir. Vincente
       Minnelli; photography Joseph Ruttenberg; artistic directors William
       A. Horning and Preston Ames; set design Henry Grace and Keogh
       Gleason; costumes Cecil Beaton; starring Leslie Caron (Gigi),
       Maurice Chevalier (Honoré Lachaille), Louis Jourdan (Gaston
       Lachaille), Hermione Gingold (Mme Alvarez), Eva Gabor (Liane),
       Jacques Bergerac (Sandomir), Isabel Jeans (Aunt Alicia), John
       Abbott (Manuel), François Valorbe (Gaston's butler), Jacques
       Bertrand (maître d'hôtel at Maxim's), Maurice Mersac (Prince
       Berensky), Edwin Jerome (Charles), Lydia Stevens (Simone), Cecil
       Beaton (gentleman), Dorothy Neuman, Monique Van Vooren, Maruja
       Plose, Marilyn Sims, Richard Bean, Pat Sheahan, Marie-Hélène
       Arnaud and Corinne Marchand.